THE FAIR FACE OF FLANDERS

PATRICIA CARSON

The Fair Face
of Flanders

lannoo

This publication appears simultaneously in English,
Dutch, French and German versions under the titles of:
The Fair Face of Flanders
Het fraaie gelaat van Vlaanderen
Miroir de la Flandre
Zauber und Schicksal Flanderns

FRONTISPIECE
Rubens house, Antwerp

First published 1969
Reprinted 1969
Third printing, revised, 1974
Reprinted 1978
Fifth printing, revised, 1991
Reprinted 1995
Cover and graphic design by Studio Lannoo
Photographs by Hugo Maertens
Maps by Dirk Billen
© Uitgeverij Lannoo, Tielt
D/1995/45/182 - ISBN 90 209 2712 4 - NUGI 644
Typeset, printed and bound by
Drukkerij Lannoo nv, Tielt - 1995

Contents

Vlaandren, o welig huis waar we zijn als genooden aan rijke taeflen !...
wie kan u weten, en in 't harte niet verblijên;
niet danke' om dagen, schoon als jonge zege-goden,
gelijk een beedlaar dankt om warme tarwe-brooden ?

Karel van de Woestijne (1878-1929)
from *De Boom-Gaard der Vogelen en der Vruchten,*

Flanders, o lavish home, where we are like guests at rich tables !...
who can know you and not rejoice at heart;
not be thankful for days, beautiful as triumphant young gods,
like a beggar is thankful for warm wheat loaves ?

CHAPTER 1

The Contours

WHAT do we see in a face ? Not only its colour, shape and expression, but also the character, experience, hopes and fears which have moulded it. The fiercer its battles, the deeper its sorrows, the more hectic its joys, the greater are the traces of life it bears. Moods, changing from one moment to the next, show also, while first impressions, acquired at the moment of meeting are never lost. Such is the face of Flanders.

To some Flanders means the quiet calm of shimmering plane trees between the white walls of a beguinage, to yet others the cheery, noisy, vulgar happiness of **Memories** roundabouts and swings, hot dough-nuts and chip potatoes of the Flemish Fairs; to some it recalls bands which blow themselves scarlet and thirsty, leading processions through town and village on every possible occasion. Some think of Flanders as the land of mighty castles, sombre and icy-cold, others are reminded of the soaring beauty of the high, airy towers or the jolly jingle of carillons. While others recall the mud and blood of the Ypres salient in 1914, and Passchendale in 1917, to some Flanders means the rolling hills of the south, to others the flat tree-filled emptiness of the Kempen, heavy with the scent of pines. To some it means the wide sandy beaches of the coast, littered with buckets and spades, the comfortable hotels and huge meals, shops packed with cream cakes and chocolates, to others, the quiet canals and winding rivers cutting up the polders. To some it means the bustle and wealth of Antwerp, or the glitter of Brussels with flood-lights picking out the delicate gables of the gild houses and town hall in the market place, to others the beautiful squares of Lier or Oudenaarde, or boat trips under the endless bridges of Bruges. Some remember Van Eyck, or Memling, others Servaes or Ensor, to some it means architecture, to others, painting. But to all

Flanders means long experience, rich historical traditions, and abundant life. It has none of the innocence and wide open spaces of new countries. Its face is marked by a long and busy life.

It is a face full of artifice. Everywhere it is marked by the works of men. To those of us used to nature untouched by human hands, empty and free to be explored, Flanders offers only one small eastern corner where sandy unfruitful soil slopes

Sophistication

gently down through heather and pines to the banks of the river Maas. Elsewhere Flanders is full of houses, farms, castles, and, above all, of towns. They are most characteristic not only of the Flemish plain, but also of the rolling hills of Brabant. They span the country like links in a chain, from Bruges, Veurne and Ypres in the west, through Kortrijk, Ghent and Oudenaarde, to Antwerp, Mechelen, Leuven and Brussels, eastwards to Turnhout, Hasselt and Tongeren. Sometimes still clothed in their medieval defences, almost always dominated by their belfries, they hold the history of Flanders in their mailed fists. Even now, when everyone is busy with supra-national organisations, with breaking down frontiers, the Fleming, while enthusiastic for all these things, feels himself above all a Gentenaar, a Bruggeling, an Antwerpenaar, a Mechelaar. He will tell you with pride of his town, and its traditions, and will feel a certain superiority in its dialect, its history, its uniqueness. What has mattered most to the Fleming has been his region, his town, or his village. Even now, in a modern state, these divisions still count for much.

England has always been England—or at least for a very long time ! This is not so simple as far as Flanders is concerned. To-day, it means the northern part of Belgium where Dutch is spoken. The other half of the Belgian state, the southern, French speaking part of the kingdom, is Wallonia. Both are ruled over by a constitutional monarchy dating back to 1831 when the throne of the new state was offered to Leopold of Saxe Coburg, uncle of Queen Victoria. The written constitution of 1831 was replaced in 1993 by a new federal one. The country's remaining unitary Parliament includes a Chamber of Representatives elected directly by the whole country by proportional representation and a Senate whose members are elected directly or indirectly by the Country. Most questions must obtain a simple majority in both houses. Changes of the constitution must have a two-thirds majority. Recent revisions have created a Flemish Region coinciding with the Dutch speaking Community. The Walloon Region which is French speaking but does not coincide with the French speaking Community (to which French speakers in Brussels belong), and a separate Brussels Region containing both the Dutch and French speakers of the capital. There are regional Parliaments and Governments responsible for educational, cultural and various specified matters including foreign relations and international treaties, for the Dutch speaking and French speaking parts of the country. There is a separate arrangement for Brussels. From 1995 onwards these regional Parliaments have been elected by their respective areas which has greatly enhanced their authority.

Flanders includes not only the Provinces of East and West Flanders, but also the Provinces of Antwerp and Limburg and the northern part of the Province of Brabant—in fact those parts of the country north of a line stretching roughly from the French frontier in the west, to just south of the town of Eupen in the east. The Belgian capital, Brussels, is a bilingual island in Brabant, just north of

Languages in Belgium

the linguistic frontier. Thus, north of the language frontier, we have one Flanders—the Flanders of the Dutch language. The official language in this part of Belgium is the same as that of the Kingdom of the Netherlands. One dictionary is common to both. There are some peculiarities, largely caused by Flanders's closeness to France, and in addition, many distinct dialects. These are not, on the whole, written, except in the sense in which a Scots accent can be imitated in print. They differ strongly from district to district and a really dyed-in-the-wool inhabitant of the town speaking his own dialect, might disclaim any understanding of that spoken in the surrounding countryside. These dialects are colourful and rich and woe-betide any foreigner attempting to speak them. The Fleming, charmingly tolerant of innumerable mistakes made by a foreigner attempting to speak Dutch, will go off into uncontrollable giggles at the same person trying to imitate his dialect. The Fleming feels strongly about his language. His history explains this. For a long time he has had to defend it. To someone coming from a unilingual country, or one in which the vast majority speak one language, it is difficult to understand this susceptibility. It is, to us, so usual to be understood by everyone, at least in our own country, that it is difficult to imagine a situation in which we are not always understood speaking our own language in the capital of our own country. Yet this can happen in Brussels to a Fleming. One may, quite wrongly, get the impression that every Fleming could speak French if only he would. This is quite untrue. In country areas his French is often not much better than that of the average Englishman ! Yet he is used to having to do his best, and there is a refreshing lack of embarrassment about using *any* language.

The Fleming, unaffected by the stupifying shyness which descends on so many of us when faced by having to speak a foreign language, always 'has a go'. He has

The Kempen in Limburg.

The Meuse in Stokkem (Dilsen).

heard, if not spoken, more than one language all his life. He is aware that Dutch is a minor language and that if he wants to widen his contacts, especially in the scientific fields, he must speak and publish in a world language as well

The Fleming 'has a go'

as in his own. He is delighted to get a chance to practise one of the world languages and will grasp any opportunity to do so, but is understandably cross when it is assumed that he has no particular attachment to his mother tongue and really no right to use it. Some Flemings prefer to speak French. This has historical roots. It complicates the issue not only for the foreigner but for the Flemings themselves. This group is Flemish by birth, and often resident in Flanders, but belongs to noble, business or financial circles among whom a process of frenchification had already begun in the eighteenth century. Most educated Flemings are bilingual, but it is a mistake to think that they do not mind which language they speak.

North of the Dutch frontier, everyone speaks Dutch! A good question to put to the Fleming may seem therefore: 'If you speak the same language as your northern neighbours, and you have aggravating and

Going north, going south

occasionally explosive, differences with your Walloon compatriots, why not join the Dutch? Why not become part of the Kingdom of the Netherlands?' Such an opinion, expressed in all innocence, is likely to provoke derisive comment. Very few Flemings want to become citizens of the Netherlands. They prefer to form the majority in a federal state, rather than to occupy a small corner of the Dutch kingdom which would look upon them also with limited enthusiasm. The Walloons, also, except for a few fanatics who mourn Wellington's victory over Napoleon at Waterloo, prefer to play an important rôle as half of Belgium, rather than to become the ninety-first French *département*. Here history and experience tell. From time to time during the Middle Ages and for a most trying time under the Revolutionaries and Napoleon, the southern Netherlands discovered what is was like to be ruled from Paris, and to be pushed, whether they liked it or not, into the French mould. It is one thing to enjoy French fashions, use the French language and dabble in French philosophy, but quite another to see all the best jobs go to officials from Paris, and to have one's sons killed for French glory in Russia. This the Low Countries discovered painfully, by experience.

The Flemings also found out from 1815 to 1830 what union with the Kingdom of the Netherlands meant. They enjoyed the experience so little that they revolted against King William I, and, with the Walloons, set up the independent state of Belgium. The Fleming no more wants to be ruled from The Hague than the Walloon from Paris. Too much has happened between the end of the sixteenth century when the northern Netherlands broke away from the southern and created their own state. Not only do basic things differ, like history and religion, but details too. Although relations between Flanders and the Netherlands are often excellent, to the Dutchman, the Fleming is showy, wasteful and irresponsible. To the Fleming, the Dutchman is pompous, too well organised, and above all, too obedient to the state. To many Dutchmen the state is a friend, to the Fleming, if not an enemy, it is at least something to be avoided as much as possible. This again has historical roots. From the end of the sixteenth century, when the Dutch fought off the Spaniards and became independent, they had their own state, built up their own institutions, fought their own battles, spent their own taxes, worked for their own prosperity. Just the opposite happened in the south. It passed from one foreign hand to another. It was not *occupied,* except from time to time, but the central government was for the most part in foreign hands, first Spanish, then Austrian, then French, then Dutch. This strengthened the regionalism of the south, and made the Belgian on the defensive where the central government is concerned. He avoids, if humanly possible, contact with authority. This applies just as much to the police as to the tax collector. Whenever and wherever the Belgian can outwit authority, he is in honour bound to do so. When roads are barred because work is in progress, the Belgian creeps past the notice; when waiting for the tram he really prefers to fight his way on to it than to wait in a queue. He is contemptuous of discipline and enjoys thwarting and getting round it.

A running battle His reaction is not to run for the police when there is a traffic jam, but to run away from them. Tax evasion is a national sport. Every one is involved to some extent in a running battle with authority on all levels—and this is the source of many of the better Flemish jokes. This national characteristic must have been strengthened by innumerable invasions. The Belgian has become used to having to fend for himself when authority is either non-existent or actively hostile. Many people are, therefore, cynical about international agreements, quick to look out for their own provisions, ready to turn up their coat collars to weather yet another storm. These are the reactions of a people who knows only too well what invasion is like, and who have lived always between powerful and aggressive neighbours who preferred to fight things out in the Low Countries rather than on their own soil. It makes the Belgian expect defeat, which only the closest human relationships, not the edicts of government, can do anything to assuage. Reynard the Fox, who lived just across the present northern frontier in the woods of Hulst, who teased and triumphed over King Noble, the stupidest ruler imaginable, is quick, cunning, lewd and vulgar. He ties King Noble and his ministers in knots, by his intelligence, his light hearted contempt for authority—which, it must be said, deserves nothing better. He, like Till Eulenspiegel, is typical of Flanders.

Difficulties between Flanders and Wallonia have led to federalism. Both communities now enjoy a high degree of independence from each other although certain powers still reside in the central government. The recent vigorous economic growth in Flanders caused alarm in Wallonia while some Flemings object to the imbalance of a social security system which favours Wallonia. Flanders' own newly won place at the fore-front of European technological advance has given the necessary confidence to cope with problems inherent in the traditional position of Brussels.

The Belgian 'Establishment'

The Fleming has not any particular affection for the central government, nor for the country's capital, Brussels. This too has historical roots. Although a Flemish town, Brussels has undergone a period of frenchification, which began in the eighteenth century and was accelerated by the period of French rule from 1794 to 1814. The Revolution of 1830 was organised and its harvest reaped, exclusively by the upper class, which was French speaking throughout the whole country, including Flanders. The economic crisis of the eighteen forties pulled the latter even further behind, and gradually Brussels became increasingly divorced from the majority of the Flemish population. Flanders was therefore not only misunderstood abroad, but even in Belgium itself.

The Catholic church played a vital role in the history of the Low Countries and was responsible in the nineteenth century to a certain degree for the solidity of Flemish society. There are a few small non-Catholic religious groups and the secular clergy of all denominations is paid by the state. The power of the church has diminished in recent years from the days when it went, in the Middle Ages, so far as to fabricate saints of its own, as did the monks of St. Baaf's Abbey in Ghent, when they felt themselves outdone in the possession of saintly relics by a rival abbey. Nowadays the saints are treated in Flanders with familiar affection. St. Anthony, finder of lost objects, peers out from a corner of every village church, often surrounded by wax moulds of the objects retrieved, St. Apollonia with a patient smile and a tooth in her hand comforts many a soul in agony, St. Godelieve helps to cure sore throats, St. Rita comforts expectant mothers, and

The Sint-Karel wind-mill in the classified Moeren landscape (Houtem parish).

The fourteenth century Maagdentower in Zichem.

St. Macharius guards Flanders against the plague. All through Flanders at the

Saints on guard corners of pastures, on barn walls, at cross roads, beside streams, stand little chapels, occupied by Crucifixes and bright painted Madonnas. On All Souls' Day churchyards are alight with chrysanthemums, as families vie with each other in honouring their dead. The countryside is scattered with big ugly nineteenth century churches put up when the old medieval ones became too small and were pulled down. Children, whose families may have no interest in the life of the church are nevertheless baptised 'just in case', make their first communion when they are seven, and their solemn communion when they are twelve, to the accompaniment of family festivities, presents, new clothes and so much excitement.

Weddings and burials still belong to the church. There is, in Flanders, a home-spun devotion, a lack of histrionics, an almost earthy intimacy with the church and her seasons and festivities. Flemish missionaries have worked all over the world. In the seventeenth century they were already at work in China, but most of their efforts have been devoted to the Congo. It often provided scope for enterprising people who found no outlet in Flanders itself. Even after the independence of Zaïre in 1960, many Flemings continued to work there in schools and hospitals, often in very dangerous circumstances. The Counter-Reformation has cut up many Gothic naves in Flanders with its black and white marble altar screens and its Marian devotions, but the Fleming is sober, unextravagant and practical about his religion. Although he goes to watch the Penitents' Procession in Veurne, with the other tourists, in the summer, and is critical of the hierarchy, he is of a northern calm, not a mediterranean exuberance. He is basically conservative, attached to the old ways, suspicious of change. But this does not mean that the average Fleming, if there is such a thing, allows the church to control every aspect of his life. When it oversteps the mark, its interference is resented. Thus the Church is not expected to insist that a Christian should in all honesty pay his taxes, or his bus fare. This is outside its jurisdiction. To many it seems an equally important duty to avoid paying them. The church occasionally reacts as if it has forgotten that the days of its greatest glory, when it wielded wide temporal as well as spiritual power in Belgium, are

Leuven University past. This happened over the University of Leuven. It angered Catholics more than non-Catholics, because their university was involved. It showed very well that the Belgian hierarchy, liberal as its views appear abroad, sometimes still reacted in the old autocratic way at home. When the Belgian bishops, in 1966, as heads of the Catholic university of Leuven to which the Belgian state pays 90 % of the amount it spends on each of the two State universities, made an ex cathedra pronouncement about the constitution of the university which completely disregarded informed advice, indignation was so vigorous that their advice was ignored. After the division of the University and the creation of the new French speaking campus their fears were seen to be groundless. Any attempt to revive old autocratic methods is immediately resented.

The church's direct and obvious influence in politics is now strictly limited. Yet it obviously supports right rather than left-wing parties. Although the old names and tendencies—the Catholic Party, the anticlerical Liberal Party, are now old fashioned and inaccurate, Flanders still stands largely behind the conservative, Christian Social Party, while from Wallonia, comes most support for the Socialist Party.

Historical Flanders

We have looked at present-day Flanders as the Dutch speaking part of Belgium. The word has, however, also an historical meaning. It meant first the County of Flanders, in the sense of an area ruled over by a count. The kernel of this county, part of the kingdom of the Franks, which had been so terribly pounded by the Vikings, emerged in the tenth century and gradually embraced an area bounded on the east by the river Scheldt, which curls down through Belgium from France northwards towards Antwerp; and on the south by the river Authie which flows into the Atlantic just north of the Somme, Abbeville and the battlefield of Crécy. The count held his fief from the king of France. This continued to be so until the sixteenth century. By the eleventh century the counts pushed across the Scheldt into the Holy Roman Empire, and so became for this part of their territory, vassals of the Emperor. For nearly two hundred years the counts settled themselves into these territories, with varying degrees of success, strengthening their hold, donating land and treasures to abbeys and churches, fostering and guarding the groups of merchants crossing and re-crossing their lands, and encouraging them to settle at fords, and in the shelter of their castles. But more ambition and power spelled trouble with overlords, especially with the king of France, who in 1191 and 1212 acquired the area round Saint-Omer and Arras, which became the County of Artois. Just one hundred years later Lille and Douai were lost for the first time. Count Louis of Male managed to regain them, in return for the hand of his only daughter for the brother of the king of France in 1369. They were finally lost to Louis XIV in 1668. This insatiable monarch also acquired other slices of the County of Flanders in 1659 and 1678. These areas—the County of Artois including Saint-

Omer and Arras, together with Lille and Douai and Dunkirk which are known as French Flanders, are thus now parts of the French state. The end of the thirteenth and beginning of the fourteenth centuries were more than usually strenuous for the County of Flanders because they coincided with social upheavals in the towns and the reign of an unusually energetic and astute king of France, Philip the Fair. He went so far as annexing the county in 1300, but two years later, at the Battle of the Golden Spurs, near Kortrijk, his knightly army was routed and humiliated by the Flemish peasants and urban militias. The County of Flanders revived and continued in the same form and with the same boundaries until 1369 when Lille and Douai were recovered. As a result of the marriage arranged between Philip the Bold, Duke of Burgundy, brother of the French king, and Margaret of Flanders, only child of Count Louis of Male, the County of Flanders passed in 1384 into the hands of the house of Burgundy. From that moment onwards it was never again alone. It formed the biggest single state in a personal union of territories under the Dukes of Burgundy, although it never came directly under the French crown. Instead, successive dukes added to their territories until one, through an unparalleled web of dynastic alliances became, not only Duke of Brabant and Count of Flanders, Hainault and Holland, but King of Spain and Holy Roman Emperor as well. This was Charles V who abdicated in 1555. After his death his possessions in the Low Countries passed, with Spain, to his son Philip II whose religious zeal caused him not only to launch the Armada but to try subdue the depravations of the Calvinists in the Low Countries with fire and sword. The unity of the Netherlands was broken for good when Philip's general failed to crush the revolt of the northern Netherlands, which under the guidance of William the Silent, gained their independence. The southern Netherlands, including the County of Flanders were not so lucky, and encouraged by Spanish lances and religious fervour, continued to be ruled over by the Spanish Habsburgs until 1715. When the map of Europe was reorganised at the beginning of the eighteenth century after Marlborough had succeeded in curbing Louis XIV's search for glory, the southern Netherlands passed to the Austrian Habsburgs. The County of Flanders, like so much else, was finally abolished by the enthusiasts of the French Revolution, when it was annexed to France and cut up into *départements.* This was the end of the county.

But it was certainly not the end of Flanders. From then onwards the term was used first for part of the kingdom of the Netherlands and after 1830 for the northern, Dutch speaking part of the Kingdom of Belgium. Thus, even to the historian, Flanders means many things. Simplicity has never been one of its characteristics.

We recognise people by their faces. What lines and colours, expression and

Subtle complications shape, distinguish the face of Flanders ? What makes the traveller aware
that he is in Flanders and not in Germany to the east, or France to the south,
or the Kingdom of the Netherlands to the north ? Of course, the language—but
in the north this does not apply. Yet crossing the Dutch frontier marks a
difference not only in the character of the people but in the appearance of the
landscape. Although much of Flanders is flat, it does not give the same
impression of being *under* sea level, which is created in the north by the towering
dikes which criss-cross through the landscape. Brabant and southern Flanders
are even hilly, while Limburg is wooded and sandy, quite unlike the lush
waterlogged pastures of Holland. Yet in Flanders water is always close.
Penetrated by innumerable streams, rivers and canals, and edged by the sea, the
air is always moist and misty. This may be why it has a peculiar glow, why
colours possess a richness reproduced by so many Flemish painters from Van
Eyck to De Saedeleer. To cross the southern frontier into French Flanders is not
in the same way striking. The landscape is a continuation of the flat Flemish
plain, while the towns with their belfries are obviously cousins of Ghent and
Ypres. Let us follow the Belgian coast southward through Nieuwpoort and over
the river IJzer, over the polders flooded to hold back the Germans in 1914, into
French Flanders. We cross the corner where the iconoclasts launched their

Flanders in France crusade in 1566, passing like Brueghel's
'Mad Meg' northwards through Flanders
and Holland, destroying as much of their artistic, religious, heritage as they
could reach. First to Bergues, where one gigantic tower reminds us of what the
Abbey of St. Winoc must have been, and where the belfry although rebuilt, is
Flemish in inspiration, and where the charming Mont-de-Piété reminds us of
another in Ghent. Still in the old County of Flanders we can pass on to Cassel,
where General Foch directed his armies in the first World War. This strange
lonely hill, although only 175 meters high, commands the flat country round
for miles on every side, while the houses in the main street are like a historical
sketch of the different periods of Flemish architecture. From there it is only a
step to Saint-Omer, where we see the ruins of the Abbey of St. Bertin and where
the learned canon Lambert composed his great encyclopaedia, the Liber
Floridus, eight centuries ago, or, further south again, we can climb round the
medieval castle of Montreuil and marvel at the tiny river skirting its foot, where
the biggest medieval ships could sail, and further to Arras, scene of so many bloody
battles, where the counts of Flanders favoured the Abbey of St. Vaast, and where

La Grande, and La Petite Place, are examples of the purest Flemish architecture. We can cross back into Belgium, without noticing any frontier, into another area terribly scarred by war, and dotted with innumerable war cemeteries and names ominous not only for the twentieth but for earlier centuries too, through Passchendale, to Westrozebeke, where the Flemings were beaten by Charles VI of France in 1382, and through the Menin Gate, unbelievably covered with the names of the dead of the first World War, to Ypres. In 1918 all that remained was in ruin. Now rebuilt, the town shows off its medieval greatness, when its huge cloth hall hummed with the negotiations of merchants from all over Europe, and its belfry called out the militia to fight at Kortrijk. From there we can cut back to the coast with its wide sand dunes and rich farms prospering on polders regained from the sea. These skies reappear in the canvases of Constant Permeke, where the same heavy, strong fisherwomen sell shrimps and plaice on the quays in Ostend. Behind the dunes with their beaches of fine sand, dream the canals and streams which used to carry the world's commerce. Along banks lined with poplar trees, where an occasional fisherman sits hoping for eels, the huge churches of Oostkerke and Damme with their heavy square brick towers, prove that this countryside was not always so peaceful and still. Damme was the bustling port where Charles the Bold, Duke of Burgundy married in 1468,

A golden litter Margaret of York and whence she set out in a golden litter for the wedding festivities in Bruges, the town which, perhaps more than any other, distills the essence of medieval Flanders. From the belfry the carillon jingles out over the cloth hall at its foot, over the bridges and canals, lime scented squares and gabled houses. Memling's paintings still hang in the Hospital of St. John, Van Eyck's panels in the Town Museum, Michelangelo's statue stands on an altar in Our Lady's church. At the town's heart we can see where in 1127 Charles the Good was murdered in his own church, or pass through the town gates closed to imprison Maximilian, the Emperor's son in 1480. Or we can watch the Procession of the Holy Blood, when the precious relic, brought back according to legend, by Thierry, Count of Flanders, from the Holy Land, is carried through the streets accompanied by a medieval pageant. From Bruges, it is perhaps fitting to pass on to its old rival Ghent, along the canal on which the poet Southey floated in a barge which was one of the chief tourist attractions of his day, famous for its *cuisine*. Ghent is no more the town of three hundred bridges, and school children can no longer claim that they are late because the bridge was shut. Now the circular canal means that no barges chug and manoeuvre through the tiny locks and round the sharp corners of canals in the centre of the town. But while the belfry with its four Stone Men, the towers of St. Baaf's Cathedral and of the church of St. Nicholas cluster in its centre, and the counts' castle overshadows St. Veerle's

Ghent the king-maker Square, while the statue of James van Artevelde dominates the Friday Market where Edward III of England was proclaimed King of France, Ghent can never lose the atmosphere of grim strength, which made her into the greatest city north of the Alps, and a thorn in the flesh of anyone hardy enough to provoke her.

Instead of approaching from the west, along the motor way from the coast, we could also follow the mysterious windings of the river Leie from northern France through Kortrijk with its memories of a mighty Flemish victory, over its medieval bridge, through the fields of flax, with its curious smell, on to Deurle and Latem and Afsnee. Guarded by the castle of Ooidonk, this landscape inspired the modern Flemish painters who lived their carefree, jolly life among these water meadows at the beginning of this century. Or, we could enter the mighty city from the south, following the river Scheldt from France through the Flemish hills round Ronse to Oudenaarde with its newly gilded town hall, and the church of Pamele, one of the first examples of the Gothic style in the Low Countries. In Ghent the Scheldt is joined by the Leie, and becomes at long last subject to the play of the tides. After a pause to wander along the Graslei, round the counts' castle, under the belfry, or to stand before Van Eyck's Mystic Lamb in the Cathedral of St. Baafs, we could continue north-east into the Land of Waas, Ghent's medieval larder, past the castle of Laarne, with its collection of fine furniture and silver, to St. Niklaas, or Dendermonde where the river Dender flowing up from Aalst, home of Valerius de Saedeleer, joins the Scheldt. Or we could take the motor way from the coast, straight as a ruler, south-east from Ghent to Brussels, passing thus from the Flemish plain into the hills of Brabant, studded with great houses. From Egmont's home at Gaasbeek, and the landscape which inspired Brueghel, it is easy to visit the church of Our Lady at Lombeek where one of the fifteenth century carved wooden altar-pieces, which Brabant exported all over Europe, still stands. In Brussels, where the Dukes of Brabant and later the Dukes of Burgundy held court, where Philip the Good's collection of illuminated manuscripts still enriches the Royal Library we are in a city of contrasts: from its medieval centre round the great Market Place, with its series of gild houses and exquisite town hall, chef-d'oeuvre of the van Thienen

'Vanity Fair' brothers and Jan van Ruysbroek, where Becky Sharp triumphed over Amelia Sedley in the whirl of 'Vanity Fair', to Atomium, typical of the World Exhibition of 1958, and the vast concrete office blocks and buildings of the European Community, with all its international flavour, gaiety and glitter. South through the Zoniën wood, where once Philip the Good disappeared after a quarrel with his son Charles, to the battlefield of Waterloo, and names for ever linked with Napoleon and Wellington. Like everywhere in the Netherlands it is only a step further to Mechelen, seat of the archbishop. His cathedral with its huge tower built by a Keldermans, one of a family of architectural geniuses whose creations soar skywards in many Flemish cities, overshadows the home of Margaret of Austria, aunt of the Emperor Charles V, to whom he confided the government of the Netherlands when he had too much to do himself, and who made Mechelen her home and built here a charming renaissance palace. More directly eastward lies Leuven, with its lively university and splendid town hall, where Henry I, Duke of Brabant, lies buried in St. Peter's church, and two triptychs by Dirk Bouts bear witness to the quality of local painters. The fifteenth century town hall escaped the fury of the iconoclasts, as did the rich altar-screen and the jolly dancing David which dominates the church of Zoutleeuw, further eastward. By making a slight curve, we can arrive in Antwerp via Lier, the town on yet another tributary of the Scheldt, the Nete, where a beautiful eighteenth century town hall clings to a medieval belfry, and which contains one of the most charming beguinages in the Low Countries. And so to Antwerp, centre of Flemish industrial life, international port with a huge economic potential and a rich and

Rich Antwerp fascinating history, linked inextricably with the river Scheldt, whose fortunes made or marred her own. Every aspect of Flemish life is exemplified in Antwerp: its richness in the Meir lined with luxurious shops, which passes the reconstructed Bourse, copied by Sir Thomas Gresham for his Royal Exchange in the City of London; its patronage of the arts, in the house built by Peter-Paul Rubens for his young wife, Isabella Brant, and the printing works set up in the sixteenth century by the Plantijn-Moretus family, where all the most modern scientific, literary and religious works were printed, on presses which still stand; its love of architecture, in the cathedral which houses Rubens's huge canvases of the 'Crucifixion' and the 'Descent from the Cross', or the Counter-Reformation Baroque style of the church of St. Charles Borromeus; or its military crises in the old castle, or Steen, in which the southern Netherlands made their last stand against the Spanish troops and their last attacks on the Dutch troops of King William I; or its future, in the huge industrial area where factories from all over the world stand beside the docks and harbour installations. Eastwards from Antwerp comes the only heavily wooded part of Flanders, in the Kempen in the province of Limburg.

Landscape near Cassel (French-Flanders).

Here the population is less dense except in the south round the old Roman town of Tongeren. Here lie Hasselt, with its monument to the peasants who died fighting against the French revolutionaries, and Bokrijk where in a beautiful park, all sorts of old local farm buildings, mills, and smithies have been reconstructed. Here the land slopes down from the sandy plateau to the River Maas, Belgium's eastern boundary with the Kingdom of the Netherlands.

If, from all this infinite variety we must pick out the characteristics of the face of Flanders, what then must we choose ? First, perhaps, its great age—it has always been open to every influence and, except for the sad seventeenth century, in the van of many. Thus it bears traces of a long history. Next its small size: it is only 135 miles from east to west, and 45 miles from north to south—and the closeness of everything. And yet more obviously, its closely-knit, human quality. Flanders is not the place to go for wide open spaces, lonely empty landscapes where Nature is more important than Man. It has no corner unknown, no acre uncultivated, no wood without path, no stream uncharted. It is an intensely human landscape dotted with farms, villages, churches and towns, like the medieval manuscripts of which it produced so many.

The Flemish tapestry

It is chequered with cultivation, from the pointed stooks of flax, beside the soft waters of the Leie, to the fields of gigantic leaks and shining cabbages of the market gardens round the big towns, to the luscious strawberry beds near Beervelde, the rainbows of begonias and azaleas near Ghent, and the huge black grapes of the greenhouses in Hoeilaart, to the corn fields of Brabant and the meadows of the polders. Under wide, moist skies this variety emerges again in the architecture of both public and private buildings. Not only is it possible to find examples of every style from Gothic to Art-Nouveau, but private houses, too, show little tendency to become stereotyped in estates, and the Fleming prefers to indulge his own fancies even if other people find them sometimes ugly. There is a curious difference between the beauty, scale and elegance of medieval buildings in Flanders, and the occasional lack of line and taste in much modern building, decoration and furnishing. It may, perhaps, be traced to the poverty of the nineteenth century, and the relative backwardness of the early twentieth which gave little time or money for luxuries.

Of the works of man perhaps the most sophisticated are the towns. They are the chief features of the face of Flanders. They embrace the essence of her public life, as the family still embraces her private life. The Fleming still relies on his family at important moments. It includes not only parents and children, but cousins, uncles and aunts in bewildering quantities. These ties count most. It is on the family, not on the state or the Health Service or the police that one can rely with confidence. It still feels itself responsible for the well-being of its older members, for the welcoming of the new, and the good send-off of newly weds. There is a certain ritual in these relationships which softens personal miseries and avoids loneliness, in the same way in which the church's rituals try to formalise and cope with birth, marriage and death. Family closeness,

The family embrace

complemented by the innumerable religious foundations coping with the sick and the old, means that life in Flanders is still more personal and less institutionalised than elsewhere. The nuns who care for the sick, the infirm, and the orphans, have *time* in a society where that, more than anything else, is lacking. The family octopus can still sometimes be too active.

The old grip exerted on young people in their choice of studies and careers has been loosened. The number of university graduates has increased dramatically especially as far as young women are concerned. Extensively improved sports facilities and attention to all aspects of diet and physical culture is obvious in innumerable schools and universities.

The land of Cockayne

With the Fleming's gift for hard work goes great gusto and ability to enjoy himself. Chronicles are full of descriptions of gorgeous feasts, pageants, processions, and jollifications of all sorts. When Duke Philip the Good gave his great banquet in Lille in 1454, when he vowed to go on Crusade, he entertained his guests with pantomimes between the courses, and on the biggest table an enormous pasty opened to reveal an orchestra of twenty-eight players ! Brueghel's 'Village Wedding' shows that country people also enjoyed a good feast, while in his 'Land of Cockayne' things have gone too far ! He is not the only artist who paints the quarrel between Carnival and Lent, between good living and abstemiousness. Food in Flanders is often excellent, cooked with care and skill, presented with pleasure. There is no puritan guilt about enjoying a good meal and it is not something to be got through as quickly as possible, but rather to be lingered over. Flemings love parties, and are sometimes even overwhelming in their lavishness. There are some regional specialities, of which most are delicious, and often demand real skill in preparation. There is less opening of tins, and use of frozen, and quickly prepared foods, than elsewhere. Who can forget the delicious pâtisserie which fills so many shop windows ! Bakers still make their own bread and it differs from one to another, and is still a matter of choice. One of the most typical scenes in Flanders takes place on a

Sunday morning, when families visit their favourite cake shop and go home each with an interesting cake-box suspended by a string from someone's finger. Sunday is a day for fun, as well as for religion. Shops, which do not employ labour, are open. Market places are full of flowers, or birds in cages, or plants, or dogs for sale. There are football matches, cinemas are open, racing cyclists zoom round corners endangering life and limb, competitions are held to see which linnet can sing the greatest number of trills, and, above all, in the summer, it is the day of the racing pigeon. From very early in the morning, weather bulletins are issued, and announcements made on the radio as to whether the different groups have been despatched from France, or even, sometimes, from North Africa. Many a cyclist wobbles along to his favourite public house with his metre stamped with the time that his pigeon arrived home. Railway stations are full, in the summer, with wicker baskets from which a gentle cooing can be heard. This is one national sport. Another is cycling. About the time of the great continental cycle race, the Tour de France, Flemish roads are hazardous with small boys, heads down over their handlebars, dreaming of past heroes. Public houses are open all day, although nevertheless only low grade spirits can be sold. Regulations are kept to a minimum. Shop-keepers who want to work long hours can do as they like, although there is one rest day for everyone. The Fleming is not a snob. He accepts the immense diversity of life and of people, and only asks to be allowed to enjoy himself as he wishes, without feeling obliged to organise others. Always at the cross-roads of Europe, he looks on foreign habits and tastes with interest, often with admiration.

For this small land bears the imprint of every important movement which has shaped European history for a thousand years. It has responded to every stimulus, tried many systems, produced some of the greatest artists and buildings the world has ever known, experimented with institutions, undergone many set-backs, reached out towards democracy, welcomed many strangers, and carried its culture and experience to many lands. It repays attention by revealing its secrets. Only when we know how this land, this society, has been beaten out on the anvil of history can we understand its present. 'If the past were ever past there would be little use recalling it; but it lives with us in never-ending variation, as if it were a magic carpet on which we travel through the middle air. The contours of our destination were long ago woven in its fading colours and half-obliterated mazes, and the time to alter or improve them passes quickly while the landscapes of our world race by below. Our future is uncontrollable if we are unable to read our past.'[1]

[1] F. Stark, *Dust in the Lion's Paw*, London, 1961.

KINGS OF FRANCE

Charles the Bald 843-877

Jud

Louis VI 1108-1137

Philip II Augustus 1180-1223

Louis IX, Saint Louis 1226-1270

Philip IV the Fair 1285-1314

John II 1350-1364

Charles V   Philip the B
1364-1380   Duke of Burgu

COUNTS OF FLANDERS

DUKES OF BRABANT

Baldwin I Iron Arm ? - 879

Baldwin II = daughter of Alfred the Great
879-918

Baldwin V 1035-1067
|
Matilda = William I of England,
the Conqueror

Robert the Frisian 1071-1093

Robert II of Jerusalem 1093-1111

Baldwin VII 1111-1119

Charles the Good 1119-1127

Thierry of Alsace 1128-1168

Philip of Alsace 1168-1191

Baldwin VIII 1191-1194

Baldwin IX 1194-1205

Henry I
1190-1235

Ferrand   =   Joan
of Portugal   1205-1244
1212-1233

Burchard = Margaret = William
of Avesnes | 1244-1278 | of Dampierre

S   S   Guy of Dampierre
1278-1305
|
Robert of Bethune
1305-1322

John I
1267-1294

John III
1312-1355

Louis of Nevers 1322-1346

Louis of Male 1346-1384
|
Margaret of Flanders

Flandria, dulce solum, super omnes terra beata.

Petrus Pictor, c. 1100

Sweet Flanders, blessed above all lands.

The Roots

ninth century to 1384

W AS it a coincidence that Baldwin of the Iron Arm visited the northern French town of Senlis in about 862 ? Or had he perhaps seen Judith, daughter of the French king, Charles the Bald, on a previous occasion ? She, although only twenty years old, had already been twice widowed. First the bride of two Saxon kings, she had then returned across the Channel to her father's court, and was held, virtually a prisoner, in the care of the Bishop of Senlis until her father needed to seal another alliance with her hand. Any such plans were, however, to be thwarted by this Carolingian adventurer. Judith's brother, Louis, may have helped. He was at that time in Senlis. Perhaps he helped her to disguise herself for the flight from Senlis to her cousin Lothar's court in the Rhineland. There Baldwin and Judith were married and there they sheltered from the fury of Charles who forced the bishops to excommunicate the couple and demanded their extradition under the terms of an agreement he had made with his nephew about the exchange of criminals. Baldwin threatened to join the Viking pirates who were at that moment

Viking menace attacking not only England but the north-western coasts of Europe also. First, however, he and his bride rode to Rome to plead their case before the Pope, Nicholas I. For him the greatest danger was of Baldwin allying himself with the Norsemen. Judith had, after all, not been kidnapped but had eloped. The Pope preferred, therefore, to recognise the marriage and to encourage Iron Arm to return to the north and to fight against the Vikings rather than for them. Charles the Bald was thus thwarted. Against the Pope he could do nothing. His bishops withdrew their excommunication. The couple were formally married with his consent at Auxerre, in France, and returned to the north to assume control, probably still rather as officials than as rulers, over these outlying domains of the king of France, and to try to protect them from the Norsemen. This was the beginning of Flanders.

To the flat marshy land at the confluence of the rivers Leie and Scheldt, where

Ghent and Bruges

the city of Ghent was later to rise, Baldwin or his son, may have added Bruges, which was already probably a tiny settlement, the land of Waas between Ghent and the wide curve of the Scheldt to the north-east, and some lands round Saint-Omer: this is the kernel from which Flanders grew.

While Alfred in England was fighting the Danes at his brother's side, Baldwin I bought them off and enjoyed a relative lull in the continual battle with them. He died in 879, leaving two sons, and was buried in St. Peter's Abbey in Ghent, but of Judith we know nothing more, not even her place of burial.

Over what had Baldwin and Judith really attempted to rule ? The floods of the early Middle Ages, when the whole of the coastal strip between De Panne and Knokke had been inundated leaving only chains of water-ways and islands between Diksmuide and Bruges, had retreated. The land provided grazing for the great flocks of sheep owned by abbeys such as St. Baaf's and St. Peter's in Ghent, St. Vaast in Arras and St. Bertin in Saint-Omer. These lands were poor and showed no signs of the rich large farms which exploit them to-day. Such land as had not been recovered from the grey sandfilled sea, was covered by scrub and heath. The Zwin, which now shelters such a variety of seabirds, still joined Bruges to the sea. The land was so poor that it was left till the last by the Norsemen. They devastated it only at the end of their violent onslaught, when the richer and more attractive lands to the south had been exhausted. This was the inheritance of Baldwin II, the young son of Iron Arm and Judith.

When the Norsemen left finally in about 883, Baldwin II was master of

Vikings retreat

a devastated, almost depopulated, infertile land of swamps, woods and heather whose wooden churches had been razed to the ground, whose crops were unplanted or unharvested, whose cattle had been stolen or slaughtered. This flat, wet, land has begun early to fulfill its rôle as the cock-pit of Europe. However, because the French king was more than fully occupied in his own defence against the Norsemen, he did nothing to deter Baldwin's assumption of control over the land from the North Sea to Artois. Both leaders began to build rudimentary fortresses. There are still traces of the seven round defensive towers surrounded by moats, built probably at the end of the ninth century against the Viking menace, at Bourbourg, Bergues-Saint-Winoc, Veurne, Oostburg, Souburg,

Middelburg and Burgh op Schouwen. They were roughly ten miles apart and linked up with the older Roman fortifications at Oudenburg and perhaps Aardenburg. In spite of the early devastation, Iron Arm and his son, centred on Bruges, restored some semblance of peace, which enabled the peasants to till their ground once more and to strengthen the slight commercial links outside the domain. In this Baldwin II was helped by his marriage to one of the daughters of King Alfred of England, which helped his cross-channel links and

Flanders expands southwards

encouraged the nascent cloth industry of Flanders, already interested in fine English wool. His eye was also on the richer lands to the south, and he managed at one time to control the abbey of St. Vaast in Arras, Boulogne, Tournai and Saint-Omer, but the French king Charles the Simple, on this occasion belied his nick-name. Baldwin provoked him too far in attempting to gain control of Saint-Quentin, and was rebuffed by losing the abbey of St. Vaast and Artois. Baldwin did not forget that in this Charles had been supported by Fulco, Archbishop of Reims. As the Archbishop rode with his retainers through the woods of Compiègne, he was set upon and murdered by one Wenemar, a vassal of the count of Flanders.

However, by the end of Baldwin's period as count, Flanders had seen the light of day, and had acquired roughly the form it was to retain until the fifteenth century. It embraced in the south people speaking a romance dialect, where the Franks had been absorbed by the local inhabitants. Others north of a line drawn

Language frontier

roughly from Calais to Eupen retained a Germanic dialect, ancestor of the language spoken there now which is called Netherlandish or Dutch. The southern Netherlands have, thus, always been the meeting ground of Romance and Germanic culture. This line was drawn rather further south than the present language frontier, through countryside subsequently taken over by French. This language frontier never corresponded with any administrative divisions of the country or with the ecclesiastical limits of the sees of Arras-Cambrai, Noyon-Tournai and Thérouanne which covered most of the county of Flanders.

Baldwin II's successors were attracted, as he had been, by the rich rolling hills of Artois, Vermandois and Boulonais. By ruse and diplomacy, but chiefly by violence, they strove to extend Flanders towards the south. But such territory as was from time to time acquired was always subsequently lost. An alternative area for expansion lay to the east across the Scheldt and towards the north and

Between France and Germany

the islands of Zealand. By the end of the

tenth century, the old middle state of Lotharingia, part of the heritage of Charlemagne, had ceased to exist as an entity. In 925 the Scheldt became the permanent boundary between France and the Empire. The quarrel at the end of the eleventh century between Pope Gregory VII and Emperor Henry IV, over the right of investiture, which meant in fact the right to control the church, had weakened imperial power until it could no longer rely on the abbots and bishops to forward its interests and maintain its control. Gradually these lands were nibbled away on the west by the counts of Flanders, until the islands of Zealand, the marshy land to the west of the Scheldt, known as 'the Vier Ambachten' (Quatre-Métiers) and Aalst, had been given to them in fief.

There is, however, one great reservation which must be made about the power of the counts of Flanders. Their rule must be distinguished from that of the kings whose lands surrounded theirs. They were vassals of the French king, for their lands west of the Scheldt, and of the emperor, for the lands to the east of the Scheldt. Standing now on the bridge over the Scheldt in Ghent, where it washes the cellars of the mighty grey fortified house of Gerard the Devil, one foot is in the territory which was held from the Emperor, the other one, on the same side as the cathedral and belfry, in the land which was held from the king of France. This meant a division of loyalty and commitment which was to complicate the history of Flanders and bedevil its efforts at unity throughout its early history. Three Flemish counts, Robert II (1093-1111), Baldwin VII (1111-1119), and Louis of Nevers (1322-

Vassals of France

1346) were killed fighting as vassals of the French king, against kings of England who should, if economic factors had been taken into consideration, have been their allies. That the country was left relatively in peace to develop along its own lines, and to amass much treasure, arose largely from the fact that in the early years until about 1180 the French crown was too weak to interfere. But almost every one seemed to have a *right* to interfere in its affairs. Every element dissatisfied with another could, and later frequently did, appeal for help to a foreign power. With an eye on the wealth and strength of the county, foreigners were not loth to give them support. By the end of the thirteenth century, the situation had become such that frequent appeals were made from the Flemish courts to the Parliament in Paris and some Flemish towns were flying the fleur-de-lys rather than the Flemish lion from their battlements.

An exceptional line of counts

Before this, however, there had been a wonderful period of development and organization which made the county of

Cassel: a French town in Flemish style.

Flanders an example of modernity, wealth and strength. This depended essentially on the count himself. The chaos which enveloped the land after the assassination in 1127 of Charles the Good who died without heirs, shows that there was really no administration independent of the count's person. Then there was a power void. But no such void had been apparent under the descendants of Iron Arm. He was perhaps little more than a legendary figure, but his descendants were, many of them, exceptional men. Baldwin V, father-in-law of William the Conqueror, so outmatched the other vassals of the French king that he was chosen as guardian of the young French prince; Robert the Frisian, the contemporary of William the Conqueror, maintained diplomatic relations as far north as Denmark, to whose king he gave one of his daughters in marriage, and as far south as Constantinople. Alexis Comnenus, ruler of the Byzantine empire, who received him on his way to visit the Holy Land, so admired his knights that he asked for a contingent to be sent to Constantinople. These he received from Robert. Robert's son, Robert II, took part in the First Crusade, as the most powerful feudal prince, and came back covered in glory and laden with holy relics. The death of Iron Arm's last direct descendant, Baldwin VII, in 1119, and the accession of Charles the Good, meant the end of Flanders' almost unbridled extension of power. After his death, the French suzerains made increasingly determined efforts to interfere directly in the county's affairs.

Brabant and Hainaut

Brabant and Hainaut developed in the same way as Flanders but emerged rather later. Before the last quarter of the eleventh century, there was little other than tradition about their history. Brabant, like Flanders contained some romance dialects, south of Brussels, and Germanic further north. Round its heart, Leuven, there gradually crystallized what was later to be the Netherlands.

The riches of Flanders

At this period, the best investment for a prince was undoubtedly land. The counts of Flanders had rather greater personal estates than many feudal princes, because after the Norse invasions, when the country was in a state of complete confusion, they acquired many of the acres which had previously belonged to the great abbeys; to this was added all that was regained from the sea. With these lands and their own personal domains, the Flemish princes were well endowed. With peace restored, and the land brought back under the plough, shipments of English wool floating in barges down the willow-lined rivers, to the nascent cloth industry in the young towns, meant income for the count. With corn, cattle, poultry, eggs, services, cloth, tolls and aids, his coffers and granaries were refilled and his chances of administering his country strengthened. The counts of Flanders had, by the twelfth century, amassed a huge fortune. Galbert of Bruges, who describes the death of Count Charles the Good in 1127, constantly reverts to the importance of his treasure, and the tremendous efforts made by everyone, plotters and friends alike, to recover it. In peace time, the wonderful central position of Flanders, between Germany, France and England, which constantly proved so dangerous in war, could be exploited. By about 1100, the groups of merchants huddled beneath the count's castles were already artificially improving communications and, thereby, trade. In these years in Ghent, they dug the first canal to join the rivers Leie and Scheldt, the Ketelvest, which once carried huge barges laden with coal, oil, or bricks from Antwerp to Northern France.

Brussels and Leuven, the chief towns of Brabant, began their development rather later, but in Flanders by 1100 Ghent covered about 160 acres, Bruges about 140, and Leuven about 120 acres.

Ghent was never completely encompassed by walls. Surrounded by marshes and water-ways, it relied for its defence on the manipulation of water levels—a plan followed successfully in Nieuwpoort as recently as 1914, when it prevented the advance of the German divisions to the Channel ports, and Cogghe showed himself the true descendant of lock-keepers of Bruges and Ghent, who could thwart each other and the king of France by a timely opening or closing of their sluices. By the twelfth century, Arras, Saint-Omer, Lille, Ghent, Douai, Ypres and Bruges in Flanders, and to a slightly lesser extent Leuven and Brussels in Brabant, had a rich and thriving cloth industry, founded on the English wool which was as yet exported rather than woven at home. Vast new markets were opening up to the Flemish merchants in northern and western Germany and England. By the end of the thirteenth century, Ghent was the biggest producer of cloth in western Europe. Arras had been lost, with the rest of Artois in 1191. Bruges had always relied less on industry than on commerce; but Ghent and to

A land of towns a lesser extent the other Flemish and Brabant towns, were weaving, dyeing and finishing not only ordinary cloth but also luxury velvets and tapestries for the gorgeous costumes and hangings of royal courts. Ghent could already look back then to a long history of trade. The Fair of St. Baafs was certainly held as far back as 1013, and probably earlier. From the wealth brought in by all this activity the count was the first to profit. No other state on the continent was as solidly based by the twelfth century as Flanders. At its head the count; next the great vassals, of whom many were the rich abbeys whose power was usually supported by him

The late gothic town-hall of Leuven.

as a valuable counter-weight to the more unruly barons. Through them much of the administration was carried on. East of the Scheldt, the abbeys and bishoprics which had exerted enormous power, and through which the emperor had ruled, had also been so influenced by the monastic reforms radiating from Cluny, that the imperial grip had been loosened.

By the middle of the eleventh century the middle states of Upper and Lower Lotharingia, fruit of the division of Charlemagne's inheritance at Verdun in 843, had ceased to exist. The emperor ruled these lands east of the Scheldt either through bishops, to whose spiritual power he added temporal jurisdiction,

Renier with the Long Neck

or through lay vassals, such as Renier with the Long Neck, from whom eventually the ruling families of Hainaut and Brabant were descended. When the Cluniac reforms, which disputed the right of lay interference in ecclesiastical affairs, and the investiture controversy, which denied to the emperor the right of nominating bishops and clergy in general, had gradually undermined such control as the emperor exercised east of the Scheldt, the piecemeal division of Lotharingia followed. There independent ecclesiastical or secular princedoms, such as Utrecht, Cambrai and Liège on the one hand and the counties of Loon, Leuven and Hainaut, on the other developed. The county of Leuven later became Brabant, largely in the Dutch speaking half of Belgium, Hainaut's count became the vassal of the prince-bishop of Liège and the county of Loon, now the province of Limburg, was held also from him and his descendants.

In Flanders west of the Scheldt, the Cluniac reforms took rather longer to appear, but many Cistercian foundations helped in the reclamation of the

Ter Duinen and Ter Doest

polders, the land gradually regained from the sea. We can visit the remains of one of these abbeys, Ter Duinen, near Koksijde and of another, the huge brick-built barn with its wonderful wooden beams at Lissewege, where the monks of the abbey of Ter Doest guarded their corn and sheep, as the farmer still does to-day.

Even at this early date, cultural life in Flanders was, like its political life, a mixture of Germanic and Romance elements. The two languages existed side by side. Eminent figures, both lay and ecclesiastical, could often speak both. Such facility made the Flemings particularly suitable to play a leading part in such an international enterprise as the crusades. According to some chroniclers Godfrey of Bouillon was chosen as leader because he could understand and speak to both the French and German contingents. Such fluency still characterises many Flemings in their dealings with foreigners.

It is difficult to get the feel of this early period of Flemish history. Later there is such a wealth of pictures and buildings of all sorts that we can get an idea of the

Churches and castles

people who painted them or commissioned and admired them. From this early, grimmer age, very little remains. Most churches were in wood: sometimes, as with the church of St. John (now St. Baaf's Cathedral) in Ghent, a rich merchant, Lausus, replaced the wooden structure with a stone church, more fitting for the worship of such a rich community. But, later, this also was too small and old-fashioned and was in its turn pulled down, although part of the present crypt probably belongs to the later twelfth century building. The same is true of the crypt of St. Hermes' church in Ronse. The lowest floor of the keep of the counts' castle in Ghent also reveals its early heaviness and solidity, but not a vestige of the castle in Bruges remains. There are a few manuscript illuminations and one great work of art by a canon of Saint-Omer, Lambert, still to be seen in its original manuscript in the library of the University of Ghent: this early encyclopaedia, called the Liber Floridus, covers all branches of knowledge—theology, botany, history, geography and also some splendid illustrations of beasts, such as a lion which still glares out fiercely from a startlingly fantastic face.

Through the great abbeys the counts could exert their authority. They also had large personal estates. But to keep order and police their whole county was an endless struggle. They tried by constantly moving about, to keep a personal hand on everything. Their court moved with them from one castle to another, from Oudenaarde to Bruges, from Ghent to Saint-Omer; formal sittings of the count's court were usually held at Christmas, Whitsuntide and Easter and sometimes on All Saints' Day. Everything depended on the count himself. He must have had extraordinary physical strength: even to lift his sword is an effort for us, quite apart from the strength needed to hit someone with it. To live in his high damp stone castles would leave us with pneumonia. To eat the huge meals and drink the tankards of wine and beer with which he regaled his followers would be just as impossible, as to exist on the incredibly meagre diet of the poor. There was no civil service, no permanent administration, although the count had a chancellor by the end of the eleventh century and his entourage fulfilled various other administrative tasks, but he was himself responsible for the government of his county and the maintenance of law and order.

Knights boiled and hanged

Baldwin VII, the count before Charles the Good,

showed his strength by boiling, in a kettle, a knight in full armour, because he had stolen two cows from a poor peasant; he also showed his ingenuity by forcing nine out of ten knights, who had disturbed the peace during the Fair in Torhout, to hang one another in succession; the fate of the tenth he arranged personally, by himself kicking away the stool on which the knight was standing with the noose about his neck.

One great factor in keeping order was the devoutness of the population. This was a time of signs and portents, of miracles and sacred relics. The counts used

Saints and relics

these to reinforce their efforts to keep the peace. Count Baldwin V, for example, in conjunction with Drogo, bishop of Thérouanne, proclaimed the truce of God, by which all persons were forbidden to resort to violence between Wednesday night and Monday dawn—the mind boggles at what must have happened on the other three days. Gradually the count's peace took the place of the truce of God. To help him to enforce it, however, the count still resorted to divine help. The bones of St. Ursmar were carried through Flanders and the inhabitants of Oostburg in Zealand, who had been in such a state of feud that they did not dare to leave their homes, were induced to throw away their arms and exchange the kiss of peace. It was estimated that St. Arnulf had saved ten thousand marks of silver by his prayers, which would otherwise have had to be paid in composing quarrels. During the uproar which filled Bruges after the murder of Charles the Good in 1127, both the traitors and their enemies stopped fighting so that the relics of the local patron saints could be removed from their highly dangerous position in the church. Even today, Flanders is dotted with wayside shrines, while until recently processions of children left parish churches on the feast of Corpus Christi.

For its time, Flanders was modern, well governed, rich and influential but it

Charles the Good murdered

depended for its stability, essentially on the personal qualities of the counts themselves. To such a society the murder, in 1127, of Count Charles the Good in his own castle-church of St. Donatian in Bruges, as he prayed and distributed alms, was therefore a more traumatic experience than many other political murders have been. It was doubly disastrous for Flanders because the count had no children and had made no provision for the succession. Standing in the Burgplaats in Bruges, we can see laid in cobbles, the ground plan of the church in which the murder took place. In this church's tower, the count's murderers barricaded themselves in with the church furniture tied together with the bell ropes. They were besieged by the barons and the citizens of Bruges, and only gave themselves up when the tower threatened to collapse under the onslaught of a battering ram. The Burgplaats encompasses what previously contained the count's castle, in which were built his church, house, the castellan's house, chapter house and provost's dwelling. It was the heart of the county. Here the provost and his clan plotted and carried out the murder. Galbert, a notary employed at the time at the count's court, recorded day by day the confusion and violence, fear and bewilderment which attacked the town and spread throughout the county, as the plotters gradually lost control of the situation and were hunted down by the barons and citizens whom they had hoped to bribe and terrorize into submission. Charles was murdered because he was hated by the clan of his chancellor, the Erembalds. His distrust of their overwheening pride and power had led him to question their free status. Threatened at the summit of their power, they struck at the count who had proved himself in fact, good for his country. His fifteenth century portrait, probably restored in the eighteenth, now hangs in St. Salvator's Cathedral, in Bruges. He had dealt with the dangerous shortages of food caused by the famine of 1125; had distributed alms from his personal fortune; had taken measures against hoarders; had persuaded merchants to store food rather than wine—in fact had proved himself a father to his people. Yet when he was murdered it became apparent that many of those who appeared to be his friends were, in reality, ready to help the conspirators, to search for his treasure, to murder his supporters, and to steal his body. We can stand on the place in Bruges where the abbot of St. Peter's Abbey in Ghent tried surreptitiously to load the count's body, roughly wrapped in a sheet, onto an improvised litter to carry it secretly

Canons fight for his body

back to Ghent, where it too would have provided a wonderful attraction for pilgrims, and in consequence a source of revenue for his abbey. He failed because the canons of St. Donatian's defended their count's body with the candlesticks and benches which they snatched from the church. Seven weeks later, the last conspirators, besieged in the tower of St. Donatian, slid down the ropes hanging from its windows to give themselves up. Once again Flanders was in jeopardy because Charles had no direct heir and had nominated no successor. The king of France, as sovereign and direct lord of the Flemish barons when they had no count, lost no time in exerting his right to interfere in Flemish affairs. He could enjoy one of the first nibbles which from time to

The heavy hand of France

time he was to take from the rich banquet laid out at his door: the moment to take a large bite had yet to come. He had the right to

Bergues Saint-Winoc, French-Flanders.

nominate the count's successor. For the first time a French king penetrated right to the heart of Flanders—to Bruges. There were at least five contestants for the title. From them King Louis VI chose William of Normandy, William Clito, sworn enemy of his uncle Henry I of England, and as such not a very attractive choice for a country which was already beginning to feel that its interests lay rather with its wool producing neighbour across the Channel than with the territorial ambitions of the house of Capet. The Flemish barons accepted the king's choice. He was after all their suzerain. They were interested more in the feudal pattern than in the mushroom growth of urban society.

The towns, sensing for the first time the possibility of political as well as economic power, had no faith in the king's nominee and gradually transferred

Success of towns' candidate

their allegiance to another contender, Thierry of Alsace. That with them lay the future power in Flanders, rather than with the feudal barons, became apparent at the moment that they forced their choice on King Louis.

Flanders was showing itself to be essentially a land of towns. Unlike the rest of western Europe, Flanders, like northern Italy, was beginning to exploit her position at the crossing of the highway from the Rhine with the barge filled rivers of northern France and Holland, as well as with the barks crossing the Channel from England. None of the great Flemish towns is a Roman foundation. All are medieval. Although now tamed they still rise like lions from the plains of the Leie and the Scheldt. And in the house of Alsace they had found a worthy champion. What they needed in their count was someone who would recognise their possibilities and give them the peace and order to transact their business, a currency solid enough to bear an increasingly complicated commercial structure, and who would realize that the future lay not in the squabbles of the feudal barons but in the commercial might of the towns. William Clito had made them extravagant promises, but had shown that he attached no importance to them, and once firmly established as count would throw them over. They therefore opened their gates to Thierry and their faith in him was not abused. The house of Alsace owed the county not to the king of France but to the towns of Flanders. This it never forgot.

Thierry and Philip of Alsace

In 1128, Thierry began, as his son Philip was to continue, the restoration of order and the encouragement of the towns. Privileges, such as freedom from various tolls and duties did not have to be wrested from him, but were rather, freely given. No favouritism marred this generosity. Bruges, Ghent and Ypres received the same type of privilege as Arras, Lille and Douai. Arras, in the mid-twelfth century, was probably the most prosperous, as the seat of the mint, and was a model for the others. Ypres' great wool hall and belfry were begun about the year 1200, and show the magnificence and wealth of this period. They were rebuilt after their destruction in the first World War. The towns of Brabant, also supported by their dukes, developed only somewhat later and, in spite of their great prosperity, never had the political pretensions of the towns further west. Within the towns, the merchants and workers were beginning to organise themselves. By the thirteenth century quality, quantity, apprenticeship, and price were not left to chance, but were stringently controlled by the gilds: of merchant gild regulations the first of which we are certain, from Saint-Omer, come from as early as the eleventh century. Parish churches, cloth halls, belfries, began to testify to civic pride and wealth. The first stone church on the site of the present cathedral of St. Baaf's in Ghent replaced the older wooden one, stone being more fitting for the place in which the rich citizens of the town were to worship. St. James's Church in Leuven received its tower about 1225 and the huge church of Dudzele, now in ruin, was built in the twelfth century. Of the belfries which still tower over the Flemish towns, the two lower rectangular floors of that of Bruges, the little watch-towers, and most of the external brick walls of the halls at its foot had already been standing for forty years when the upper wooden tower (which was only to be constructed in stone in the fifteenth century), caught fire in 1280 and its bell fell through to the chambers beneath (and reduced the town's charters to cinders). In the Gruuthusemuseum in Bruges we

Bruges' belfry ablaze can still see one of the coffers with its seven locks in which the town's archives were kept safe. Earlier on, the coffer must have been further protected in special niches, in the belfry, by means of thirteenth century cast iron doors. In Bruges the tower still rises over the quiet, swan haunted canals and cobbled quays; then, the banks of its waterways were cluttered with cranes, littered with bales of merchandise, resounding, as they still do with many different tongues—merchants from Lombardy and Champagne, from Frisia and East Anglia, from Aix-la-Chapelle and Genoa. In 1198, we hear for the first time of wine from Bordeaux appearing beside Rhine wine in Flanders—a tradition which was to last a long time. The bells which now entertain the tourist with folk tunes, in those days sounded the hours and brought out the citizens, to defend their rights against the aggression of a king, a count or a neighbour. When a furious Charles V punished the town of Ghent for its revolt against him in the middle of the sixteenth century, he ordered that the bell Roland should be removed from the belfry. It bore the inscription:

> *'Mijn naem is Roelant*
> *Als ik kleppe dan is't brand*
> *Als ik luyde, is't storm in Vlaanderland !'*

which means that when Roland tolled there was storm in Flemish lands.

On the Graslei in Ghent, the Staple House where merchandise waited transhipment by the boatmen of the town is still reflected in the quiet Leie— its dark-grey, hard stones from Tournai were first mirrored there around 1200. At about this time also, the merchants and craftsmen no longer depended for their defence on retreat into the counts' castle, at the approach of danger, because they were already too numerous and their possessions too bulky and valuable. Instead, they surrounded their settlements with walls: in Leuven some of this first twelfth century wall still remains, in Antwerp there is also a small remnant, while in Brussels the lower half of the Black Tower in St. Catherine's Place is part of the first wall.

Town walls In Bruges the first wall was replaced at the end of the thirteenth century by new walls of such extent that the ground inside was not used up until the end of the nineteenth century; four of the contemporary gates still exist, although they have been reconstructed. In all this activity and development, the counts were at this time invariably the allies and supporters of the towns. They provided peace and good administration. Philip (1168-1191), Thierry's son and successor, reformed the criminal and fiscal law as well as creating an entirely new official, the bailiff, capable of much greater efficiency than the often unruly baronage had provided.

Tournaments and crusades For Thierry, Philip, and their immediate circle, all this practical activity took place against a background of knightly tournaments and crusading zeal. Their lives were dominated by the quest for the holy grail written about by Christian of Troyes, by the desire to die serving in the Holy Land in order to free the home of Our Lord from the hands of the infidel. Thierry went to Palestine four times. On the third occasion his wife, Philip's mother, accompanied him and remained there in the east. Philip himself went twice, and on the second occasion died in the siege of Acre in 1191. His mighty castle, in Ghent, has the cross of a crusader above its main entrance.

At home an atmosphere of the troubadours and patronage of poets, although not yet on the same scale as it was later to assume under the dukes of Burgundy, nevertheless attained an unequalled standard of culture for the period. Philip

The three towers of Ghent: St. Nicholas, the belfry and St. Baaf's cathedral.

was the patron of the poet, Christian of Troyes, who wrote of him:

> *'Qu'il le fet por le plus prodome*
> *Qui soit an l'Empire de Rome*
> *C'est li cuens Phelipes de Flandres*
> *Qui mialz valt ne fist Alixandres'*

'For he was the noblest prince in Christendom and worth more than Alexander'. Philip had, nevertheless, a very practical streak of character which stood the towns in good stead. In spite of his crusading zeal he was not averse from taking back some of the land which he had earlier donated to the church in order to establish upon it the town of Nieuwpoort on the river IJzer; he founded also Gravelines on the Aa, Biervliet and Damme. The latter were intended to support the growing trade of Bruges and to act as ports for the Flemish navy. The huge church in Damme gives some idea of what the town must have been like during its prosperity. The present town hall is now only half the size of the previous one. The canal linking Veurne to Diksmuide and the IJzer, which he built, opened up the sea for the west of the county, while the markets of Duisburg and Aix-la-Chapelle, were persuaded to open their gates to Flemish merchants. Gradually Philip brought the smaller territorial units under his direct control; and therefore reduced the number of troublesome barons who could claim independence from law and order. His domains were very large. From his wife, Elizabeth, he had gained control over Vermandois and the powerful towns of Amiens, Péronne and Saint-Quentin. The county stretched from the North Sea to near the walls of Paris, and from beyond the Scheldt to the Channel. It was the greatest area over which a Flemish count ever held sway.

Flemish rule from the North Sea to Paris

This, Philip Augustus, King of France, could not bear. He had, as a minor, been under the control of his most mighty vassal, the count of Flanders, but, once free of this tutelage, he put in hand the policy of subduing his northern neighbour, which he was to continue throughout his reign. Philip Augustus was no mean foe. He beat a king of England, John, in 1214 at Bouvines. Before that he had taken Normandy from England.

Philip Augustus turns against his tutor

Against his might, skill, determination and resources, the count could not, even with the support of his loyal towns, maintain his position. For he too had no heir. His marriage to Elizabeth of Vermandois, who had brought him such a rich inheritance, was childless. On her death, her lands should have been returned to her sister. This the count refused until he was forced to do so by Philip

Augustus. The count having sat, with his army, for three weeks face to face with his suzerain, suddenly gave way without striking a blow. Never averse from increasing any influence which he might have in France, Philip had, in his successful days, arranged the marriage of the young French king with his niece, Isabelle of Hainaut. Her dowry was expensive. It consisted of Artois. Thus in 1191 when Philip died miserably of fever before Acre, control over Vermandois and Artois fell to Philip Augustus. Even the splendid towns could not maintain such a structure in face of the power of France. Philip Augustus had already bared his teeth before the death of Philip of Alsace. His aim seems to have been to swallow Flanders completely, as he was already doing with other fiefs of the French crown. The death of the count of Flanders before Acre seemed to present

Death before Acre

the tasty morsel to him on a platter. But he was not quite quick enough. As usual, the Italian towns, always at the forefront of the crusading business, received the news first. And the faithful retainer of Baldwin V, Count of Hainaut, who was count of Flanders as Baldwin VIII, Gislebert of Mons, got hold of the news and transmitted it to his master. Baldwin beat Philip Augustus to it in the occupation of the county to which he was heir. But, although he had obtained possession, it was clear that the new count must have help against his threatening suzerain.

Richard the Lion Heart

The obvious ally was England, supplier of wool and enemy of France. Richard the Lion Heart may have been less astute than the king of France, but as well as being one of the foremost clients of Flemish bankers and money lenders, he had the enormous Plantagenet inheritance in France with which to harass his powerful enemy. Unfortunately for Flanders however, he was not alone in his crusading preoccupations. Baldwin IX of Flanders, infected by the prevalent crusading epidemic, left his county, alledgedly for three years. His success in winning the lottery for the crown of Constantinople, which the crusades had chosen to attack, rather than their more obvious enemy, the infidel, meant a more prolonged stay than he had contemplated. He did not, in fact, ever return. In a bloody battle near Adrianople in 1205 he fell victim to the Bulgars. For years his people waited hopefully for his return, and certain impostors had some success, but the county lay really at the mercy of Philip Augustus. For, not only had Baldwin disappeared, but his wife followed him to

Baldwin of Flanders rules in Constantinople

the east and died there in her turn. Two small daughters remained— a golden opportunity for the wily

The gothic town-hall of Bruges (1376-1420).

old fox of France. It looked as if he were going to achieve his aim without violence. He was aided and abetted by the regent of Flanders, who delivered the two little girls into his hands. Later the latter was said to have regretted this step, and to have begged the monks of the abbey where he lay dying to drag him through the streets by a rope tied round his neck to die like a dog, as he had lived like one. By that time however, it was too late. Joan and Margaret of Flanders were brought up at the court of the French king until such time as he should arrange marriages for them which would satisfy his aims in Flanders.

In Ferrand of Portugal, king Philip seemed to have found the ideal match for Joan. A stranger to Flanders with no following there, it seemed unlikely that he would branch out on an independent policy inimical to France. Philip, therefore, saw him depart after his marriage in Paris to Joan, with a calm, even

Philip's marriage plots

triumphant, mind. It looked as if this time Flanders was going to be totally swallowed by the insatiable Augustus. A moment of very uneasy balance had been reached in relations between Flanders and France. Under the house of Alsace, Flanders had been, on the whole, the dominant partner: then a period of balance, and then one of increasing aggression and interference in Flemish affairs, which would only be beaten off by the 'goeden dag's' of the Flemish town militias at Kortrijk in 1302.

But the French overdid it. Ferrand found a French prince in possession of two of his southern-most towns. His barons had been got at with French gold; they

French gold

were beginning to form the pro-French party which was to bedevil the political structure of Flanders throughout the thirteenth century. There was, however, one ray of light. John, king of England also had every reason to dislike Philip Augustus, and was also busy buying himself a following in the Low Countries. It seemed a chance worth taking. Ferrand threw in his lot with John and his well endowed agents. He

Sack of Damme and Bruges

defied Philip. But he was dreadfully punished. What followed was the invasion of Flanders, the sack of Damme and Bruges and flight to the island of Walcheren. Mercifully, the English fleet sank the French pay ships in the mouth of the Zwin, and Philip had to return home in search of more silver. But it was only a momentary respite. In 1214, at Bouvines, Philip revealed how puny the efforts of his adversaries really were. He defeated a coalition of the Emperor, the Count of Flanders and the King of England in the first of the series of international battles—Oudenaarde, Waterloo, Passchendale—to be decided with such devastating frequency on Flemish soil. Ferrand returned to Paris, this time a prisoner. The day when Philip of Alsace had boasted that he would plant his standard on the bridge over the Seine, seemed a terribly long time ago.

Flanders' punishment was terrible. Hostages taken, town fortifications destroyed, French sympathizers given all the best positions. French domination in the country seemed complete. Brabant seemed to be similarly ruined. But her

Schemes of Henry of Brabant

Duke Henry I was so devious, so unscrupulous in changing sides, too set on one purpose and one purpose alone—the consolidation of his lands and the control of the valuable trade routes between Flanders and the Rhine,—that he managed on the whole to wriggle out of the consequences of his unfortunate alliance. No wonder he looks rather self satisfied as he lies on his tomb in St. Peter's in Leuven ! But for Flanders it looked, as so often, as if the end were in sight. Count Ferrand, after twelve years in captivity, and the payment of a huge ransom, returned to his county and his wife as the most servile vassal of France. His only child was placed in the tutelage of the king, his suzerain. But, favourable as the whole affair seemed for France, the county escaped yet again. The little princess died before she could wed the king's brother, and for the next seventy-five years France had to be content with what she had. A certain equilibrium had been reached—between king and count, between barons and towns, between merchants and craftsmen. And the opportunity which such a balance offered for economic and artistic development was enormous.

Bruges became the metropolis of the north. The clever policy of commercial encouragement and freedom which the Flemish counts had followed paid off in golden showers. Flemish merchants penetrated to every possible corner of the known world. They carried cloth and wool, leather and grain from the Baltic, luxury products from the east and Italian wine. Busily they travelled between

Bruges half-way between Italy and the Baltic

the Fairs of Champagne and the Hanse towns, Lübeck and Bremen in north Germany.

Bruges' quays were piled high with merchandise from all over Europe and the East.

Merchants from the countries which the Flemings had largely opened up for trade began themselves to take over their commerce. And for them Bruges was an easy, convenient place of negotiation. There they could be sure to obtain the cloth, which most often they wanted in exchange for their more exotic wares. In 1277 the first galleys from Genoa penetrated the Straits of Gibralbar to sail to the north and were soon followed by those of Venice. From every side,

Venetian galleys commercial links met in Bruges—from England, the Hanse towns of Germany, the Fairs of Champagne, Gascony, Italy and the East. The floods which in the eleventh century had opened up the Zwin, had made Bruges' communication with the sea very easy; the canal through to Damme gave her additional space for unloading. The town was at the peak of its development and prosperity. It had not yet to cope with the rivalry of Antwerp or with the political troubles of the fourteenth century. A merchant's handbook from the end of the thirteenth century mentions thirty different countries whose merchants worked in Bruges. The remains of the economic network which this activity engendered can still be traced in the great churches of Damme, Lissewege and Oostkerke. Many of the other buildings have disappeared, but the great size of these churches, disproportionate to the village which they now serve, reveals the importance of the communities for which they were built.

Such prosperity led to the construction of many important buildings which were intended not only to house the merchant communities and provide facilities for their work, but also to be a sign of civic pride and wealth. Many of these buildings can be visited: one is the immense reconstructed cloth hall and belfry of one of the most important weaving towns of Flanders, Ypres. This was started in 1200 and finished about a century later. In Bruges the cloth hall and the lower stories of the belfry are those built by the rich citizens of several

Belfries and cloth halls hundred years ago. Many of these buildings were in brick, sometimes, as in Bruges, decorated with hard white stone. Others, such as the church of Pamele in Oudenaarde, or of St. Nicholas in Ghent were entirely in stone brought along the Scheldt from Tournai. Much of the artistic inspiration in the Low Countries followed the course of the Scheldt from France, and acquired there local variations of the Gothic style of building, such as the Scheldt-Gothic of Pamele and St. Nicholas, Coastal Gothic such as in Lissewege or Oostkerke, and Brabant-Gothic such as in St. Michael's in Brussels. Watching over its citizens since the fourteenth century the dark grey belfry of Ghent rises crowned by its firebreathing dragon. When Charles V, later to be emperor, was born in

Fire breathing dragon the town in 1500, its mouth was filled with fireworks. According to one legend it had been stolen by Ghent from Bruges whither it had been brought back by Crusaders, who, in their usual manner, had taken it from the cupola of St. Sophia's in Constantinople.

Yet the merchant's life was often hazardous, and his profits doubtful. It was all

The house of the Dukes of Brabant in the Market in Brussels.

too easy for quarrelling princes to confiscate goods and throw merchants into prison: in Scotland, in 1292, thirty Flemings lost their merchandise in this way; two from Ypres and Poperinge had been thrown into prison in London the year before. But on the whole they were much too necessary to the princes of the time to be victimised too often. The Plantagenets, constantly short of money, resorted to Flemings for loans. One of these, Hugh Oisel of Ypres, was rewarded by John, with the freedom of the City of London. At first participation in trade was not, however, confined to such dominant figures: wax and wool merchants, bakers who had married well, craftsmen and workmen also took part in all this flurry of commercial activity. They came not only from Bruges and Ypres but from Lille, Aardenburg, Diksmuide and Poperinge. They reached not only London, but as far as Dundee, Perth and Berwick-on-Tweed.

Such a society not only built churches and public buildings but also provided for the poor, and the sick. Some of the most impressive thirteenth century buildings were charitable in origin. One of Ghent's hospitals, the Bijloke, now a mixture of all architectural styles, still retains its great thirteenth century sick room. Its foundation is interesting. It was the inspiration of a lady of good family, Ermentrude Utenhove, who began to care for the sick in her own home in about 1200, near the church of St.

The social services Michael. The work was too much for her and was transferred to its present site in about 1230, and the Cistercian sisters installed to care for the sick. Later an abbey was added for them, and it is this fourteenth century building which now houses one of the town's most interesting museums. The great refectory still bears some traces of the original wall paintings of the Last Supper and St. Christopher. This hospital's old buildings contrast with those of the large modern university hospital on the other side of the town. Even earlier, such a building was started in Bruges: the hospital of St. John. Its sick-room now houses a marvellous series of paintings by the fifteenth century artist Hans Memling, including the shrine of St. Ursula. Many other similar foundations began in the thirteenth century. In Douai, sixteen orphanages, hospitals and almshouses date back to between 1200 and 1300; in the following century there were only three. The western facade of the refectory of the abbey of the Bijloke in Ghent shows the richness of architectural style which could be achieved in brick; it is similar to that of the church of the Great Beguinage of Leuven. It houses, among many fascinating exhibits, the tomb of Hugh II, Castellan of Ghent which is, in its turn, a rich example of what thirteenth century sculptors could achieve in stone. Strong, confident, well armed and bearing above his head a defended town, Hugh must have been typical of the local knights who occupied castles such as that of Laarne, or Vorselaar, where the square central and round corner towers date from about 1250. Near Hugh, a further successful, confident, pair appear on a splendid fourteenth century brass, William Wenemaer and his wife Margaret de Brune. William died defending the bridge over the Leie at Deinze against Bruges in 1325. Both William and Margaret and Hugh contrast with the stone faces on the bosses supporting the vaulting of the Bijloke's refectory roof. They typify perhaps the more strange, mysterious element in Flemish culture which runs throughout beside the confident, successful mercantile element.

Flemish mysticism This mystic, withdrawn, profound strain in the Flemish character found its medieval expression in the work of Hadewijch, a lady from near Antwerp, who at the head of a small group of nuns, wrote mystic poetry of extraordinary richness. In the following century, the same thread appears again in the work of John of Ruusbroec. A quite different, but equally typical, more Chaucerian work recounts the amusing cunning exploits of Reynard the Fox, who with very Flemish astuteness manages to escape the results of his actions and to cock a snook at authority.

Reynard the Fox Sometimes the urban vision was too ambitious. New parishes in Flanders, often occupied by texile workers, had developed outside the original walls or the other defences. It looked as if nothing could stop urban development: no one could foresee the political troubles or the Black Death lurking ahead. Bruges' new walls were constructed at the end of the thirteenth century; Ghent's successively in the fourteenth, in spite of the troubles of the fourteenth century, Ypres finished its new defences only at the end of it. Leuven conceived her future rôle on so large a scale that the ground enclosed in the fourteenth century was not fully built up until the nineteenth. In Brussels the lower parts of the Halle Gate, now an arms museum, date also from the fourteenth century.

Within the walls or canals, the great mass of weavers and small craftsmen lived in wooden houses. Some of them show, through arched windows, in paintings by Van Eyck and Memling. Of these wooden houses few remain. Richer families built, however, in stone. Some have escaped the town-planners, and they often have a castle-like appearance, useful in the frequent revolts and riots of those years. The house of the Templars in Ypres, the thirteenth century house of the Van der Sickele family in Ghent, with its battlements and crest of sickles over the door, the vast town dwelling of the lord Gerard the Devil, so-called because of his dark complexion, with its hall of justice and vaulted crypt

The Atomium, part of the Great Exhibition of 1958 in Brussels.

exemplify this. Many more appear in the backgrounds of paintings by Memling, Van Eyck, Van der Weyden and Van der Goes.

Franco-Flemish brinkmanship

Bouvines meant triumph for France and danger for Flanders. After 1214 it looked as if her absorption was only a matter of time. For a further eighty years brinkmanship was successful. And then, suddenly, the whole fragile balance of relationships collapsed in violence and slaughter. The king of France could no longer bear the tempting and unsubdued northern vassal. The count could no longer tolerate his suzerain's interference, pretensions and the gradual sapping away of his authority. The Flemings could no longer put up with the French. The weavers, dyers and fullers could no longer bear the overwheening pride and French sympathies of the urban magistrates. Although the outcome was a violent revolt against all things French, it was not simply a patriotic outburst. It is too early to look for a purely national reaction. Hatred of the French combined with social tensions caused by the gradual but certain widening of the gap between the ruling citizens in the towns and the craftsmen in the gilds. The days when a weaver or an inn-keeper might trade on the same footing as a rich merchant were over. And in the search for allies there is no fixed pattern. Even hatred for the French was not universal: to the urban ruling class they seemed the only hope. Further complications arose because of the still essentially feudal reactions of the counts. Flanders was breaking out of the medieval pattern but, as usual, not at the same pace in all spheres.

After the death of Ferrand in 1233 and of his wife Joan, the county passed to the latter's sister, Margaret. She had had a colourful career, marrying first the lord of Avesnes by whom she had two sons. The rather late discovery that her husband was in holy orders and could therefore not marry, led to a second marriage with William of Dampierre and to the birth of two more sons. This implied more trouble for Flanders. Who was to succeed to the county ? Saint Louis IX of France attempted to solve the problem by awarding Hainaut to the Avesnes, and Flanders to the Dampierres. Neither was content. Both houses spent the next eighty years trying to overcome the other, and this circumstance provided a wonderful excuse for constant intervention by France and others in their affairs. Only France really profited, as Hainaut was separated from Flanders.

What were the important pressure groups in Flanders in the thirteenth century ?

Pressure groups

What held certain of them together and made enemies of others ? From a twentieth century point of view what we look for is patriotism, the united feeling of loyalty towards a well-defined territory, a sentiment which, particularly in difficult times causes the inhabitants of such a territory to sink their differences and make common cause against the enemy. To look for such a sentiment in thirteenth century Flanders would be a waste of time. Occasionally something almost like it appears, as in 1302 at the battle of the Golden Spurs, but even then one important class of Flemings was on the other side—the urban patriciate, the Leliaerts, wanted a French victory. Not vertical divisions, but horizontal ones were relevant. Each group or interest felt itself perfectly justified in allying with anyone who would support it, as was the case in international politics. And two of the protagonists at least seriously misunderstood the position of the others. What really interested the counts, who were after all peers of France, was the maintenance of their feudal rights, the extension of their dynastic power, and the quarrel with the Avesnes family. Sometimes it suited them, with these aims in view, to ally with the towns against the king, their suzerain, when the latter seemed to be going beyond the bounds set down for feudal manoeuvre. They certainly had no understanding of, or sympathy for, the pretentions of the towns towards political and financial independence. They, like the towns, were anxious to break the power of the Francophile sympathising urban patriciate, but they did not care in the least what happened to the ordinary people. They saw the patriciate, quite rightly, as the ally of their bitterest enemy, the king of France, who had begun to behave much more like a modern despot, than a feudal suzerain. When therefore, the towns had helped the count, and expected their reward, they found that it consisted in the loss of some of their autonomy. When the town charters of Bruges were destroyed in the Belfry fire of 1280, Count Guy refused to renew them. In Ghent he disciplined the magistrates but quickly pocketed the town seal and the keys of the treasure chests rather than turning them over to the gilds. The very great urban prosperity of the twelfth and thirteenth centuries had gradually widened the gap between the rich merchant-drapers and the workers whom they employed. This urban ruling class was patriotic, at least so far as its own town was concerned, hence the great number of charitable foundations and civic monuments. But they became more and more proud and exclusive in their direction of urban affairs. The magistracy became hereditary. It lost contact completely with every day affairs. The mass of weavers, fullers, dyers, and all the other crafts who paid the urban taxes had no say in how they were spent. In the second half of the thirteenth century conflicts broke out in the towns on purely social grounds: in Bruges, Ypres, Douai and Tournai. This feeling of social frustration, identified in the popular mind with France and the French, combined in 1302 with the struggle of a great vassal to maintain his feudal independence from his suzerain, the king of France. And what a suzerain ! Cunning, intelligent, autocratic, violent and completely

Appetites of Philip the Fair

unscrupulous, this Philip the Fair was capable of the cold judicial murder of the Knights Templars, or of allowing his envoy to slap the Pope, Boniface VIII, in the face. He was certainly no mean adversary and the web which he span to catch the blundering, if courageous, Dampierre, was tougher and of a different substance from anything which the latter could imagine. Philip, for all his readiness to rush to the support of his vassals, when it suited him, and his insistence on his feudal rights, had, in fact, for a suzerain most unappropriate aims. He wanted to absorb the county of Flanders, to make it another royal province, and completely to swallow the appetising fly he had in his web. But in spite of his unwavering advance towards this tempting meal, it is only at the end of the thirteenth century that his aim was recognised, at least by the count. The patricians never saw it at all. They continued to run for help to the man who in his own domains was destroying urban charters and the belfries which proclaimed urban independence as fast as he could.

What could Guy do against the gradual infiltration of his county by French officials, by their insistence at being present at trials which had then to be heard in French, a language which the parties could not always understand ? How could he stop the constant appeals of the Flemish towns against judgments in his courts, to the Parliament of Paris ? His only hope seemed to lie in an alliance with England, as his predecessor Ferrand had thought at the beginning of the century. Edward I of England, as John before him, was briskly searching for allies against Philip. Flanders was an obvious place from which to launch an attack on Philip's northern frontier. Guy took the most provocative step by announcing his daughter's engagement to the son of the English king. He was immediately summoned to Paris. That he went, shows his faith in the feudal relationship. There, however, he was kept in prison until his little daughter was delivered to Philip to be educated in the Louvre. Crushing taxes were imposed on Flanders and Philip was cunning enough to insist that they should be collected by the Count's own officials. The importation of wool from England was forbidden and Guy was given the job of catching the smugglers. Currency reforms struck at the wealth of the great towns. Royal officials took charge of Ghent, Bruges, Ypres, Lille and Douai. Such measures were impossible to enforce. The towns appealed to Paris. Guy was again summoned to appear there; not before his peers, as he demanded, but before the lawyers of the Parliament. His county was confiscated and only returned to him at the king's pleasure. Such a humiliation could leave Guy with no illusions about his suzerain's intentions. His last desperate struggles involved renewed promises to Edward of England, and renewed concessions to the town gilds which were beginning to see in him a possible ally against their own patricians. After a solemn proclamation in St. Donatian's church in Bruges, Guy's defiance was submitted to his suzerain.

In spite of the efforts of Guy's sons, the French invasion was quick and thorough. Edward of England arrived too late to help, quickly

France invades Flanders

made a truce with Philip in which no mention at all was made of his ally, Flanders, and sailed back to England. After the expiration of the truce in 1300, the conquest was completed. In May, Guy capitulated and once more took the road to Paris, this time as a prisoner. After two weeks in the Châtelet during which his suzerain refused to see him, he was transferred permanently to Compiègne. Flanders, both royal and imperial, was annexed to France. It looked as if her independent history was over.

Philip seemed only to have to consolidate his victory, and to extend northwards into Flanders the centralisation which he was enforcing elsewhere in his kingdom. Perhaps, in spite of his cunning and ruthlessness and ambition, he never really understood the nature of the independent, rich, proud, northern cities. This would explain his subsequent actions. A cruel, ruthless and stupid governor, Jacques de Châtillon, rode north from Paris; and although the urban administration was reformed, the bill for a royal progress by Philip and his queen through their new northern territories was unwisely sent to the Flemish towns themselves. Touched on their rawest point, the citizens of Bruges rioted under their popular leader Peter de Coninck and massacred the patricians who, like the murderers of Charles the Good, were hunted out of the castle. An appeal to Paris, so well received when it had been against Guy, proved useless against Philip's own envoy. De Coninck, banished by the Châtillon, returned. He and Bruges were ready to lead the revolt. The governor's actions were almost as maladroit in Ghent. The tax on that favourite Flemish drink, beer, which had been remitted by Philip, was re-imposed. Rioting broke out. Here too the patricians, seen as the ally of France, were attacked and banished from the town through the Hoogpoort where they had to run the gauntlet of the citizens armed with swords.

William of Julich, Guy's grandson, young and popular, assumed the lead in the revolt. For the first time, a real alliance was made between prince and people, both with identical motives, to rid the country of the French.

St. Carolus Borromeus church in the Conscienceplein in Antwerp.

Bruges, momentarily frightened by its own temerity, approached de Châtillon for terms. Surrounded by a menacing armed company, he entered the town, obviously rather as a conqueror than an appeaser. Terror struck the citizens and surreptitiously a message was smuggled out to the leaders hiding in the woods and ditches outside the walls. Through the cracks in the partially destroyed defences, through the alleys and paths which they knew so well they crept back into the town. As the French sleepily emerged they were set on and slaughtered unmercifully. It was the night of May 17th 1302. As the 18th dawned and the church bells rang out for Matins all the French occupants were butchered. Anyone speaking with a foreign accent, unable to say 'schildt ende vriend' was a victim. Only de Châtillon, with a handful of followers escaped. The Matins of Bruges meant war.

Flanders retaliates

Throughout the early summer days the Flemings collected their army and their weapons. Workmen from Bruges, Ypres and Ghent, peasants from the polders, carpenters, masons, fullers, dyers, shop-keepers and wine sellers, all the hundreds of craftsmen and traders, collected their pikes and 'goedendags' and gradually assembled from all the villages and towns of Flanders. About seven hundred crept from French controlled Ghent, under their leader, John Borluut. There were about five hundred from Ypres. The greatest number came from Bruges: about 2,500. From the Franc of Bruges came about the same number. The total Flemish force was between 8,500 and 11,000 men. The great majority were foot-soldiers. A handful of local knights remained loyal to the count and they were mounted. To them must be added a few knights from Zealand and a handful of mercenaries. Their most popular leader was William of Julich. Perhaps the best soldier was John of Renesse. No contrast could have been greater than that between this motley collection and the glorious, aristocratic, feudal host which entered Flanders on July 1st, 1302. Two thousand splendid heavily armoured French knights on magnificent chargers crossed into the Flemish mud. The list of their names—Robert, Count of Artois, Raoul de Nesle, Constable of France, Louis, Count of Clermont, the king's cousin, the lords of Tancarville and of Estouteville, John of Avesnes, Henry of Luxemburg—read like a roll of chivalry. Their behaviour did not live up to their names. Once across the frontier they pillaged, burned and destroyed to such an extent that they certainly gained recruits for the Flemish army.

The Flemings were drawn up on a sort of island, guarded in the rear by the town moat of Kortrijk, its left flank against the river Leie,

Battle of the Golden Spurs

its right defended by another stream, and before it the Groeningerbrook. The right wing consisted of men from Bruges, the centre of those from the polders and the surrounding countryside, both under William of Julich. To the left stood the mercenaries, East Flemings and the men of Ghent, under the orders of Guy of Namur, the count's son. The men of Ypres and Kortrijk itself crowded at the foot of Kortrijk castle to stop a French sortie. John of Renesse commanded the reserves. It must all have looked very ludicrous to the flower of French chivalry, to be faced by half-armed, apparently undisciplined peasants and craftsmen, on foot ! Robert of Artois could not wait to get at them and to finish the day. Before his infantry, which had been drawn up in front of the cavalry, had withdrawn according to his orders, he signalled the knights to advance. They crashed through the ranks of the retreating foot soldiers, who scattered or were trampled underfoot. The horses thereby lost their momentum, and slithered into the mud of the Groeningerbrook. The shock of their charge was however enough to make John of Renesse throw in his reserves and they managed to stand firm before the second French attempt. A third charge met a solid wall of goedendags and in three hours the remnant of the fine French army was fleeing before the triumphant Flemings. The rules of the medieval code of war were not observed. Fallen French knights unable to remount were summarily despatched instead of being taken prisoner. When the Flemings could not reach the knights, they attacked the horses. No prisoners were taken. When Robert of Artois attempted to surrender his sword, he was struck down by thirty blows. That evening, sixty-eight French lords were found to have perished on the battle field, as well as eleven hundred knights. Seven hundred golden spurs were collected and hung in Our Lady's Church in Kortrijk as a thank offering. Nothing like this had ever happened before. France was stupified. Pope Boniface VIII rose from his bed in the middle of the night to enjoy the news to the full.

One town after another opened its gates to the Flemish army, now on the offensive. Lille, Ghent, Douai and Ypres flung out the Leliaert sympathizers and joined up with their compatriots. On the splendid wooden coffer conserved at New College, Oxford, the whole history of the battle of the Golden Spurs was carved, perhaps by a contemporary. There it all is: the Matins of Bruges, the town keys being offered to Guy of Namur, the crafts and peasants with their banners and weapons, the castle of Kortrijk, and the despatch of the French army after the battle.

In three hours the whole direction of Flemish history for the last ninety years had been, it seemed, reversed. The grip which, since Bouvines in 1214, had been tightening on the administration, on justice, on the economy of Flanders was loosened. Even a statue of St. Louis of France in the church in Thérouanne, was

Flemish disillusionment

taken out and decapitated. It looked as if nothing could stop the Flemish triumph. But, gradually, complete success seemed to slip further and further from their grasp. Philip the Fair managed to beat Guy of Namur in a sea battle off Zealand. His troops fought again at Mons-en-Pévèle and both sides tried to claim victory. The first glorious élan gradually diminished. The new count Robert of Bethune saw that the fighting could not be allowed to go on. The economy of the country was becoming exhausted. The peace terms left Flanders once more as a semi-independent country. The prisoners in France were released. But an enormous fine was imposed on the Flemish towns, they were threatened once more with an interdict, and Walloon Flanders, Lille, Douai and Béthune were finally surrendered to the French crown. But Flanders had escaped annexation. The towns had tasted political, as well as economic power. The gilds would never again sit down under an urban government which was socially and politically alien to them. Although, economically speaking, their greatest period was passing, politically the fourteenth century came near to seeing the establishment in Flanders of a system of city states similar to those which were developing in Italy. This is still important to-day. The immensely strong local feeling is a sentiment which gives the present day Fleming from the town a feeling of great superiority over the Fleming from the countryside. The local differences in a very circumscribed area, still lie at the core of the Flemish character.

After the victory of the Golden Spurs, the towns seemed to have the county at their disposal. But the superstructure was still essentially feudal. The counts, although their lands were returned to them, were still vasals of the French king. The peace of Athis of 1305 was more a condemnation than a treaty. The towns were ordered to destroy their fortifications, to pay huge indemnities to the French king, to swear to abide by the treaty, to send three thousand citizens from Bruges on an expiatory pilgrimage and to restore the Leliaerts whom they had so enjoyed chasing away, while any contravention was to be followed by an interdict. The towns felt that they had been betrayed. Those negotiating the peace had all been from the nobility. None had represented the towns whose gilds had won the battle of 1302. The count, Robert of Béthune, and his towns found themselves once more looking at the situation from entirely different points of view. He was free once more to fight the house of Avesnes. The towns gradually returned to their peaceful occupations. All might have been well had

Philip of France really intended to leave things as they were. But he had never given up his intention of annexing Flanders. The events of 1302 were for him an additional reason for crushing this northern county. His infiltration began again. Attemps were made to force the count's successor to resign his rights to the king. Enthusiastic clergymen in Paris preached a crusade against the Flemings as being as worthy as one against the infidel, and not nearly so far away. But the French king did not want to lose yet another army in the Flanders mud. Robert, plagued by difficulties with his towns and with his sons finally accepted the peace terms: Walloon Flanders was abandoned to the French crown; but the rest of Flanders had escaped from the French web.

Flanders had not become another French province, but the counts were still vassals of France and feudal princes. They had nothing in common with the 'blue-nails', the great mass of workers, in their Flemish towns. They combined only at rare moments when the same danger threatened both of them. What had changed was the position of the Leliaerts, the supporters of the French, and the

Power changes hands

artisans or Clauwaerts, so-called because of their loyalty to the clawed Lion of Flanders. The year 1302 saw the end of the monopoly of power of the rich bourgeoisie. The next hundred years were scarred by the Clauwaerts' attempts to replace this monopoly by their own and to organise their own future. The Flemish towns were quite exceptional for the fourteenth century. They were modern in an economic sense but still medieval in their social and political structure. They were extremely large. Only Paris north of the Alps had a bigger population than Ghent with its 62,000 inhabitants; Bruges had about 35,000, while London after the plague, had about 40,000 and Cologne, 30,000. In Ghent more than 50 % of this population was employed in one industry— the production of cloth. Their market was not local. Their interests were not limited to a small hinterland. Flemish cloth was sold throughout the known world. The ordinary weaver could not go to sell it in Novgorod ! He had to rely on professional merchants. For his raw material he was also dependent. It had to be bought in large quantities, and for the most part abroad, in England. The weaver had in fact, no control either over the provision of the wool which was essential for his work, or over the disposal of his finished cloth. What made the situation even less comfortable for him was that these two functions were often in the hands of the same merchant, however successful the artisan was in extracting places in the urban government, or vague privileges from the count. The production of cloth was enormous. But the social organisation necessary to deal with industrial capitalism had not yet evolved in the fourteenth century.

The capital involved was very large. The rich became richer and the poor stayed poor. The artisans who had won the battle of

Weavers thwarted

Kortrijk and had chased away the old urban governments, could still not wriggle free from this economic dependence. As victorious veterans they still found themselves living in slums divided from the residential quarters of the towns. One of the first measures they took in Bruges after the battle of the Golden Spurs was to obtain the agreement of John of Namur to a new charter. Three weeks after winning the battle, when they had just got home, the first thing they demanded was freedom to work and dispose of their products as they wished. Theoretically they could have immediately embarked for Novgorod, instead of having to sell their cloth to merchant middlemen. In fact, they observed crossly that the situation was not improving. They were still dependent on the merchant drapers. They may have slaughtered the flower of the French chivalry in the bogs of Kortrijk, but they could still not dispose of more than a few pieces of cloth without someone else's help.

This situation was unbearable and insoluble. The fourteenth century is filled with attempts to find a solution. The Flemish plain saw numerous and bloody experiments. The men who did the work wanted to have the profit. They fought for economic independence, and almost invariably failed to get it. The towns of Flanders were the testing ground for the new capitalist society which was springing up there earlier than anywhere else except in the Plain of Lombardy. What hung in the balance was whether the county of Flanders would break up

Flemish city states ?

into independent city states as had happened in Italy. Flanders in the fourteenth century was a country in turmoil. At every moment it threatened to disintegrate. For not only did the towns have economic pretensions, they had equally strong political ones. In every £ 100 of the national taxes Bruges contributed £ 15.4.3; Ghent £ 13.17.0; Ypres £ 10.14s.7d; Franc de Bruges £ 13.6.9; together this totalled more than 52 % in 1309. They felt therefore, entitled to political power. Unlike in England, there was then no effective supreme territorial power in Flanders. The counts cannot be compared with the English kings. Their loyalties were sometimes divided between their county and their feudal obligations. Exceptional men like Philip of Alsace had painstakingly begun to build a central administration at the expense of the local baronage. Troubles with France had, however, diverted the counts' energies. The towns had never been integrated in any system. They were, more often than not, literally at daggers drawn with the counts' officials, the bailiffs. And their power was enormous both financially and humanly speaking. No-one could say that the count had won the battle of Kortrijk. He was in prison in Compiègne at the time. His sons and nephews had provided leaders, but the whole affair had really been organised and carried out by the towns, especially Bruges. Her militia had provided the greater part of the fighting force. She had payed most of the wages. She had led the pursuit of the Leliaerts. She might have expected to enjoy the fruits of her efforts. Instead she found herself obliged to foot the bill. The terms imposed by France at Athis in 1305 certainly implied that the French rather than the Flemings had won at Kortrijk. Huge fines were the price which followed the restoration of Flanders as fief of the French crown. This was coupled with economic disappointment. The Clauwaerts of Bruges must have begun to wonder what they had been fighting for. At least they saw no reason why they, rather than Ghent or Ypres, who had also profited from the victory, should pay for it alone. The unity between the towns shown at Kortrijk began to crack. They began to struggle between themselves for predominance.

Strife between towns

Another of those dominant characteristics of the history of fourteenth century Flanders was emerging.

Three threads in the complicated design of the fourteenth century become obvious: the struggle between the towns themselves; the efforts of society to cope with a new economic situation caused by capitalism and an international market; and the political pretensions of the towns which aimed at independence from the counts and complete control of their own affairs. One element is common to all of these threads: the weavers. They were extremely numerous. They had chips on their shoulders. If provoked, they were extremely violent. Their aims were never really defined and understood. They always failed to solve the real problem partly because they never understood its cause. The new economic situation which was developing in the fourteenth century lay at the base. Yet the weavers strove unceasingly to attain political power which they felt ought to liberate them from humiliating economic dependence. Sometimes their feeling of unity disregarded urban loyalties. In the eighties, weavers from Bruges joined their attackers from Ghent, in turning out on the other crafts and the bourgeoisie of their own town. They never understood that they were the victims of international trade fluctuations rather than of other classes among their countrymen. At this time none of the

Weavers of the towns unite !

social or economic padding existed which was later fabricated to dull the blows of the trade cycle.

Although the new Count, Robert of Béthune did not want to restore the old

The Groenplaats and cathedral of Our Lady in Antwerp.

The only town gate-way still existing in Tongeren, the Moerepoort (1379).

political situation, when the towns had been dominated by cliques owing allegiance to his enemy the French king, he did not wish to be dominated by revolutionaries. Odious old taxes were not reimposed but there were enough odious new ones to provoke one riot after another. The huge sums imposed by Philip the Fair at Athis infuriated everyone. The towns had on several occasions tasted the fruits of political power. They had defeated France's candidate for the county, William Clito, after the murder of Charles the Good. They stopped French interference after the death of Philip of Alsace. Guy of Dampierre had been forced to rely on them to curb Philip the Fair. Such tastes of power had given them a good appetite for more. The authority, which counts such as Philip of Alsace had gradually acquired over the countryside, was to a large extent lost to the towns in the fourteenth century. As they began to sense this, and to try to extend their political power, they needed to dominate the surrounding farms and pastures to be sure of ample food supplies. In times of trouble they needed manpower. They also felt obliged to limit, so far as possible, the spread of clothmaking outside their walls. Astute farmers bought citizenship in order to have at least some say in the organization of affairs. Nevertheless, the

Country looms destroyed countryside suffered terribly. Exasperated bands of weavers had a nasty habit of roaming about, whenever a recession affected their earnings, and breaking up the country looms which they thought had caused it, just as during the industrial revolution in England the weavers broke up machinery. The polders were an exception to this pattern. Since they had been reclaimed from the sea, they had belonged to independent farmers, often direct tenants of

Peasant rising the abbeys or of the counts themselves. They were, on the whole, richer than farmers elsewhere in Flanders. This area was now also caught up in the general unrest. These farmers objected also to the payments which they had to make towards the French fines. This was not the limit of their rebellion however. It was not a desperate fling by a famished band of beggars. Unlike the revolts of the Jacquerie in France and Wat Tyler in England, these Flemish farmers could carry on the struggle for four years from 1324 to 1328. They attacked not only the land owners, but also the church. This was almost unheard of. They demanded that the vast grain stores of the abbeys—such as might be collected in the enormous barn at Lissewege— should be distributed to the poor. Under leaders like Nicholas Zannekin and James Peit they were so successful that the count began to see it less as a rebellion and more as a war. Bruges joined in. Ghent, at that moment undergoing a pro-Louis reaction, after a period of rule by the weavers, supported the count. Once more Bruges and Ghent were on opposing sides. Count Louis of Nevers appealed to his suzerain. Philip of Valois advanced from the south, and Ghent threatened from the east. Hopes ran high that it was going to be another Kortrijk. But this was very different. Ghent and Bruges were opponents. The count was fighting with, rather than against, the French. The countryside had already sustained four years of war. The spirit of 1302 was missing. The Flemings drawn up on Cassel Hill were too impatient to wait for the French attack as they had done so successfully at Kortrijk. Instead they tried to attack,

Defeat at Cassel

but they were too heavy and too slow. Out-manoeuvred by the more experienced and swifter French troops, they got in a terrible muddle and were thoroughly beaten. William de Deken, burgomaster of Bruges was carried to Paris to be executed as a traitor. Fines, executions, banishments and confiscations of goods, lands and privileges, were painful warnings for the Flemings of what revolt could mean. But it did not deter them. Instead, it built up a store of hatred and resentment which burst out again and again.

Bruges was for the moment rather out of breath. However, Ghent was ready to take over the leadership. Louis of Nevers depended on France. This was the eve of the troubles between England and France, which prefaced the Hundred Years' War. The count was on one side, his subjects on the other. Unfortunately, Louis's enemy was the source of his subjects' livelihood. The Flemings had realised what could happen without English wool. Before 1302 the supply had been interrupted once or twice with very unpleasant results for all who depended on it, rich and poor alike. Flanders could not join in a war against England. Yet this was exactly what the count was determined to do. He felt himself under an obligation to repay Philip of Valois for the help he had received at Cassel Hill. He started to repay his debt by putting an embargo on the import of English wool. King Edward III of England, who arrived at this moment in the harbour of Antwerp having sailed from Yarmouth, realised that this was his chance. The count was playing into his hands by giving his subjects a foretaste of what would happen if they dutifully followed him. Edward quickly made the pill even more bitter by adding a prohibition on the importation of cloth from

English raw materials cut off

Flanders too. Unemployment immediately followed. The 'blue-nails' were wage-earners. They had no opportunity to save. Everyone was brought up short by a sharp taste of what a real quarrel with England would mean.

Ghent did its best to make Louis listen. He was adamant. The embargo must

The ruins of St. Baaf's Abbey, in Ghent, founded in the seventh century.
The farm of Ter Doest in Lissewege, property of the Cistercians.

stay. If his feudal obligations meant ruin for his people, they would have to bear it. Ghent however had never felt any obligation towards France, and very little towards the count. The idea of negotiating in their own right appealed to their feeling of independence. Not only would they have a say in the affairs of the county, they would have their own foreign policy as well. The bourgeoisie and the weavers, both threatened, drew together and set up a revolutionary administration. Louis fled again to his suzerain. And at this juncture either the events produced the man or the man produced the events. Ghent found a leader. James van Artevelde was not a popular demagogue. He came from a well-to-do

James van Artevelde

merchant family with a house in the centre of Ghent. He possessed farms in the polders and had married a rich wife. He was reasonable and intelligent with a gift for inspiring and controlling his very mixed band of supporters. When the town was in a state of crisis in 1338, he took over the leadership of affairs in fact, although not in name. He did not love the workers. But he and his colleagues were prepared to put up with them, if in so doing they could preserve their town's prosperity. So, Van Artevelde, in Ghent's name, approached Edward III. The king was, of course, extremely pleased to see him. This signified that his policy had worked. The French king saw just as well as Edward, what a very favourable jumping-off ground Flanders could become for launching an attack on northern France. Did he perhaps find Louis of Nevers' intransigence rather trying ? At least he forced the count to make some conciliatory gestures towards Ghent, but could not make him agree to a marriage between his son and Edward's daughter. Anyway it was too late. Ghent was in the delicious position of seeing its leader hobnobbing with the king of England.

Van Artevelde may have become rather inebriated by his own power. He may have felt that this was the moment to exert Ghent's claim to the leadership of Flanders. His first steps showed great economic insight as well as a feeling for public relations. He arranged an economic agreement between Brabant, Flanders and Hainaut. But the real peak of his power came on January 26, 1340,

Ghent proclaims Edward III King of France

when Edward III of England was proclaimed king of France, on the Friday Market in Ghent, where Van Artevelde's statue now stands. Ghent felt triumphant.

Edward had promised anything and everything: subsidies, Walloon Flanders and Artois, a common currency for France, England, Flanders and Brabant. All this seemed due to Van Artevelde. To make the situation even more gratifying for Ghent, Edward III on a return visit from England met the French fleet at the mouth of the Zwin and promptly sank it. Everything seemed to be going splendidly. Ghent and Van Artevelde could not, however, let sleeping dogs lie. They undertook the siege of the French royal outpost of Tournai on the Flemish frontier. Van Artevelde became so overbearing that the Duke of Brabant who was also involved in the operation, threatened to go home. Edward returned to England. The smaller towns were getting sick of being sacrificed to Ghent's foreign policy. Their drapery was being crippled, their privileges trampled under-foot. Even in Ghent itself things were not going well. The uncomfortable collaboration of the weavers and the merchants was beginning to waver. Within the gilds themselves, all was not in order. On May 2, 1345, Black Monday, the weavers met the fullers head on, on the Friday Market and cut one another to pieces. What was now necessary was a really impressive success by Van Artevelde to rally his supporters. Just when he needed to be able to show off as the intimate friend of the English king, Edward let him down. He was not nearly so dependent on Flanders as Flanders was on him. Although he crossed the Channel and met Van Artevelde at Sluis, he refused to disembark. His promises were unfulfilled. His soldiers and his subsidies were unpaid. The disillusionment for Ghent and especially for its leader must have been very hard to bear and to explain.

When Van Artevelde returned home, alone, after his meeting with Edward, he

Van Artevelde murdered

was set upon, in the Kalanderberg where the event is now commemorated by a plaque, and murdered. The weavers blamed him because he had tried to force them to share power with the other groups and gilds. They wanted it all for themselves. His murder had nothing to do with the alliance with England. That continued after his death.

The weavers had now got what they wanted. They had power. The question was what to do with it. Over the one thing that really counted, the international economic situation, they were in fact powerless. They did not even recognise that any such problem existed. Therefore they used their power to dominate all the other groups in the towns and surrounding countryside. Other gilds, the fullers, and the country drapers were gradually sacrificed. This resulted in increasing hatred and revolt against the weavers. This flared up in one town after another. They were massacred in Bruges and in Ypres, at last only Ghent remained in their hands. Oudenaarde, Dendermonde, Geraardsbergen opened their gates to the new count, Louis of Male. The weavers of Ghent, not numerous enough to defend the walls of the city, withdrew to the Friday Market, that new centre of urban affairs, and in the middle of the winter of 1349 were subdued there. Ghent had had its chance. Its attempts to dominate the Flemish plain ended in yet another bloodbath on the Friday Market.

The new count was less vicious in his reprisals than his father had been on similar occasions. He was much less involved with France than Louis of Nevers who had died on the battlefield of Crécy in 1346. He felt under no obligation towards his suzerain. What he needed was to find some system of government which would reconcile all the different groups in the country. But the second half of the fourteenth century was a difficult time for reconciliation. The Black Death had swept through Europe like a scourge. Queer heresies—the Dancers, the Flagellants—were making their appearance. Something inexplicable was wrong with society. The wage-earners were, as usual, the first to feel the pinch. In spite of various periods of power, and of minute regulation of the urban administration, they had not been able to evolve anything to cope with the economic depression of the second half of the fourteenth century. They, therefore, blamed the count, and his friends, the bourgeoisie. The riots which broke out all over the country, in Ypres, Bruges and Ghent, were confined to the towns. The countryside was much too happy to see the towns restrained by the count, to take any part itself. Louis protected the countryside against the towns because he could then tax it himself. The country drapery, which he did nothing to restrain, grew gradually more prosperous. Competition which had hardly existed in the cloth industry, except within the towns themselves, now began in the Flemish countryside, as well as in Brabant. In the Flemish towns, costs were becoming far too high because of restrictive practices and very high urban taxes. In order to pay them, the price of cloth in the towns was ceasing to be competitive.

In Brabant the towns were both freer from the gilds and less severely taxed. Development there had been slower and more peaceful. Towns, such as

Brabant catches up Antwerp, Leuven, Brussels and Mechelen were much less thickly populated. From as early as the reign of Duke Henry I, the princes had acted less as vassals of the empire than as territorial rulers. In contrast to Flanders they had not had to cope with strong and ambitious suzerains, but with powerless Emperors. They had identified themselves from early times with the interests of their people, had extended their territory and had gradually established themselves on the highroad to the Rhine. John I and John III, poets, astute politicians, had carried on where Henry I had left off. While Flanders was resisting the threat of disintegration only with difficulty, Brabant had already a feeling of unity and loyalty towards its territory. Of course it did not escape the general economic changes of the fourteenth century. But their effect was less violent. The dukes came gradually to need more money. The towns were in a position to provide funds. They preferred to do so, rather than to have their goods confiscated and their merchants molested abroad, because their dukes had failed to pay their debts. In return, however, they demanded a say in their own affairs. Gradually, the towns, nobility and clergy, the Three Estates, obtained guarantees of a share in the government. As early as 1312, the duke had granted the Charter of Kortenberg, which set up a council of fourteen representatives of the towns and of the nobility, which was to meet every three weeks to assure the maintenance of the customs and privileges of the duchy. If the duke refused to abide by the decisions of the council, the people were released from their duty to obey him. This charter was not obtained as a result of violence but in return for the payment of debts. It left no feelings of bitterness and hatred on either side. Had such a measure been drawn up and accepted in the neighbouring county, might it have avoided some of the uproar which occurred there over each concession ? Many of the disturbances in Flanders certainly broke out over mysterious 'privileges' which were never defined. Had some of them been committed to parchment, might reference have been made to them before arms were snatched up ?

Joyeuse Entrée The failure of the male line in Brabant in 1355, gave the towns an opportunity to obtain an even greater share in the government. The duke's daughter, married to a foreigner, Wenceslas of Luxemburg, was accepted—at a price. The new duke was made to feel that he would receive the dukedom only if he agreed to the terms set out by the towns. These were incorporated in 1356 in a further charter, known as the Joyeuse Entrée, which continued to exert great influence upon the constitutional development of the Low Countries. It so established the indivisibility of the land of Brabant, insisted that government was to be carried on only by citizens born there, and demanded that the consent of the three Estates should be obtained before alliances were concluded, war was declared or money minted. Those two charters, of Kortenberg and the Joyeuse Entrée, have much in common with Magna Carta even in their phraseology. Were they perhaps modelled to some extent on it ? They continued to be the basis for development towards representative government in the Low Countries, as Magna Carta was for England. Constitutionally they placed Brabant far ahead of her neighbours.

In Flanders there was no comparable step. In 1369 in Ghent, Margaret the daughter and heiress of Louis of Male, married Philip the Bold, Duke of

Burgundy enters the Netherlands Burgundy, and brother of the King of France. In return for his daughter's hand, Louis had obtained the return of Walloon Flanders—Douai, Lille and Orchies—and thus reconstituted the heritage of the Dampierres. It was as if the gains of Philip the Fair had never existed. Yet the French king must have had the agreeable impression that he was solving the irritating Flemish question and obtaining peacefully what his predecessors for the past hundred and fifty years had been fighting for. It looked as if Flanders would at last fall into the hands of the French loyal line. It did. But into the hands of the younger branch of the Valois under whom, instead of being firmly bound to the French crown, it proved to be the corner stone of an entirely new ruling house in the Netherlands—the House of Burgundy.

In spite of Count Louis's dynastic plans, he was not drawn into the French camp in the Hundred Years' war. The French marriage, however, helped to avoid the other danger—that too close an alliance with England might have made Flanders into a battleground where England and France would settle their differences. On this occasion, Flanders was not a 'rendez-vous des guerres'. The county had enough internal conflicts on her hands. In spite of Louis's efforts to widen his jurisdiction, to insist on the definition of privileges, and to curb urban pretensions, the towns still took justice into their own hands when their immediate interests were concerned. Ghent was, for instance, determined to defend her grain staple. All corn passing down the river Leie from northern France had to be transferred onto her boats. The toll houses still stands on the edge of the Leie on the Graslei. There, too, is the boatmen's gild house. Such a monopoly was extremely lucrative. It was also very irritating for Bruges. She regularly attempted to by-pass Ghent and to obtain a direct supply of grain by digging a canal direct to the Leie. Such plans always enraged Ghent. In 1379,

New canal provokes Ghent Bruges began to dig again. As soon as the canal reached Ghent's boundary at St.-Joris-ten-Distel, the town militia fell on the workmen and destroyed their work. This was the excuse for a general uprising. The boatmen's leader John Yoens went on to kill the count's bailiff and to destroy his newly built castle of Wondelgem. Under Ghent's inspiration, the weavers immediately joined the revolt. It ceased to be a row between Ghent and Bruges, but became rather another weavers' rebellion. Louis was forced to come to terms. He allowed the appointment of twenty-nine commissioners to investigate abuses. They only made things worse. The revolt broke out again. It was no longer sure, however, of complete support. The smaller gilds, even the fullers, tired of the weavers' excesses and pretentions, turned against them and chased them from power in Bruges, Ypres and many of the smaller towns. Finally only Ghent remained. It became the symbol, once more, of urban independence. Mechelen revolted; Liège sent supplies. One excited poet saw Ghent as a virgin defended by Christ and His Apostles. Van Artevelde's son, Philip, was called upon to lead the town's resistance. The unbeatable enthusiasm of the weavers, in spite of food shortages, provoked them to attack Bruges. Louis of Male was using it as his capital. His much restored castle of Male still lies a little east of the town. The militia of Ghent arrived outside Bruges, on the field of Beverhout, on May 3rd 1382, just as the citizens were celebrating the Holy Blood procession. More or less overcome by the festivities they were disorganised and thoroughly defeated. Louis escaped only by swimming across the moat.

The weavers, joined by their colleagues from Bruges, hunted down everyone else, burned and pillaged the belongings of the bourgeoisie, and retired, leaving control of the town in the hands of the weavers of Bruges. Only Dendermonde and Oudenaarde remained loyal to Louis. He had fled to France and there had to ask for suzerain's help against the rebels. Charles VI, nephew of Philip of Burgundy, the heir to Flanders, was persuaded by his uncle to deal with these dangerous neighbours. They were setting a most alarming example. It provoked riots in Amiens, Rouen, even in Paris. Philip was

Riots in Paris anxious that the expense and opprobrium of a punitive expedition should be borne by Charles rather than by himself. Thus once more a French army invaded Flanders. At Westrozebeke, on November 27th, 1382, the Flemish army, under Van Artevelde's leadership, was beaten in a few minutes. While the French hurried off to burn Kortrijk, hated souvenir of their astonishing defeat, Ghent gathered

Kortrijk revenged another army and re-occupied Oudenaarde and Damme. It looked as if, even then, Ghent might gain control of the whole country. England was once more ready to help. Charles VI of France was supporting the anti-Pope, Clement VII. Under the bishop of Norwich, an English expedition disembarked in Calais, in support of Ghent's candidate for the Papacy, Urban VI. This peculiar crusade advanced as far as Ypres, besieged the town unsuccessfully, as a painting in the church of St. Martin shows, and went home again. It had not helped Ghent very much.

Philip the Bold was, however, determined to put a stop to the troubles. After Louis's death in the winter of 1384, he persuaded his nephew the king of France to advance once more into Flanders, and assembled a French fleet near Bruges.

Such a show of force coupled with the offer of favourable terms convinced Ghent at last of the wisdom of making peace with the new count. During the negotiations, in Tournai, Ghent's representatives showed their city's metal once more. Unlike Philip's delegates, they were not provided with cushions on which to sit during the discussions. Coming from the town which produced the finest cloth in the world, they were, however, sumptuously apparelled and with their great cloaks they made themselves cushions. On leaving they left these expensive and gorgeous garments behind. Their reply to a messenger sent to warn them of this omission was that it was not their habit to take their cushions with them when leaving a meeting. Philip's terms were, however, more generous than his provision of furnishings. A general amnesty, the confirmation of all Ghent's privileges, permission to support the cause of whichever Pope they chose—it appeared almost a capitulation. In fact, Philip was willing to pay such a price for the entry of the house of Burgundy into the Netherlands.

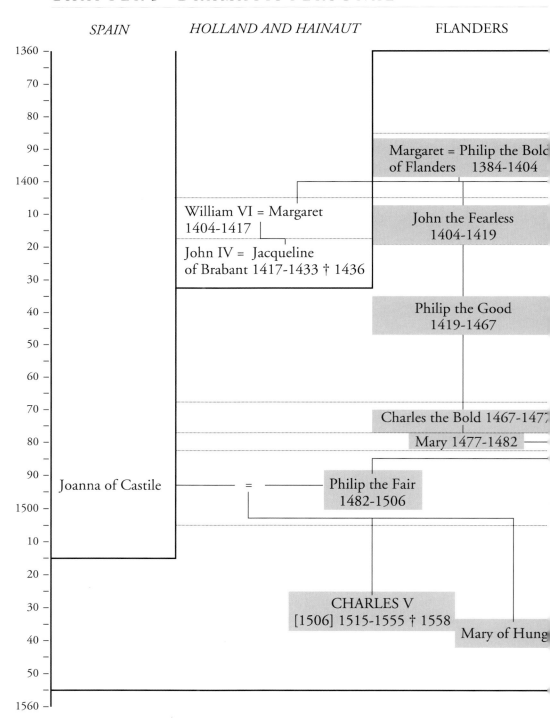

SPAIN   HOLLAND AND HAINAUT   FLANDERS

1360

70

80

90   Margaret = Philip the Bold
                                                  of Flanders   1384-1404
1400

10   William VI = Margaret   John the Fearless
              1404-1417 | 1404-1419

20   John IV = Jacqueline
              of Brabant 1417-1433 † 1436

30

40   Philip the Good
                                                    1419-1467
50

60

70   Charles the Bold 1467-1477

80   Mary 1477-1482

90
              Joanna of Castile   Philip the Fair
                             =   1482-1506
1500

10

20

30   CHARLES V
                                                [1506] 1515-1555 † 1558
40   Mary of Hung

50

1560

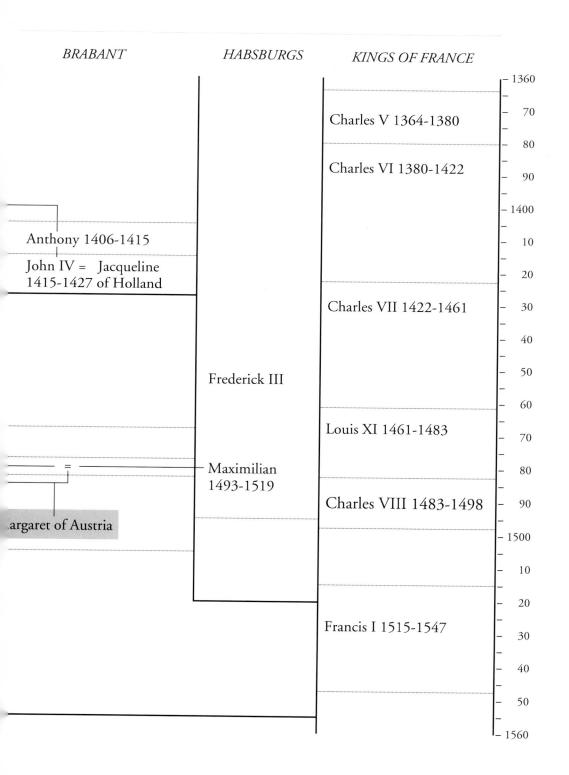

BRABANT   HABSBURGS   KINGS OF FRANCE

Anthony 1406-1415

John IV = Jacqueline
1415-1427 of Holland

Frederick III

Maximilian
1493-1519

argaret of Austria

Charles V 1364-1380

Charles VI 1380-1422

Charles VII 1422-1461

Louis XI 1461-1483

Charles VIII 1483-1498

Francis I 1515-1547

1360
70
80
90
1400
10
20
30
40
50
60
70
80
90
1500
10
20
30
40
50
1560

Me semble que pour lors ses terres se
pouvoient myeulx dire terres de promission
que nulles aultres seigneuries qui fussent sur la terre.

Philip of Commynes writing in 1465

I believe that this country deserves more to be
called the promised land than anywhere else on earth

The Flowering

1384-1555

U NDER the rule of the house of Burgundy it looked as if the Low Countries would become part of a new and independent monarchy stretching from Holland in the north to Burgundy and Franche-Comté in the south. Yet this did not happen. It seemed probable in 1384 that the dukes of Burgundy would gradually be transformed from their rôle of great princes of the house of Valois, into national sovereigns, ruling over a conglomeration of lands which they had gradually acquired and which were slowly submitted to some system of centralised administration.

Prospects This process was going on in France itself. In England it had already been accomplished. The general tendency during this period was towards territorial unification and absolute rule. There is no question that the first of the Burgundian dukes, Philip the Bold, had this as a conscious aim. He remained always essentially a French prince. His acquisitions were intended to increase the power and importance of his house. But by the early fifteenth century his son, John the Fearless was already involved in a ferocious feud with France, and Charles the Bold died in the battle of Nancy trying to bridge the gap which divided his possessions in the Low Countries from Burgundy. Significantly, in 1482 Burgundy and not the Netherlands was lost. The ruling house had completely re-orientated itself. When Burgundy was re-absorbed by the French crown in 1482, what was left roughly covered what is now contained in the kingdom of the Netherlands, Belgium, and the French *départements* of Pas-de-Calais and Nord. Unfortunately for the Low Countries, the marriage of Charles the Bold's only child, Mary of Burgundy, drew them into the wider net of European politics. They became a pawn in the long drawn out struggle between France and the Habsburgs. When Louis XIV, *le roi soleil,*

The ruins of the abbey of St. Bertin in Saint-Omer (French-Flanders).
The belfry and statue of Jan Breydel and Peter de Coninck in the market in Bruges.

Town-hall and belfry of Aalst.

'Voilà le berceau de toutes nos guerres'

visited the tomb of Mary in Our Lady's church in Bruges, he remarked 'Voilà le berceau de toutes nos guerres'. Events fully justified the remark.

Already much earlier, during the reign of the Emperor Charles V, the Netherlands had ceased to be anyone's principal concern. Charles had Luther and the New World to cope with. He had, however, been born in Ghent. He spoke the local language, and felt at home in the Netherlands. But with Charles's son Philip II, it was a very different matter. His responsibilities were enormous, 'duty flowed in his veins instead of blood'. For him the Netherlands were an inconsiderable part of his preoccupations, a seed bed of heresy which had to be dealt with, quickly, efficiently and without sentiment, by the Duke of Alva and his troops. Philip was, after all, busy converting the American Indians and organising the conquest of England. The vivid flowering of the distinctive, rich culture of the southern Netherlands, comparable to that of the England of Shakespeare and Elizabeth I, disappeared in the flames of religious intolerance and military occupation. Diplomacy and international affairs at this time depended very largely on a complicated system of dynastic marriages. The Low Countries owed to them their greatness and their downfall.

What was in fact the situation after the death of Louis of Male, count of Flanders in 1384 ? His only child, Margaret, had married, in 1369, Philip of Burgundy, brother of the French king. To obtain such a rich bride for his brother, Charles V had returned Walloon Flanders (Lille, Douai and Orchies) to Count Louis. When he died, they formed part of Margaret's inheritance. Part of the dowry of her grand-mother, a princess of France, had been the counties of Artois

A rich inheritance

and Franche-Comté. They, too, passed in 1384 to Margaret. Philip the Bold himself held the duchy of Burgundy.

He devoted his life to the acquisition of the surrounding principalities. Of these, the most significant for the future of present day Flanders, were Brabant and Loon. They had for a short time in the middle of the fourteenth century been joined to the county of Flanders in the economic union negociated by James van Artevelde, but this did not last. The childless duchess, Johanna, agreed as early as 1390 to the succession of Philip, but the Estates of Brabant only gave their consent in 1402. Philip's second son Anthony had been brought up in the duchy and it was to him that the succession passed on Johanna's death in 1406. By 1430 this cadet branch of the house of Burgundy was extinguished and the duchy added directly to the possessions of the dukes of Burgundy. These territories—the County of Flanders, parts of Brabant, and the County of Loon or Limburg—together form present day Flanders. Further north the romantic exploits of the Countess of Holland, Jacqueline of Bavaria, had led, by 1433, to her renunciation of her rights in favour of Duke Philip the Good. Her possessions had included Hainaut, Zealand and Frisia as well as Holland itself. By his usual mixture of diplomacy and bribery, Philip the Good had, by 1451, been accepted as ruler of Luxemburg. He had bought, in 1421, the county of Namur, and in 1435 made the Somme towns his southern frontier. His son, Charles the Bold, temporarily added both Liège and Gelderland. Liège had always been a difficult proposition for the marriage makers. It was, until the

Liège the stumbling block

end of the Ancien Régime an ecclesiastical principality ruled over by prince-bishops. It fell, therefore, outside the normal scheme of dynastic marriages. The only way to control it was to obtain it for a protégé or by armed force. The latter solution was adopted by Charles the Bold in 1474 and in spite or because of his savagery, it did not last. Until the end of the Ancien Régime, the Prince-bishopric formed an arrow piercing the eastern flank of the Netherlands. When, however, Charles the Bold attempted to link up his possessions in the Low Countries with Burgundy and Franche-Comté, and so resuscitate the old middle kingdom of Lotharingia, he met his defeat and death at Nancy in 1477, and the gap was never filled. Instead Burgundy was lost. In 1482 it returned to the French crown, while Charles's descendants concentrated on their northern lands. On Charles's death in 1477, his only child, Mary of Burgundy, brought with her a far greater inheritance than her ancestor Margaret of Flanders had done in 1384. But her marriage with Maximilian, the son of the Habsburg Emperor, meant that, instead of becoming an independent kingdom, the Netherlands would be treated, to an increasing extent, as a part of the immense Habsburg Empire.

Was this new, broader, land a better place in which to live ? Did these princely marriages really make any difference to any but the few at the top ? Did the changes mean that there was more to eat, and that life was less precarious ? Who profited from the change, if anyone did ? Philip of Commynes, writing in 1465, calls the Netherlands 'a land of promise'. Yet we know that the number of paupers was rising.

A land of promise

Commynes describes the rich apparel, the sumptuous banquets and the long period of peace. But we know that it saw also the dreaded, inexplicable visits of the plague, nightmares of famine and flood, and merciless war.

Where must we try to draw a line ? No period is, after all, one of continuous progress. Is there really any justification for thinking that the Burgundian period was different from the years which preceded and followed it ? Dynastic alliances, the great medieval diplomatic tool, usually affected the ordinary folk very little. The house of Burgundy's widening of her frontiers was, however, more than a mere change of ruling house.

The drama of the twelfth and thirteenth centuries had unrolled on the Flemish plain. It was there that the lion had shown its claws, there that France had been rebuffed, that the gilds had won their power, that the patriciate had lost its grip on the urban administration. It had set the pattern for the future. But by 1384, its very strength was becoming burdensome. To fight the French and the Leliaerts, the towns had relied on the food and the strong arms of the countryside. But the French and the Leliaerts had been beaten in 1302. The dominance of the towns did not, however, then come to an end. They continued to sacrifice their neighbours, when this was no longer necessary. Louis of Male tried, with some success, to curb the excesses of the towns, but it was under the House of Burgundy that rural interests were predominantly considered.

Thus for the great thirteenth century giants, the advent of Philip the Bold was not an improvement, but for the Flemish countryside, his protection was priceless.

And there is no doubt that it, rather than the towns, was the land of promise. The Flemish cities were, after 1302 in the hands of the gilds. The interests of the masters lay in the maintenance of a small élite who could lay down rules for the fabrication of the cloth of superb quality which had made them famous all over the known world. But by the fourteenth century the demand was changing. More people were in a position to buy cloth, but what they needed and could afford were the cheaper qualities manufactured in the countryside and in new textile centres. The gilds could not, or would not, see this. They tried, by even more stringent regulations to banish their com-

Recession of the old cloth industry

petitors. But this did not work. Their raw materials were no longer so abundant. They had to cope not only with country industry but with the products of their great international rival, England, who was gradually taking over the manufacture of her own cloth, from her own wool. About 1300, 35,000 sacks of English wool were imported into Flanders. Between 1400 and 1425 this had fallen to about 14,000 and later in the century to 10,000. However, cheaper Spanish wool had come to take its place and it was perfect for the new lighter cloths. By the mid sixteenth century between 36,000 and 40,000 sacks were entering the country—more than the quantity of English wool at its peak. So although the classic cloth industry of the Flemish towns was certainly undergoing a recession, it was replaced by a flourishing, vigorous alternative. Such terms as recession, and statistics about wool and cloth imports seem to be rather far removed from our enquiry into Philip of Commynes' claims about the prosperity of the Netherlands. They are however in fact relevant, because such a high proportion of the population lived from industry. Flanders had the most highly developed capitalistic society north of the Alps. In bad times this could be a weakness. Many of the country folk grew industrial crops such as flax, and in times of bad harvests and high grain prices had little home produce to fall back on. Yet this was a characteristic of the life of all but the very rich at this time. The court, the nobility, the church, the rich bourgeoisie would never starve. But for the rest of the population the bread-line was never far removed. On the whole, it was the poor, who paid the taxes. The rich generally managed to be exempt. The poor's chances of saving were very slim. They were, therefore, still

Flood, pest and famine

extremely susceptible to the effects of natural phenomena—such as flood, pest and famine. Life was intensely precarious and inexplicable. This had not improved in the fifteenth century. Life was still full of unreasonable risks—unrecognisable dangers—inexplicable catastrophes. The terrible grey rat, infested with plague, brought not only the Black Death of 1348-50, when one third of the population of Europe was wiped out, but recurrent bouts of varying degrees of intensity. On the whole its ravages seem to have struck less violently in the Low Countries than elsewhere, but nevertheless in Brabant the number of families had fallen from 94,000 in 1437 to 75,000 in 1496 chiefly owing to the plague. Population may have fallen in certain regions for other reasons also. Ypres, for instance, whose cloth trade had been of enormous importance in the twelfth and thirteenth centuries, saw a fall from between 20,000 and 30,000 inhabitants in 1300 to 7,600 in 1491. This seems to have been largely because of her dependence on the decaying Fairs of Champagne.

Such falls in population seem, however, to have been accompanied by improvements in the standard of living of the ordinary folk. They ate less bread, but what they did eat was more likely to have butter on it. Cheese, meat, milk, eggs all became more attainable. Important improvements in agriculture, in which the Low Countries were pioneers, meant more to eat. Brueghel's peasants are certainly not suffering from under-nourishment, as they prepare the wedding party or lie under the trees at harvest time while their wives sit cutting slices of bread and cheese. Yet the number of paupers had risen enormously. In the countryside round Leuven in 1526 it was as high as 41.5 % of the population. All this could perfectly well have occurred in the separate principalities and was not affected by their inclusion in a bigger territorial unit. The Netherlands were experiencing the same economic currents as the rest of Northern Europe. But the territorial expansion of her boundaries did, in fact, bring about at least one change of great moment. It ensured that the future lay rather with Brabant than with Flanders.

Brabant takes over from Flanders

The old drama was over. France was repulsed. The Netherlands were no longer threatened from the south.

All the old reflexes which had made the Flemish towns fight, and which had brought them to the brink of urban political independence, were no longer really relevant. Yet they could not be cast off. Ghent was one of the most impassioned enemies of the centralising tendencies of the new rulers. Brabant, on the other hand, was not encumbered by these out-moded reactions. She had had the good luck to be ruled by an intelligent line of dukes whose aims—the extension of their power over the east-west trade routes to the Rhine—had coincided happily with those of their people. They had been the vassals of powerless Emperors, unlike the Flemings, who had had the powerful, cunning and astute Capetians to deal with. The towns in Brabant had acquired administrative control over their own affairs rather late—Leuven only in 1378 and Antwerp in 1445. They had never, therefore, been the victims of the unscrupulous and ambitious feuds of the gilds. Their constitutional development, as the charter of Kortenberg and the Joyeuse Entrée of Johanna and Wenceslas show, had gone smoothly. Brabant had not had to settle the vital political questions by fighting. She had not been wrecked by the struggles which had shaken Flanders. While Flanders had been using up her energies on the struggle which threatened to make her into a land of city states, Brabant had quietly and, on the whole, peacefully followed a continuous line of constitutional development. Violence, animosities, feuds and endless riots had not divided the towns of Brabant, as had happened in the case of Bruges and Ghent. They could take over the chief rôle under the Burgundians without the bitter memories and out-dated habits of their western neighbours.

One of the victims of the shift in the centre of power was Bruges. Its position was gradually weakening for both economic and political reasons. Yet until the fifteenth century it remained of paramount importance. The days when merchants from Bruges had themselves ventured throughout the world in search of business were over. The defeat of the rich traders, sympathetic to France, on the field of Kortrijk had seen to that. Everyone instead flocked to Bruges: Venetians, Genoese, Florentines, Catalans, Portuguese, Parisians, English, Scots, Germans from the Hanse towns—Lübeck, Hamburg, Bremen, Danzig, Stettin—all brought their wares there. Many were highly organised. They had their own headquarters. One of these, built in 1478 for the Easterlings by J. Van de Poele, although now less extensive, still rises in the Memlingplaats.

Bruges: European metropolis

Another, rebuilt in 1720, had belonged to the Genoese since 1399. St. George attacks the dragon above its door. Each group was organised under its own director who coped with legal difficulties which arose in such complicated business transactions. All dealings had to be carried out through citizens of the town. In this way they kept the threads of trade nicely in their hands. Often these middlemen started as inn-keepers, lodging the numerous foreigners in their midst. One such family was called Van der Buerse, whose name is recorded for the first time in 1257. Before their house, which was rebuilt in 1948 in the Grauwwerkersstraat, the merchants came together to carry out their negociations. Hence the name 'beurs' or 'bourse' which came gradually to mean 'exchange' or a place where financial transactions are carried on. But the market which these foreign merchants served was largely a regional one. Commodities like honey, wood and skins from Novgorod, grain from the Baltic lands, herring and stockfish from the North, wine from Bordeaux and the Loire valley, spices and silks from the East brought by the fleets of Genoese and Venetian galleys, and copper and silver from the Carpathians and the mountains of Bohemia were intended for the rich consumers of Flanders and Brabant rather than to be exchanged in Bruges and to be carried later to more distant markets. The density of population, and the wealth of the area gave it an appetite for consumer goods. Families and institutions, such as monasteries, orphanages, almshouses, beguinages, came to buy their provisions in Bruges. As return cargo, merchants asked for nothing better than a good supply of good quality Flemish cloth. This at least was the case in the good old days of Bruges's prosperity. But when the supply of raw materials for the production of this cloth diminished, because England started to produce her own cloth from her own wool, it became more difficult to find a suitable exchange cargo in Bruges. The Germans looked outside Bruges, and they found an excellent alternative in the cheaper qualities produced in the new textile centres.

Others, requiring cloth of high quality, such as was now produced in England, could not buy it in Bruges. The town grasped at protectionism to try to combat

The Broel towers in Kortrijk: a good example of medieval fortification.

English competition, and forbade the import of such cloth. So the foreign merchants turned elsewhere—to Brabant, and particularly to Antwerp where the importation of English cloth was free and where much of it was finished. Between 1350 and 1550 the amount of English cloth imported into the Netherlands increased thirty times. In Bruges one after the other the various nations closed their houses, and went elsewhere. The last to go was the Hanse—in 1546.

Unfortunately for Bruges, her inability to satisfy her clients concided with practical difficulties of transport.

Bruges left high and dry

The Zwin and the canal from Damme and Sluis, the harbours of Bruges, were gradually and irremediably silting up.

Innumerable schemes were tried to remedy the damage caused by the tides and currents, but they were all ineffective. The tonnage of foreign shipping which in one day in 1457 had amounted to 66 boats with a total of 6,500 tons, had fallen by 1486 to a total of 75 for the whole year, and in 1499 to as low as 23. Customs' duties received in the Zwin ports tell the same sad story.

Antwerp at the cross-roads of the world

Yet the sea had played just the opposite trick on Antwerp. Changes in tides and currents had there widened and deepened the Scheldt on which the town's trade depended. At the level of the town the river is nearly half a mile wide. A glance at a map shows Antwerp's strength and weakness. She is admirably placed to receive the traders coming from several parts of Germany. The approach by sea from England across the Channel, or from the Baltic, is easy and safe while the mouth of the Scheldt is in friendly hands. The land routes from Italy over the Alps are shorter to Antwerp than to Bruges. Her own hinterland of Brabant was developing fast during the fifteenth and sixteenth centuries. Trade in the Netherlands doubled during this period. Most of this increase was centred on Antwerp. Yet her weakness lay in her dependence on the Scheldt. When once its mouth was commanded by enemies, her position would be even more untenable than that of Bruges. By the end of the sixteenth century this had happened. Antwerp's decay was complete.

Yet she had not only taken over Bruges' role, but had expanded it also. Antwerp was an international port and market. Everything was on a much larger scale than it had ever been in Bruges. Her trade spread over ever widening circles. Her responsibilities grew heavier and heavier. At first she coped with the trade of her own hinterland—Brabant. To this she soon added the immensely lucrative

English cloth trade, and established connections with the southern German towns like Ulm and Augsburg. She became the centre of the Baltic grain trade, of the trade in minerals from the Carpathians and Bohemia, and then of the apparently inexhaustible riches of the New World. While Bruges floundered in the political difficulties after Charles the Bold's death, Antwerp offered peace and hospitality and a sophisticated commercial structure capable of coping with the complications of world trade. For foreign merchants, lured away from Bruges, she built new headquarters, such as the magnificent new Hanse house built by Cornelis Floris de Vriendt. In 1531 she added a fine and imposing new Exchange—the Beurs—which the Englishman Sir Thomas Gresham admired and copied for the new Royal Exchange in London. Its motto 'in usum negotiatorum cuiuscumque nationis et linguae' 'for the use of all merchants, of whatever nationality or language' might have served for the whole town. Yet the complexity and scope of Antwerp's commercial rôle were dangerous.

After the absorption of the southern Netherlands by the Habsburgs, her rôle as an international financial centre became more and more complicated. The large

Antwerp: world financial centre

quantities of silver imported from the mines of Bolivia upset the traditional relationship of prices and wages.

Antwerp was called upon to provide huge foreign loans. Merchants from Antwerp were disastrously involved in the bankruptcy of Spain in 1567, and again three years later, of Portugal. Confidence was shaken. Political troubles threatened at the same moment. The unwillingness of Elizabeth of England to surrender a tempting quantity of Spanish silver, on which she had laid hands, led to the rather abrupt removal of English merchants from Antwerp to Hamburg. The Germans followed. War between Sweden and Denmark upset the Baltic grain trade. The year 1566 saw the iconoclastic rage sweep through the Netherlands, to be followed by the equally terrible vengeance of the Spanish Duke of Alva and his mercenaries. Brigandage, war, piracy ravaged the land. In 1576 came the Spanish Fury when the town was destroyed, burned and pillaged by the unpaid mercenaries. For nine years Antwerp held out against Spain in alliance with the Northern Provinces but in 1585 the end came. She was forced to surrender to Spain. For two hundred years her life blood was cut off. The Scheldt mouth on which all her prosperity had depended was closed to her,

The Scheldt closed

for its control lay in the hands of the Northern Provinces. Spain never managed to subdue them, and Antwerp paid for their success.

Did, then, the Netherlands become a land of promise ? Were they different from the Flanders of the twelfth and thirteenth centuries in any really important respects ? Were there compensations for the decline of some of the old traditional sources of wealth ? The answer is that the general prosperity doubled. There seems little doubt that for many classes of the population there was a distinct improvement in the standard of living. Losses in one sector seem to have been more than adequately compensated by gains in another. Bruges declined but Antwerp flourished. Urban industry contracted but rural industry increased. The lead lost to Flanders passed to Brabant. The great luxury and magnificence of the Burgundian court compensated for the decay of some of the old means of livelihood. Society became more complex, technically more skilful, and until the disasters of the end of the sixteenth century, more peaceful.

National feeling ?

Is there anything which distinguished this group of territories from other blocks which had been formed from time to time, by previous dukes or counts ? In the first place, this unification under the House of Burgundy lasted longer. Its effects must not be exaggerated. Under Philip the Bold there was probably little to give a farmer from West Flanders any common feeling with a townsman from Antwerp except that both spoke Dutch. But gradually the dukes created institutions common to their different lands in the Low Countries.

The Burgundians enter the Low Countries

In February 1384, the body of Louis of Male, count of Flanders was laid to rest, with great ceremony, in the family tomb in St. Peter's Church in Lille. The last male descendant of the Dampierres had disappeared. His only child, a daughter, Margaret, inherited the lands which Louis had ruled with great shrewdness and comparative success for thirty-eight years. One of his diplomatic successes had been her marriage in 1369 to Philip, son of the French king John II, brother of Charles V of France, and uncle of Charles VI. Philip himself held the fief of Burgundy. In 1384 he was 42 years old. He had earned his title of 'the Bold' on the field of Poitiers, and had already given numerous signs of his astuteness, far-sightedness und unflinching loyalty to the French crown. His greatest ambition was to extend the possessions of the house of Valois and to obtain for himself the dominant position at the French court, as the greatest peer of France. What he most certainly never suspected was that when his wife entered into her inheritance, the first step had been taken towards the creation of a new power in northern Europe, and of a group of lands ruled over by a branch of the Valois which would gradually assert its independence from the French crown.

That Philip came from outside the Netherlands was, in 1384, probably an

The university library in Leuven.

avantage. He was not personally involved in the internal quarrels which were still rending the country. He had accompanied his nephew, King Charles VI of France, on the punitive expedition of 1382 which had ended in the Flemish defeat at Westrozebeke, but had been careful to let the responsibility rest on the shoulders of the French king. Ghent had been provoked to even greater efforts by the

The old lion roars

defeat, and was still capable of asserting her political independence. Instead of receiving its new countess and her husband, the town raised the English flag and allowed Richard of England to nominate its governor. Trade was interrupted, and the countryside of Flanders repeatedly destroyed. Guerilla warfare had become such a habit that no-one could have been surprised to see the militia of Ghent appear before the walls of Bruges. Philip, enjoying the festivities accompanying the marriage, in Amiens, of the French king, was interrupted by the news that this new subjects had turned aside from Bruges and were holding Damme.

The tournaments, dancing and feasting came to an abrupt end and the king's uncle left with a French army to try to bring things under control. In 1385 while Frans Ackerman and his fellow citizens defended themselves in Damme, Philip cut off their water supply from the sources of Male—which was piped to Damme along the same lines followed now by the cobbled road—and also attempted to reduce his subjects by starvation. Twenty days later he was still there. The men of Ghent had had enough, however, and in the middle of the night, after shutting up the women and children in the church, they crept away, unbeknown to the French—back to Ghent. Neither side could really claim to have won. Both were anxious for peace. Ackerman was frightened by the approach of winter and the shortage of provisions. Philip saw that Flanders needed peace rather than the settlement of old scores, and so an armistice was signed in Tournai. Philip was ready to grant almost everything which the delegates from Ghent demanded, but insisted that they should kneel to ask his forgiveness for their revolt. When they refused Philip's demand, because, they said, they had not been empowered to kneel, negotiations were only maintained because of Margaret's intervention. On December 18th peace was made and a month later Philip and Margaret entered Ghent and swore there, in the church of St. John (now St. Baaf's) to maintain the town's privileges, while the town promised obedience. Philip then took his precautions. New castles were built. The defences of towns such as Kortrijk, Oudenaarde and Sluis were strengthened.

Unlike so many of his predecessors, Philip the Bold was not threatened from the south. He acted always as a French prince. He passed most of his time at the French court. All his attention could, therefore, be given to the east and north. The most obvious field for manoeuvre was Brabant. The duchess, Johanna, was childless. She was the aunt of Philip's wife, Margaret. What could have been more obvious that that she could choose her niece as successor ? The decision did not rest with her alone. The Estates of Brabant had also to agree. Philip gradually extended his influence in the duchy, on the one hand by helping Johanna to recover the estates which she had been forced to pawn, and on the other by a show of generosity and splendour towards the ordinary folk. When, for instance, he visited Brussels, Philip was accompanied by an extravagant retinue of 112 knights and 240 other retainers, who made large purchases of velvets and saddles and provisions from the local shop-keepers, and so pleased everyone ! Gradually the idea of Margaret's succession came to be accepted, and by 1402 the Estates had formally agreed, provided only that Flanders and Brabant were not united. Such a reaction shows the danger of exaggerating the growth of a 'Burgundian feeling' in the Netherlands. It was, however, agreed that Brabant should pass to Philip's younger son Anthony, while Flanders would be the inheritance of John. Johanna's rights over Limburg had been ceded to Philip in 1396. It must

The next step: Brabant

have seemed most improbable that either branch would die out, as was in fact the case under Philip's grandson. In 1406 Anthony, who had been educated in Brabant, inherited the duchy. The Valois were one step further in the Netherlands.

To the north and south there were also interesting possibilities. Holland and Hainaut were in the hands of the Wittelsbach family, and there were marriageable children there, as in Flanders. A double marriage, celebrated with great splendour of the Sunday after Easter 1385 in Cambrai, united Margaret of Burgundy with William of Holland and Margaret of Wittelsbach with John, heir to Flanders. According to the chronicler Froissart there had not been such festivity for five hundred years. In the presence of the King of France, the crown jewels were removed from their iron coffers, and the guests at the banquet were served by the highest officials in the land in their most gorgeous raiment. In fact, it was an ominous moment for the king. He was helping to lay the foundation stone for a very powerful independent Burgundian block on his northern frontier.

Under Philip the Bold's sons, John the Fearless, Count of Flanders, and Anthony, Duke of Brabant, these two parts of the Netherlands loosened the bonds which still bound them to France and the Empire. Philip the Bold died in Halle on April 4, 1404 and was buried, not in the Netherlands but in the family tomb in Dijon, where his statue was later erected. It was now the turn of the counts of Flanders to stir the French political brew rather than the reverse. During the 171 years between the accession of Philip the Bold and the abdication of Charles V, the policy of the rulers of the Low Countries gradually turned from wholehearted identification with France and French interests, to open hostility. Each ruler widened and deepened the gap between the two countries which was beginning to show under John the Fearless and which had become a chasm under Charles the Bold. In 1404 Charles VI of France already showed the symptoms of madness which were to complicate European politics for twenty years. The great vassals were all anxious to fill the gap made by his inability to steer the ship of state. One obvious contender was John, another his cousin, Louis of Orléans. The struggle was of no interest to the count's Flemish subjects. The following years saw too an unending flow of petitions and exhortations from them, begging him to keep out of it, for all sorts of reasons. The beginnings of the murderous struggle between the Burgundian and Armagnac factions in France were quickly recognised by the Netherlands as dangerous to their interests. They wanted a prince who would put their affairs first, not last. When John made his Joyeuse Entrée in Ghent, the town's

John the Fearless

representatives asked him to remain neutral in the war between England and France; to honour their privileges; to use the Flemish language in his dealings with the county; to fix his exchequer on the Flemish side of the Leie; and to reside in Flanders. He agreed. Whatever his intentions were at the time, he certainly did not carry out his promise. Even more significantly, the representatives of Ghent were joined by those from Bruges in their negotiations with the count. They were together insisting that John should act not as a French prince but as Count of Flanders. As throughout the whole of Flemish history, they were trying desperately hard to get a ruler of their own. They did not want to see Flanders the scene of later battles between English and French, as would happen if their prince became too preoccupied with French affairs. An English expedition had already attacked Sluis, and raided the coast round Sint-Anna-ter-Muiden and Kadzand. Flanders was a political pawn as she so often was, in the hands of her more powerful neighbours.

The murder of Louis of Orléans on a November evening in 1407 by the supporters of John of Flanders meant the end of any hopes of a Flemish policy. New taxes were demanded to pay the bill for a struggle in which the Flemings had no interest whatever. Veurne, Ghent and Bruges protested. The urban militias packed up and went home whenever they felt inclined, leaving John in the lurch. Luckily they were not asked to take part in the battle of Azincourt as their count was at that moment sulking in Flanders after an unsuccessful attempt to enter Paris. John personally paid the price for his attempts to cut a

Murder at Montereau

dash in French politics. He was in his turn murdered, on the bridge of Montereau, in September 1419, in revenge for his own dark deed of twelve years before.

For John's brother Anthony the succession of Brabant was in some ways more complicated, for he had to deal not only with his family connections with the French crown, but he also held his lands from the Emperor. He met his death at the side of the French King at the battle of Agincourt. But during his life-time he had to deal with the enmity of the Emperor Sigismund towards the house of Burgundy which he saw, quite rightly, as a threat to his western lands. The Emperor tried to stop the gradual infiltration of Burgundian power between Brabant and the Rhine, and towards the north. Events seemed always to play into the hands of the Burgundians. Jacqueline of Holland, the only child of one of the marriages arranged so judiciously by Philip the Bold in 1385, married

Jacqueline of Bavaria's romantic progress

Anthony's son and successor, John IV of Brabant. The danger now was that Holland, Hainaut and Brabant would be united in the hands of their heirs. Sigismund rushed to the support of Jacqueline's uncle and rival. The princess's adventurous career had begun. Her husband was not capable of ruling either Holland, or Brabant. In Brabant, he was deposed in favour of his brother. In Holland, Jacqueline had to defend herself. Even before her marriage to John could be annulled by the Pope, she married the brother of the English king, Henry V. He, however, was not much help in her efforts against John of Bavaria, her uncle, who was supported by the Count of Flanders. Gradually Philip the Good forced her into a position where she had to give up her rights over Hainaut, Holland and Zealand. Her last effort to exert herself, after escaping from Ghent where she had been imprisoned by Philip, was to marry the governor he had placed in charge of her lands, Frank van Borselen. Philip threatened the latter's life if Jacqueline did not give up her rights. To save her husband's life, she renounced all her rights to Philip, Count of Flanders and Duke of Burgundy.

When, in Shakespeare's play 'Henry V', the Duke of Burgundy appears as the mediator between England and France, his rôle as elder statesman is historically justified. Philip, the son of John the Fearless, was acting as mediator between

St. Nicholas's church in Ghent: thirteenth century.

Jacqueline and her uncle, John of Bavaria, even before the death of his father. After the death of Henry V of England he was offered the title of Regent of England which he refused. But that he was offered such a title is significant in two respects: firstly that the bonds between France and Burgundy were weakening, and secondly that he had become one of the most important rulers in western Europe.

Philip the Good: conditor Belgii ! What sort of man was this greatest of the Burgundian dukes ? He ruled Burgundy and the Low Countries for a very long time—from 1419 until 1467 and the greater part of this period was peaceful. This was of immense importance for the Netherlands. They had, for the first time, a Burgundian ruler who put their interests first. Because of the murder of John the Fearless, Philip's father, the son's relations with France were naturally not cordial. At least until 1435 he was tempted neither to play any direct part in French affairs, nor to sacrifice the English alliance—so dear to the hearts of his Flemish subjects. Philip was born in Dijon and brought up in the Ghent Prinsenhof. For the first sixteen years of his rule he abandoned the traditional alliance with France, and even after the Treaty of Arras in 1435, when relations were resumed, the French crown had to renounce all feudal rights over him personally. As the same time, he acquired the famous Somme towns, so often fought over in the history of western Europe, as his southern boundary. Even more interesting, in the light of thirteenth century Flemish history, is the stipulation contained in the treaty of Arras by which the French king besought his vassals to punish him if he failed to carry out its stipulations. All the humiliations of Guy of Dampierre by Philip the Fair seemed to be coming home to roost. Until 1435 relations between the English and the Flemings had been good. Cross channel trade continued uninterrupted. This may have arisen more from Philip's fear of an Anglo-Armagnac alliance than from real care for the Netherlands, but whatever the motive, the results were excellent. He even went so far in 1420 as to take the extraordinary step, for a Valois, of accepting Henry V of England as heir of Charles VI and Regent of France. Yet Philip refused to bind himself personally to England. He would never accept the Order of the Garter. That might have involved him in questions of personal honour about which he was particularly strict. He did not want to impede his freedom of movement. That he found such bonds important led him to found his own

The Golden Fleece order of chivalry—the Golden Fleece, with which he bound his great nobles and landowners in a personal oath to the house of Burgundy. By 1435 he had had enough of the English alliance. The complications caused by the ceaseless struggle between England and France, and between Burgundians and Armagnacs, seemed endless. For the Flemings, his treaty with France was unfortunate. Flemish merchants in London were set upon and slaughtered and the Duke of Gloucester raided the coast and damaged the villages between Saint-Omer and Poperinge while the navy blockaded the Zwin. The urban militia was called out to besiege the English in Calais, but the men of Ghent at least had no heart in it and returned home with their nice new weapons. The whole thing was very trying for both sides and was finally taken in hand by Philip's third wife, Isabelle of Portugal, who was herself a very experienced and able diplomat. She arranged an armistice. Philip had been hankering after a hand in French affairs, but in spite of the treaty of Arras and the sacrifice, if only temporary, of Flemish trade, he never really obtained any effective power there. Relations with Charles VII were always strained. The French gradually cleared the English out without his help. His attempts to arbitrate between the king and the dauphin were unacceptable. Everything seemed to compel him to look east rather than south for a field of influence.

There was in fact more room for manoeuvre in Philip's relations with the Emperor than with the king of France. Sigismund always responded to the Burgundians as if they were French princes rather than independent rulers. He remained constantly hostile. But luck was against him. Imperial fiefs seemed to fall almost unasked into Philip's lap.

In 1421, he managed to buy the County of Namur. Jacqueline of Holland's adventures were over by 1433, and Philip had inherited her lands. Philip of Saint-Pol, Duke of Brabant, died in rather suspicious circumstances, just as he was threatening to ally with France against Philip and his Duchy fell into Philip's hands. The Estates of Brabant had to accept the previously almost unimaginable fact that Flanders and Brabant were united under one ruler—a fact of very great importance for the future. Threats from the Empire could achieve nothing against Philip when he was accepted by the Estates themselves. He knew the strength of his position and sent a strongly worded memorandum to the imperial princes and the Kings of Denmark and Poland setting forth his case, insolently questioning the Emperor's right to ally with the murderers of John the Fearless, and, much more cogently, threatening to cut off their trade from the Rhine if they took a step against him. The German princes rushed to assure him of their neutrality.

Political patience pays

Gradually the boundaries were being pushed back. The Burgundian

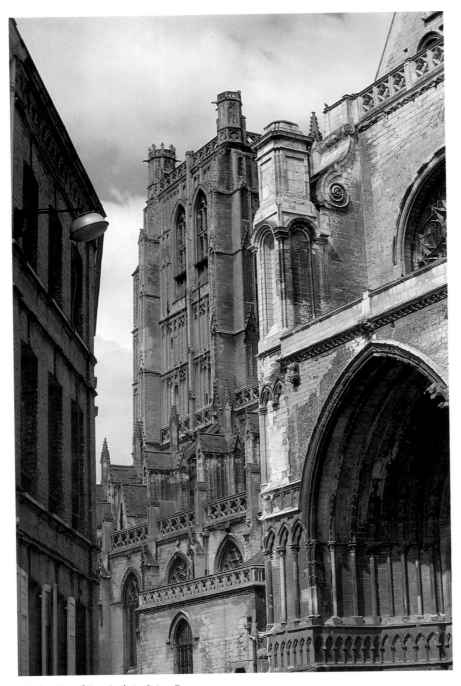

The basilica of Our Lady in Saint-Omer.

Netherlands were a very different proposition under Philip the Good from what they had been under his grand-father Philip the Bold. And these very important territorial acquisitions had been accomplished on the whole peacefully. No large-scale war had been provoked. Unlike his son Charles was to do, Philip never attacked lands where his rule was undesired. He rather took advantage of every favourable movement and did not provoke violent opposition. Sigismund's attempts to exert his own rights in Brabant were repulsed, not by Philip, but by the inhabitants themselves. Philip still had occasional crises with the old Flemish lions. Bruges and Ghent never accepted the centralising tendencies of the Burgundians. He never supported the particularism and monopoly which these towns loved. When, therefore, he tried to loosen Bruges's grip on Sluis, Philip was attacked as he entered Bruges, and although he was unhurt, several of his followers were killed. For this, the citizens—bare-headed and bare-footed—had to beg their duke's forgiveness. Ghent made a more serious attempt to regain her old political independence. A tax on salt, the gabelle such as was paid in France, was proposed as an alternative to the old piece-meal aids and dues, but this did not appeal to Ghent. The duke's argument that it would be more equably distributed did not tempt the town council, who worked on the principle that taxes should be paid, not by the rich, but by those too poor to avoid them. Philip did not insist. He seems to have had an affection for the great Flemish town where he had passed his youth. But when Ghent went on to nominate her own council without the participation of the ducal representatives, Philip withdrew his legal officer, a step rather like the breaking off of diplomatic relations by the withdrawal of an ambassador. A revolutionary and violent government controlled Ghent, but received only enforced support from the surrounding countryside. Nevertheless the rebellion was kept up for two years before the urban militia was once more heavily

Ghent once again

defeated at Gavere in 1453. The struggle was over once again. Many of the precious privi-leges were re-defined and severely pruned. The count regained control. Two thousand citizens clad not in rich clocks, but in their shirts, kneeled to beg his forgiveness. There were fines, and the curtailment of liberties but no bloody reprisals. Philip dealt mercifully with one of the final antics of the old rebel trying to put back the clock. There had been no question this time of independent alliances with the count's enemies as had happened between van Artevelde and Edward III of England. Henry VI of England reminded the Flemish towns of their old loyalties but without success. Ghent's militia helped in the duke's attack on Calais, as in van Artevelde's day they had helped the

English. They pitched their tents in the same place. But this time they had neither the ability nor the desire to execute their own foreign policy.

We may ask whether, under Philip the Good, the Low Countries took an appreciable step towards becoming the land of promise described by Commynes. We have described the substantial territorial gains of the first three Burgundian dukes. We have discussed the undoubted prosperity of most of these lands in the possibly declining western European economy of this time. How far was Philip himself responsible for this state of affairs ? Several portraits of him still exist. The fifteenth century copy of one by Roger van der Weyden hangs in Bruges. A manuscript miniature shows him receiving the translation of a manuscript from Simon Nockart. There are others. In all of them he is dressed soberly, but richly, in black and wears the collar of the order of the Golden Fleece. Contemporaries commented admiringly on his dignified bearing and his prominence in European diplomacy. Some remarked that he was lazy, others that the had he gift of leaving his able officials in peace. With the great range of his responsibilities, he could never have hoped to do all the work himself. One of the symptoms which beset his son Charles, and which helped to bring about his ruin, was his insistence on supervising every detail of government. Philip, at least until the last few years when he was ill, showed great skill in choosing first class diplomats and civil servants, such as the great Nicholas Rolin, and leaving them to get on with the job. He seems to have been a kind man. His numerous illegitimate children were all brought up at court and many filled important positions. He certainly had an eye for an attractive face.

A duke surrounded by artists

When after the death of his second wife, there was talk of a possible marriage with Isabelle of Portugal, Philip sent John van Eyck to Lisbon to paint her portrait, and bring it back to his master, before he committed himself. Her portrait in the Louvre, by an unknown Flemish artist (the one by van Eyck is lost) shows that Philip was probably right in being pleased with van Eyck's report. The duke was constantly on the move. His court impressed everyone with its luxury. He was an impassioned bibliophile and left the greatest contemporary collection of nearly nine hundred illuminated manuscripts, most of which are now in the Royal Library in Brussels. In certain miniatures we can see the duke himself visiting artists' studios to order new works—for example from David Aubert. The numerous miniatures in these manuscripts provide a wonderful commentary on the scholars, artists, courtiers and religious life of the fifteenth century. Philip certainly had good taste. It has been suggested that the Burgundians loved to show off—that they were a sort of fifteenth century 'nouveaux riches'. Such a view seems to ignore their origin as Valois princes. It was certainly fortunate that they were rich enough to patronise artists like John van Eyck, the painter of the triptych of the Mystic Lamb in the Cathedral of St. Baaf's in Ghent, Hans Memling, who painted the beautiful Shrine of St. Ursula in St. John's Hospital in Bruges, and Roger van der Weyden who made numerous court portraits, such as those of Philip's son and heir Charles, and possibly of his illegitimate son, Anthony. Philip patronised the weaving industry by ordering a series of tapestries—the 'History of Gideon'. In Memling's 'Mystic marriage of St. Catherine' we have a portrait of Margaret of York, wife of Charles, as St. Barbara, and of his daughter Mary of Burgundy, as St. Catherine. Such artistic glory was possible only in peace. This most valuable and most unusual ingredient in the history of the Low Countries had a great champion in Philip the Good. He had much good luck. Often his schemes seemed to accomplish themselves. But he had great patience and was without the uncontrolled ambition of his son, Charles. He had an eye for the possible, and did not exhaust his people in hopeless and costly pipe-dreams. His very long period of power gave the ordinary citizen time and funds to patronise the arts. His councillors commissioned beautiful pictures, very instructive for the history of the fifteenth century. His great chancellor, Nicholas Rolin, gazes calmly across John van Eyck's 'Virgin of Autun' in the Louvre; George van der Paele, a canon of the chapter of St. Donatian in Bruges, holding his spectacles and his prayer-book, is obviously very much impressed by the sight before him. Ordinary citizens appear in many of these detailed pictures—in the crowds in the 'Mystic Lamb', in Dirk Bouts's 'Justice of Otto' in Brussels, on the misericord stalls in St. Salvator's in Bruges, where

The blossoming of a culture

they sit comfortably at table, eating. Innumerable examples illumine the peaceful, prosperous, artistic and comfortable life of the fifteenth century Netherlands of Philip the Good, when a distinctive and rich culture blossomed. Compared to other European societies at this time, the Burgundian Netherlands showed an unparalleled level of artistic and cultural achievement. This is one of the peaks of western European civilization, such as England was to see in the time of Elizabeth I. A fascinating comparison can be made between a picture such as van Eyck's 'Virgin of Autun', and some Spanish paintings of the same period such as that of King Ferdinand and Queen Isabelle praying before the Virgin, which hangs in the Prado in Madrid. Both artists have painted glorious cloaks and draperies. In one, the fur around the wrists of Nicholas Rolin makes one almost stretch out a finger to feel its softness; in the

other the clothes hang stiffly from the figures. In one the faces are like wax models, in the other lined with the experience of great affairs. In the Spanish picture the view through the windows, so often a feature of the Flemish primitives, is flat and dull; in the Rolin picture, tiny details of trees, meadows, and houses stand out with jewel-like clarity. That artists such as van Eyck were given such commissions and had the peace in which to carry them out, was certainly in some measure due to Philip's peace and patronage.

Almost to the end of his life Philip seems to have had a great fund of common-sense. But in one special respect he himself provided the exception which proved the rule: his ambition to go on Crusade. His court was organised on a basis of chivalry and personal honour. The foundation of the Order of the Golden Fleece fitted into this tradition, although it may also have had practical advantages. A crusade was just the sort of plan to which such an Order should be dedicated. The Byzantine Emperors were always busy trying to enlist western support against Islam. Philip sent galleys to help John Paleologue's defence of Rhodes against the Turks. But this was not enough. The Pope continued to exhort the princes of Christendom personally to embark for the east, and Philip seems to have been serious in his intention to go. At a meeting of the chapter of the Order of the Golden Fleece in Ste Waudru's church in Mons in 1451 the crusade was preached by the Bishop of Châlons. However, in the same year the revolt broke out in Ghent, ant Philip had to stay in Flanders. But three years later

The Pheasant Banquet

at a sumptuous banquet in Lille, known as the Pheasant Banquet, Holy Church, in the person of a lady dressed as a nun, carried in the 'Castle of the Faith' on an elephant led by a giant in a turban, appealed to him again. The Herald of the Order of the Golden Fleece, carrying a live pheasant decked out in a golden collar studded with precious stones, and accompanied by two of Philip's daughters, pleaded with the duke to promise the ladies and the pheasant that he would go. Philip agreed to follow his suzerain Charles VII of France, or any other leader designated by the King of France. One hundred and three enthusiastic nobles promised on the spot to accompany him and, after reflection, a hundred and twelve more agreed to go. Following this burst of enthusiasm Philip set off to Ratisbon to discuss crusading plans with the Emperor Frederick III. The trouble was that no one dared to set off leaving one of the others behind, for fear of what he might then do! Philip and his entourage made such a deep impression on their German neighbours that Frederick decided it was more prudent to stay away from the Diet, in case Philip tried to force his hand to obtain a royal title for all his imperial fiefs. Had this once been given Frederick would have lost his last bargaining counter. Philip next appealed to his suzerain, Charles VII, to be confided with the banner of France. Charles, who hated him, refused. He saw, however, in Philip's need for money to equip his expedition an opportunity to buy back the Somme towns, whose loss, in the Treaty of Arras, had always rankled. Philip was involved in a bitter quarrel with his son Charles who accused his father of being too much influenced by the de Croy family. They were in their turn in the pay of the French king. Philip, in a weak moment, probably already ill, agreed to France's purchase of the Somme towns. Tremendous scenes with his son led at one moment to Philip riding off into the Zoniënwood, near Brussels and losing himself there for twenty four hours, much to the court's alarm.

And still Philip could not leave for the east. In 1456, the Dauphin, Louis, fled from his father's palace and sought refuge in the Burgundian court. Philip found the situation delicate but allowed the young man to stay, and in fact lodged him royally in the castle of Genappe. Philip still hoped for a say in French affairs, and to succour the dauphin seemed a good way of going about it. Louis's behaviour on his father's death must have seemed a little odd, as the prince immediately left for Paris, without making his farewells and taking with him Philip's wife's horses. However, Philip rode to his coronation in Rheims in high spirits and surrounded by an enormous company. His treasure, 400 fat sheep and some 80 horned beef for the kitchen, accompanied him. His reception in Paris and the obvious intrigues of the new king with his son Charles gradually disillusioned Philip. His departure for the crusade was once more complicated by the thorny problem of who was to rule the Netherlands and Burgundy while he was away. He had quarrelled with his own son. If Louis once got his foot firmly into the Netherlands he was most unlikely to withdraw it again voluntarily. Nevertheless, Philip went on collecting a fleet at Sluis, gathering treasure, and he despatched his son Anthony to Marseilles to await him there. Louis, who certainly hated Philip as much as his father Charles VII had done, and whose whole life was dedicated to destroying the house of Burgundy, went rather too obviously about the business of buying himself a following in the Netherlands, and even went so far as to summon Philip to appear before the Parliament of Paris to answer some charge brought against him by a private person. The de Croy party became too overpowering and were suddenly dismissed by the duke. The Estates General, called by Philip, put the case of the young prince Charles so vividly before his father, that the two were reconciled. Philip, furious at having given up the Somme towns, determined to get them back by force. This was, however, to be the task of his son. Philip, worn out by his immense responsibilities, in 1465 made over the government to him and retired from public life, to his court, either in Brussels or in Bruges, where he died in 1467 at the age of 71. Charles, however, in spite of inexperienced soldiers and rusty

Charles the Bold invades France

armour had triumphantly invaded France, crushed Louis XI at Monthléry, and recovered the Somme towns. It may have given him an unfortunate taste for battle. In about a hundred years the wheel had gone full circle. From being among the most loyal vassals of the French king, the house of Burgundy had invaded France at the head of an army, advanced as far as Paris, and enforced a crushing defeat on its suzerain.

Twelve years later in 1477 near Nancy, on the hills of Lorraine, the frozen corpse of Charles the Bold, Duke of Burgundy, was identified by his doctor from an old wound and its long finger-nails. It bore three recent wounds and had been partly eaten by wolves. How, and why, had Philip's son met such an end after ruling for only twelve years?

A glance at a map of the Burgundian possessions at the time of Philip the Good's death in 1467 shows what a temptation lay there for such a man as Charles.

Charles aims at a royal crown

To him, it must have seemed as if just one or two more small acquisitions would mean the rebirth of the old Lotharingian state between Germany and France. The ruler of such a state would be on an equal footing with king and emperor: he could not be refused a royal, and perhaps even an imperial title. It all looked so simple. Between him and his heart's desire there lay only a handful of Liégeois, a few Alsatians and a few Swiss peasants. If only the rich towns of the Netherlands would open their bulging coffers to pay a few more Italian mercenaries, what a triumph it would be for Charles! Yet each of these elements was individually dangerous to him, and, when united, they were fatal. The solid towns did not wish to use their hard earned wealth to equip armies for a ruler who did nothing but tear up their charters and let bands of hired troops ravage their lands. The men of Liège enjoyed the special status by which they were ruled over by a prince-bishop, nominated, in theory at least, by the Emperor. Yet their land cut like a sword through Charles's domains, dividing Luxemburg from Brabant and Namur. Further north, the Bishopric of Utrecht and the Duchy of Gelderland stopped any advance towards Frisia and threatened the frontiers of Holland. South of Luxemburg, Lorraine blocked communications between the north and the duchy of Burgundy itself. Alsace threatened Franche-Comté, and the Swiss lurked menacingly in their mountains. Taken separately, each of these lands

The port of Ostend.

seemed to present small problems for the strength of Burgundy. But together they were overwhelming. Charles managed to arouse such hatred in them that other enmities seemed trifling by comparison. Once they had united against him, he could not fight on all sides at once. He showed an extraordinary ability to unite his enemies against him. The despotism typical of the fifteenth and sixteenth centuries became in him so overwheening that it defeated itself. In complete contrast to his father, Charles never managed to recognise reality. He never saw the limitations of the possible. Beneath his demands, the administrative structures common to many of the Burgundian lands and built up so painstakingly by his predecessors, were broken up and the particularism which always threatened the Netherlands again burst out. Charles could not afford both to continue the modernisation of the administration and to fight innumerable wars.

Louis XI seemed to have been dealt with at Monthléry. Charles next turned his attention to Liège. It had been an annoying problem to the Burgundians throughout the fifteenth century. They had tried to put their man in as bishop, but Philip's choice of Louis of Bourbon was unfortunate. He did not want the job and was always packing up and going home at critical moments. Louis XI could not resist such a promising chance of undermining Burgundian power, and when Liège chose its own governor he promised help. Rather over-confident the Liégeois then harassed Brabant, one of the Burgundian lands. Charles fought them in Brustem and imposed humiliating terms—very unlike those dictated elsewhere by Philip the Good. Liège was occupied in October 1468, by Burgundian troops, all its privileges revoked, walls, gates and arms destroyed, and one of Charles's most loyal lieutenants, Humbercourt, put in as governor. It looked as if Liège was dealt with, but he had underrated the efforts of which such a community was capable, under such circumstances. Charles returned to his endless running fight with Louis XI, who always managed to slip through his fingers like quicksilver. On this occasion it looked, however, as if Charles really had got hold of him at last. Louis wanted summit talks, and was given a safe conduct to meet Charles at Péronne. Just at that moment the Liégeois attacked Tongeren. Charles had no doubt that this move had been provoked by Louis and encouraged by French gold but was badly synchronised.

The narrow escape of Louis XI

The French king was put in a most delicate position. With a very small suite, he was virtually Charles's prisoner. Luckily, his safe-conduct had some significance for the duke, and by promising anything and everything as was his habit in awkward situations, Louis at least saved his own life. He was forced, however, to accompany Charles to the punishment of the Liégeois. On Sunday October 30th, 1468, the Burgundians entered Liège and deliberately and systematically destroyed it. For seven weeks the town burned. Only the churches were spared. For seven years no rebuilding was allowed. Only in 1475, when Charles was desperate for soldiers, did he allow rebuilding to begin—in return for six thousand archers. Louis XI was forced to watch his triumph. Two hundred and fifty years before, Ferrand of Portugal had been forced to walk in Philip Augustus's triumph in Paris.

One of the chinks in the Burgundian armour had been filled, but at what a price! Other possible thorns in Charles's flesh trembled and took their

Charles's military adventures

precautions. He turned south. Alsace belonged to Sigismund of Austria. His constant need of money to fight the Swiss led him to pawn it to Charles. No thought was given to the preferences of the inhabitants, who found themselves under Pierre de Hagenbach, a Burgundian noted for his fidelity and his cruelty. He ruled so harshly that the Alsatians could hardly wait to return to the pleasant laxity of Habsburg rule. After five years they were more than ready to bury their differences with the Swiss and to receive back Sigismund with open arms. De Hagenbach, left in the lurch by Charles with no money to pay his mercenaries and attacked on all sides, was tried and executed. Burgundian domination there had been shortlived. Further north, a similar train of events took place. Family quarrels between the Duke of Gelderland and his sons led him to accept the Duke of Burgundy as his heir. The Estates of Gelderland were horrified at such a prospect and refused to accept this arrangement. Charles enforced his rights by force of arms. He left this dangerous possession to turn to the bishopric of Cologne, where troubles between the prince-bishop and his chapter gave the Duke an excuse to interfere. The episcopal lands were defended against the invading Burgundian army by the town of Neuss. Remembering the fate of Liège, Neuss held out against the besieging army from July 30th 1474 until June 15th 1475, and in spite of prodigies of military organisation, Charles was in the end forced to withdraw without ever entering the town. One further gap remained wide and obviously open - Lorraine. It still divided the Netherlands and Luxemburg from the Duchy of Burgundy. Accordingly in 1475, the Burgundian army entered Nancy, and Charles talked grandly of making it his new capital. Duke René fled. Other towns trembled with fear. The Swiss tried to join Sigismund and Louis XI in approaching Charles. But he was provoked at long last to attack the mountains. The castle of Granson fell and its defenders were hanged from the

Village of Sint Anna ter Muiden in Zealand.

battlements. It was obvious that he could not be stopped by diplomatic means. The Swiss turned and fought Charles outside Granson and, to the stupefaction and delight of Europe, won. Everyone immediately rushed to take advantage of this unexpected and incomprehensible luck. René of Lorraine returned to his lands; a revolt broke out in Gelderland; the towns of the Netherlands refused new taxes and supplies; the Duke of Milan and the King of Provence allied themselves secretly with Louis XI, who rushed to Lyons to be at hand to enjoy his enemy's discomfiture. Charles still refused to accept reality. Philip of Commynes, who had deserted him for the service of Louis XI, remarks 'Dieu lui avoit troublé le sens et l'entendement'. Before Morat, Charles's army, discouraged, unpaid, and undisciplined, was again heavily defeated and the treasures of the Burgundian camp, as well as most of its artillery, captured. This is the treasure which can be seen in Berne museum. All that was left for Charles was to retreat to Luxemburg. But Duke René entered Nancy, and in his turn hanged the 120 defenders, draped in black, from the battlements. This time, however, they were Burgundians. Charles, deaf to all advice, desperately collected yet another army, which deserted him at the critical moment, and he was again defeated and this time killed. In the icy new year of 1477 in a hopeless attack on the advancing Swiss, his dreams ended.

The machinations of Louis XI

Like a wicked wizard, Louis XI had always hovered on the edge of Charles's grandiose schemes, pricking the bubble, intriguing with the enemy, encouraging another revolt, or infiltrating his informers and supporters into the Burgundian court. His ambition was just as firm as Charles's, but his methods were quite different. He was subtle, wily, dishonest, pliable and astute, but relatively weak. Charles was stubborn, cruel and fanatically incapable of delegating authority and had an outstanding talent for alienating absolutely everyone. In a Europe not yet characterised by strong national feeling he succeeded in arousing it. The defence of Neuss by the Germans, the brutalities of Hagenbach, the agony of Liège welded previously intangible emotions into invincible weapons. Even in the Low Countries, where Charles had the core of his support, all favourable feeling was gradually crushed by his endless demands for arms and money, and by his complete indifference to the real interests of his people. Ghent saw her precious privileges torn up before her eyes. Trade suffered because of the endless tramping of military feet. Yet Charles would not see the impatience and exhaustion of his homeland. His fanatical ambition recognised in every criticism a personal attack. He played into the hands of his enemies by uniting all opposition against himself. No previous Duke of Burgundy had come out so obviously on the English side in her struggle with France. Philip the Good had always maintained some reservations. Charles however threw himself into the English alliance. He married Margaret of York, sister of king Edward IV, in Damme in June 1468.

Festivities in Bruges The festivities which followed in Bruges had never been outdone, and probably set the pattern for many of the processions which we still enjoy in Flanders. After being received at the town gates by the clergy and court and stopping at street corners to watch 'tableaux vivants', the foreign merchant communities were presented to the Duke and his bride—the Venetians in rose coloured velvet, the Florentines and Spaniards in black satin, the Genoese in white damask and the Hanse in purple cloth. In a specially built hall, its ceiling draped in blue and white, a tapestry depicting Jason and the Golden Fleece, and splendid candelabra in the form of mountains topped with castles, a huge meal was served on the Burgundian gold and silver plate from vessels shaped like boats. Eight days of tournaments followed. Louis XI quickly took advantage of the opportunity to invade Brittany, which was allied with Charles. Whenever Charles's back was turned, Louis always managed to make the most of it. In December 1470 he took back the Somme towns and invaded the Netherlands while in 1471 the duke retaliated with an invasion of France. But on the only occasion when such an invasion might have produced substantial results, Charles was too late. Stubbornly sitting before Neuss he allowed Edward IV of England and his army to wait, until the English begin to think he was uninterested, and then to make peace with Louis. With the Emperor, his relations were more varied, but even in Germany by 1477 he had built up a mountain of hostility. Frederick had in fact had the pleasure of making Charles the laughing stock of Europe. On September 29th 1473, he met the Emperor at Trèves. For two months the two courts enjoyed a luxurious holiday while the two heads of state conferred in secret. The fact that Charles had ordered a sceptre seemed to point to negotiations about a royal title. He had already spoken of the possibility of a renaissance of the old kingdom of Burgundy or of Lotharingia.

The Emperor sneaks away Europe was frightened at such wild talk. Frederick quietly left Trèves, having committed himself to nothing and Charles had to pack up his sceptre and go home. One very strong diplomatic pawn, however, still remained to him—the hand of his only child, Mary of Burgundy. He promised it successively to seven princes. Even his choice of husband for his daughter caused nothing but trouble. The alliance with the house of Habsburg, through her marriage to Maximilian, son of the Emperor, deprived the Netherlands of any chance of having a ruling house of its own, for three hundred and fifty years. When the news of Charles the Bold's death came from Nancy, Europe was incredulous. Louis XI had waited and schemed for this moment. Yet, when it occurred, he seemed bewildered by its possibilities. He could choose between destroying the Burgundian Netherlands and controlling them through a marriage between a French prince and Mary of Burgundy. The Duchy of Burgundy in the south was immediately absorbed by the French crown. In the north, the young princess Mary and her stepmother Margaret of York, waited in the Prinsenhof in Ghent, shattered by the frightful news from Lorraine. Although promised to Maximilian of Austria, Mary was not yet married. Would she not be a splendid catch for the dauphin ? Then the Netherlands would come under direct French domination. There was then, however, the awful possibility of a situation similar to that when Philip the Bold inherited Flanders in 1384. Would it not be better to put an end to the threat from the north and east, once and for all, by doing everything possible to divide it up into small parts, none of which would be strong enough to move against France ? Gelderland and Liège asked for nothing better than to get rid, as quickly as possible, of Burgundian domination. Ghent and Bruges were ready to revolt against the centralisation and taxes of recent years. There were many candidates ready to

The Burgundian inheritance threatened

take over any morsel of the Burgundian heritage which might be going. Louis did not like war. He preferred diplomacy. He seems to have decided to give full rein to the disintegrating tendencies within the Burgundian lands. Agents were sent north to encourage everyone who was dissatisfied. The most obvious place on which pressure should be exerted was Ghent. It was known to be anti-Burgundian, ferociously independent with a tradition of intransigence, and anxious to wipe out the humiliations which it had undergone at the hands of Charles the Bold. It seemed an excellent point of departure for a policy calculated to disintegrate the Burgundian Netherlands.

Yet Louis had miscalculated. He had badly underestimated the unifying force of the ruling house and the dynastic loyalty of all these dissimilar lands. As many others had done, and still do to-day, he could not understand why all these apparently disunited regions should stay together. Yet he soon learned his mistake. Mary's first action on hearing the news of her father's death was to call the States General to ask for their support. At the end of January 1477, these representatives of the provincial Estates met in Ghent. All of them, Brabant,

Flanders, Hainaut, Namur, Holland, Artois and Zealand, proclaimed their loyalty to the house of Burgundy. Whatever their separate ambitions, they never considered breaking up the personal dynastic union built up before 1467.

The administrative institutions of this union were, however, a very different matter, and each group of delegates had its own pet aversions among the governmental machinery hammered out by the dukes. This was a golden **Regionalism run riot** opportunity, too good to be missed, to break up the centralising institutions which had threatened the regionalism so dear to every heart in the Low Countries. The price which the States General demanded for their support of Mary was the destruction of the central institutions and a return to the good old days of privileges, monopolies and regionalism. What they wanted was to put back the clock. They would not succeed in the long run. But the defeat of Nancy showed that the Netherlands were not yet used to life in the more sophisticated framework set up by the Burgundian dukes. What were the changes, which had gradually been extended throughout the later fourteenth and fifteenth centuries ? They arose largely from two factors. In the first place the extent and dissimilarity of the Burgundian lands; in the second, from the fact that the ruling house came from abroad. Both these factors led to the creation of new institutions common to all these lands, and led to their being foreign, or French in conception. Also they were put into effect, at least at first, by the Burgundians and Frenchmen who had accompanied their duke to the north. It was in their interest to discourage particularism and to create new, common, institutions dependent on them. Such changes fitted into the general European pattern. Strong monarchies were emerging in France, Spain and England. Society was becoming more complex and the old lines of division were breaking up. Science was no longer the sole province of the church—this was to produce Erasmus and Thomas More. War could no longer be waged by the feudal host, but was becoming professionalised, with complicated weapons and hired mercenaries. Government was no longer controlled by the princes of the blood, but by professional civil servants who could come from any layer of society and who were dependent on their own efficiency and on princely favour. Prosperity and economic innovations no longer belonged exclusively to the old towns, but had spread to the country-side and to new towns. The old European world no longer confined men's view. From across the Atlantic all sorts of exciting possibilities, markets and raw materials came flooding. All these tendencies appeared with peculiar intensity in the Netherlands because of their history and geography. Nevertheless, particularism too still tempted the Netherlands in spite of

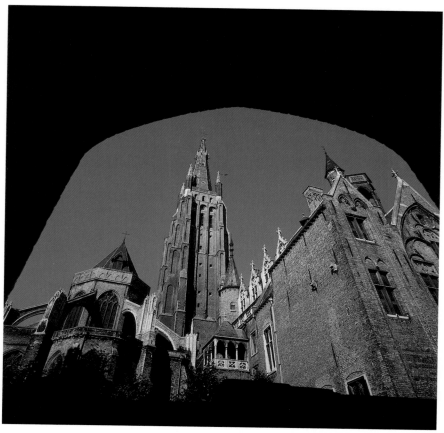

Church of Our Lady in Bruges: one of the most beautiful gothic churches in the Low Countries.

Burgundian attempts and successes in providing common institutions. Regional government remained basically the same under the common ruler.

New institutions But the Burgundian achievement was two-fold. On the one hand new institutions were created. On the other, the old were reformed and many of the worst malpractices cleared away. In order of time, the first reform was the creation of the Council of Lille. This dealt not only with Flanders but with all the possessions of Philip the Bold with the exception of Burgundy itself. It was responsible for the dukes' financial affairs throughout their possessions and also for judicial business. It was sedentary, instead of following the court about from place to place, had a competent and specialised staff, its own records and a degree of impartiality which was comforting for the under-privileged but exasperating for the big bosses of the towns. Under John the Fearless this Council was divided into two parts: the first, the Exchequer (Chambre des Comptes), remained in Lille and continued to be responsible for all the ducal financial affairs and for the book-keeping for all their territories except Brabant, Holland, Frisia and Burgundy; the second, or judicial section, was moved and finally settled, in 1498, in Ghent. This was the Council of Flanders. Pleas were heard in the language of the parties involved. Gradually it overcame hostility because it provided a refuge from the biased justice of the urban courts. In Brabant and Holland, a similar line of development was followed. Each received its Council and its Exchequer.

The new institutions were of very great importance because they continued in the southern Netherlands, with a temporary set-back at the end of the fifteenth century, until the French Revolution, and formed the basis for the constitution of the United Provinces. They were, at least at the beginning, in the hands of the duke's own entourage who were, for the most part, French, Burgundian or men of Picardy. They were professional civil servants, mostly jurists, and many had been members of his council in Burgundy. They had acquired much responsibility and experience in the duchy while Philip was busy in Paris. This experienced group of lawyers, nobles and men of affairs followed the duke north to the Low Countries and devoted themselves to his interests. This was not a one-sided affair. They received rich rewards and favours—for example one of the sons of the Chancellor of Philip the Good, Nicholas Rolin, became a cardinal, the bishopric of Tournai fell successively to two of his Heads of Council, John Chevrot and William Fillastre. There were also rich ducal wedding-presents and new year presents. In return they advised the duke, whispered information in his ear at audiences, fought at his side, governed his provinces, and acted as his ambassadors. The most important official was the Chancellor. He had great personal power, enormous wealth and was, in fact, responsible for state administration. Nicholas Rolin, whose portrait appears on a painting by Van Eyck, was chancellor for forty years—no wonder he could kneel before the Virgin entirely robed in cloth of gold. Round this secret, powerful figure was grouped the Great Council, which, from 1446 onwards, became permanent and fixed. It was both a law court and a council of state. Under Charles the Bold these two attributions were separated into the Council of State, and the Parliament of Mechelen, which was not a chamber of representatives but a Supreme Court. Charles seems to have upset his subjects with this reform, humane as it may have been—there was legal aid for paupers—by introducing it too abruptly and too early. They hated and distrusted the civil law which it administered, in the place of their customary law. The Parliament of Mechelen, as well as the unified Exchequers of Lille and Brussels, which Charles brought over to Mechelen, were swept away in 1477.

Whatever innovations the Burgundian dukes brought into the central machinery of government, the provinces always retained the upper hand when it came to voting the funds. Although the ruling house was immensely rich—contemporaries were constantly awe-struck by its treasures—nevertheless taxes had to be voted by the Estates. By careful house-keeping, and peace-time conditions, the dukes built up substantial savings, but when projects of the size of those indulged in by Charles the Bold had to be financed, even the funds built up by Philip the Good were insufficient. To vote new taxes, the provincial Estates met. Philip the Good found it convenient to call representatives of each of them together, at the same time. Their meeting in Bruges was the beginning of the States General. Its five hundredth anniversary—it took place in 1465—was officially celebrated in 1965 in the Netherlands. At first meetings were infrequent, and they were called only by the prince himself. But after the disaster of Nancy and the destruction of much of the central machinery of government, the Estates forced Mary of Burgundy to agree to their meeting whenever they wished, and not to go to war without their consent.

Centralisation under attack

The Great Privilege which the Estates forced on Mary destroyed the Parliament of Mechelen while a mutilated Great Council was to accompany the ruler. Local privileges, urban freedoms and even the provincial law courts were left more or less intact, but much was undefined. Nothing was stipulated about the authority of the States General, except that they might meet whenever they liked. The Great Privilege, in fact, only destroyed. It created

The seventeenth century exchange in Lille.

nothing to replace the central institutions created by the dukes. Regionalism had triumphed. On the same day that she signed the Great Privilege, Mary was forced also to agree to the re-assertion of the independence of Flanders, which refused at the same time to be drawn into wars in which other Burgundian lands were engaged. Similar privileges followed for Holland and Zealand. So much for Burgundian unity.

The miseries which followed the disaster of 1477 showed two important things. Firstly that the Netherlands were right to keep out of wars whatever the possible prizes. Secondly, that once the country fell back into regionalism and privilege, it was incapable of defending itself, and quickly became a battlefield. The Burgundian possessions in the Netherlands did not, in fact, fall apart. The Duchy of Burgundy was quickly absorbed by France, but Louis XI's invasion of Flanders did not provoke the support he expected. The towns wished not to exchange Burgundian for domination by France, but wanted urban independence. Yet there was a great hidden danger in the means adopted to thwart Louis. If the Netherlands were to resist, Mary had to have help and

The Habsburgs enter the Low Countries

support. Her marriage to Maximilian of Austria was rushed through, by proxy, in April 1477 in the chapel of the Prinsenhof in Ghent, and four months later formally. She could no longer be forced to marry the dauphin. But her husband was the only son of the Emperor Frederick III, and the Low Countries were not to escape from the Habsburgs until 1794. For three hundred years they were never to have their own ruling house. They would never be the centre of their ruler's preoccupations, never the exclusive object of his care. Until the reign of Philip II, they were, at least, to retain their own internal government. Although Charles V had gradually subordinated their foreign policy to that of his empire as a whole, it was only under his son, that a systematic attempt was made to hammer this cold, complex, sophisticated land into moulds made in the hot, fanatical south. Between 1522 and his abdication in 1555, Charles spent only ten years in the Netherlands on five visits. His son Philip came only once. Between the latter's reign and that of Joseph II, in 1781, no Spanish or Austrian ruler of the Low Countries ever set foot in them.

Nevertheless in 1477 the worst was avoided. At least those provinces brought together by the Burgundian dukes before 1467 remained together. This was thanks mainly to the huge fortune amassed by Philip the Good and not entirely wasted by his son. Maximilian had these resources to oppose the particularism of the towns. Bruges, Ghent, Brussels, Leuven and Ypres saw in the weakness of the ruler a wonderful opportunity to throw off the new central institutions which they hated, and to dominate the country as they had done in the fourteenth century—in fact to take a step backwards. Mary, as well as having to agree to the Great Privilege, was forced by Bruges to suppress the right of the

Steps back Franc of Bruges to be considered as the Fourth Member of Flanders, to submit the countryside to renewed urban domination, to forbid weaving in the villages, to re-establish the staple for foreign imports, and to refuse citizenship to anyone born outside Flanders. This was typical. The gilds tried to re-establish their violent control over the urban administration and, by more and more stringent regulation, to stem the economic changes which were becoming painfully apparent at the end of the fifteenth century. Such increased control only aggravated the situation when in fact freedom was the step which might have helped. Antwerp saw this and never supported the reaction of the older towns. Violent frustrations exploded in riots

Executions in Ghent and bloodshed. The chancellor Hugonet, and Humbercourt were caught in Ghent and paid for their loyalty to the central institutions with their heads. Louis XI's flattery of the towns, and his claim that his only desire was for their peace and independence, was unmasked when his troops advanced north. Luckily his behaviour and that of his soldiers was so outrageous that the towns managed to shut their gates in time. Mary's marriage to Maximilian of Austria seemed the best way of defending her territory against the French. She wrote secretly to her fiancé asking him to hurry, because of the danger she was in, virtually imprisoned by the citizens of Ghent. Hence the wedding by proxy, while Maximilian laboriously gathered enough cash to make a show on entering his new lands. Unlike Philip the Bold on his marriage with Margaret of Male in 1369, Maximilian was not a younger son. One day he would inherit the Habsburg domains. He could never devote himself entirely to the Low Countries. Unknowingly, the Netherlands were thrust into the Habsburg empire.

Mary's subjects suspected none of this. Maximilian seemed a desirable alternative to domination by France. Hence he was given ample credit to help him to bolster up his wife's authority. She had been forced in the Great Privilege to give in to regionalism. Her husband resisted this out-moded form of government, with the help of the savings of Philip the Good. Things began to improve. Louis XI was beaten at Guinegate, and went back to surreptitious encouragement of the enemies of the Low Countries, rather than provoking a head on collision with them. Mary's death, as the result of a riding accident in

The death of a young princess

1482, left a young prince four years old, as had happened after the disappearance of Baldwin IX in the battle against the Bulgars. This time, however, the child's father was still alive, and although young Philip's sister was sent to be educated at the French court, the government of the Netherlands was placed, for the time, in Maximilian's hands. As so frequently in their history two diametrically opposed forces were at work. On the one hand, regionalism and separatism exemplified by the gilds and the return to urban privileges; on the other the centralising tradition, already a hundred years old, of the Burgundian dukes with their new institutions and dislike of privileges and exceptions. For a hundred years the latter had gained ground: the death of Charles the Bold looked like the end. But for Maximilian it was the only hope of holding together his wife's inheritance. So he gradually forgot the promises made in the Great Privilege: he did not consult his subjects about his every movement; and he nominated foreign members of his council. It was a dangerous policy. The Flemish towns would certainly ally with Louis XI, in order to crush any symptom of a revival of centralisation. Ghent even negotiated a treaty with the French king. This second Treaty of Arras was as disastrous for the Low Countries as Philip the Good's first Treaty of Arras had been favourable. Much territory was given up, and worse still, Maximilian's little daughter, Margaret, was engaged to the dauphin and until she had reached a suitable age, was to be educated at the French court. Louis XI had not got hold of Mary of Burgundy, but it looked as if nevertheless one day his son would rule the Netherlands.

Maximilian's position seemed hopeless. Ghent dominated both internal and external affairs. As quickly as possible, she was busy putting back the clock to the time of van Artevelde, except that she was relying on France rather than on England. Luckily for Maximilian, Ghent, as so often, overdid it. The other provinces began to see that Flanders was not aiming so much at regional independence as at domination over them. In an attempt to resuscitate the dying industry of Bruges, for example, a barrier was built in the mouth of the Scheldt to stop traffic proceeding to Antwerp. This could not really be interpreted as a friendly gesture. Flanders was trying desperately to stop the shift in the centre of things from Flanders to Brabant, which had got well under way under the Burgundian dukes who chose Brussels and Mechelen as the centres of their government, rather than Ghent and Bruges. Antwerp never doubted that its true interest lay with a strong central government. Gradually the rest of the provinces came to the same conclusion. Ghent was forced to allow the young prince, Philip, to leave for Mechelen, and Maximilian was free to leave for Germany to be crowned as King of the Romans and so assure himself of the Imperial succession. On his return he was visited by his father, the Emperor. The Netherlands were flattered. They were not yet used to being ruled by a king, visited by an emperor, and being part of the Habsburg inheritance. These halcyon days were soon over. Maximilian's return meant war with France, and the Netherlands had a foretaste of their rôle as battle-ground for France and the Habsburgs. Destruction of the countryside under army boots as well as economic depression and rising prices in the towns, made a violent mixture. The explosion came when Maximilian was imprudent enough to confide himself to Bruges. He rode there from Ypres just before Christmas, 1487 in order to convoke the States General. His retinue of about 200 Germans did not appease the citizens. The local tradesmen were restless because they had seen their clients diminish at an alarming rate. Many foreigners had left partly because Bruges's regulations were smothering enterprise, and partly because of the continual threat of pitched battles. Ghent, led by the demagogues Adrian Vilein and John Coppenholle was under French protection. Early in January Maximilian called a meeting in the market place in Bruges and requested money and men to tackle

Maximilian at the mercy of Bruges

the French. This was touching the town on the raw. The citizens demanded that the guard on the town gates should be formed entirely from their number. This was an ominous sign for Maximilian. Eight days later representatives from Bruges left for Ghent to admonish that city in the ruler's name. However, they were quickly converted to the opposite point of view, and came back determined that Maximilian, rather than the French should be their target. By the end of the month, Maximilian felt that he needed some comforting German support, and went to the town gates to let his troops in. One guard after another refused to allow his reinforcements to enter. Maximilian was forced to return through hostile streets to his lodging. The town was in uproar. The gilds assembled on the market place and set up the town artillery. The ice on the moat was broken to cut off any possible means of escape. All the grievances of the townsmen against their own administration, against their ruler, and against Antwerp erupted in an orgy of trials, torture and executions. Maximilian was moved to the Cranenburg on the market place whence he had an excellent view of the treatment of his supporters. Until April 5th the commune held a reign of terror there. But they did not know what to do next. Suspicious of Ghent which showed itself too anxious to get hold of Maximilian, the gilds rioted themselves to a standstill. Frederick III could not

The Counts' Castle in Ghent, partially built by Philip of Alsace in 1180.

allow such flagrant ill-treatment of his son to go unnoticed and moved west into the Netherlands with a German army. Maximilian promised to comply with all the demands of the commune, if only they would let him go. After a solemn oath to this effect and a Te Deum on the market place from which the scaffold had now been removed, Maximilian at long last saw the gates opened. As soon as he was safely outside, he quickly revoked his oath, as it had been given under duress. The whole incident had revealed the abysmal poverty of the towns as far as any constructive contribution towards the government of the Low Countries was concerned. All they could do was to indulge in a blood-bath in the name of their sacred, undefined, privileges. Their day was done. When Coppenholle, the leader of Ghent, mounted the scaffold four years later, it was only a question of time before the idea of a centralised state won the day. But in some respects it was already too late.

The failure of the Netherlands

In one essential at least the Netherlands failed. They never succeeded in defending their frontiers. The result, half a century later, was the invasion of the Netherlands by the Spanish army and their permanent division, along the present frontier, into two separate states. Of these two states, one, the United Provinces, asserted its independence. The other, the southern Netherlands passed from one foreign ruling house to another for the next two centuries. Under lawful, but foreign rulers, they were sacrificed miserably to the dreams of world domination in which the Habsburgs and the Roi Soleil indulged. The promise of unity and independence, so rich at the accession first of Philip the Fair, and later of his son, Charles V, came to nothing. For seven years it looked as if the Netherlands would achieve their heart's desire—a prince of their own. On 9 September 1494, Philip the Fair, the son of Mary of Burgundy and Maximilian was declared of age, and took over the government of the Netherlands from his father, Maximilian, who had succeeded to the Imperial crown. Born and educated in the Netherlands, speaking the language, surrounded by native advisers, attractive and peace loving, Philip could rally to himself a wealth of personal loyalty which had always been denied to his father. He could reconcile the centralisation so harshly imposed under Charles the Bold, with the regionalism of the Great Privilege. He could soften the harsh demands of both and give in to neither. He reconstructed the Parliament of Mechelen, under the name of the Great Council, reclaimed the royal domains, and above all, insisted on peace. In spite of his father, Philip managed to placate Charles VIII of France, and to re-tie the commercial knots with England in the Magnus Intercursus which released

Anglo-Flemish trade from many of its crippling regulations.

But all this was too good to last. The probability that Philip would one day inherit the Habsburg lands from his father had been disregarded by the Low Countries. What they could not have foreseen, and what was in fact just as bad, was that an unimaginable series of royal deaths would leave the throne of Spain in the hands of Philip's wife, Joanna of Castile. After the death of Joanna's mother in 1504, Philip took the title of king of Spain. This was an ominous moment for the Low Countries. As the bells tolled for one Spanish Infant after another, so sounded the death knell of an independent, united Netherlands.

The rule of Charles V

Two years later Philip died at Burgos in Spain. He left a mad widow and six children of whom the eldest son, Charles, was six. This boy was the heir not only of his father Philip, ruler of the Low Countries and of Spain, but also of his maternal grandfather, Ferdinand of Aragon, and of his paternal grandfather the Emperor, Maximilian of Austria.

A completely unforeseeable train of circumstances had deprived the Low Countries of their ruler. Even under Margaret of Austria, sister of Philip the Fair, who became Regent of the Netherlands, there was already a change. Although devoted to the interests of her young nephew, and a skilled diplomatist of great culture, she regarded the Netherlands essentially from a dynastic point of view. They fitted into the greater pattern of the Habsburg dominions, and her foreign policy was orientated towards furthering her family's aims. Margaret was never at home in the Netherlands, as Philip had been. She had been brought up at the French court. Her home in Mechelen in the house of John Laurin opposite the Court of Burgundy where Charles lived, became a glowing centre for the encouragement of the arts of all kinds. Yet she never gained the affection of her people, as her near contemporary Elizabeth I of England managed to do. Her policy was disliked and distrusted because it was seen as a threat to peace with France. The nobility of the Netherlands, with whom she was associated in government, objected to her power and attempted to release the young prince Charles from her influence. Only after her resumption of authority as Regent for her nephew in 1522, did the two see eye to eye, because the nobility felt by that time that they had more or less taken over the Habsburg inheritance themselves. In 1515, however, they could not get rid of Margaret quickly enough. Charles was declared of age and seemed entirely under the influence of his Burgundian advisers. But one year later his grand-

The Spanish inheritance

father, Ferdinand the Catholic, king of Aragon, died, and Char-

The market in Hasselt.

les came into his Spanish inheritance. Another three years passed, and on Maximilian's death, Charles became Emperor. In April 1521, Martin Luther appeared before him in Worms and refused to withdraw his opposition to ecclesiastical discipline. The three great cares of Charles' life had already made their appearance—the Empire, Spain and the Protestants. By 1519 the Netherlands had become part of an Empire which stretched from the snowy peaks of the Carpathians to the orange groves of Granada. The Netherlands were the most complex, highly developed and above all, the richest of these possessions, and Charles was careful that they should be cared for to ensure for him the vast financial credit needed to run such a huge enterprise. At first there seemed no danger. Marvellous opportunities opened up before Charles's entourage from the north. The poorer, simpler, Spanish court was dazzled by the gorgeous pomp of the Burgundian splendour. Charles's companions

Charles's followers exploit their opportunities

behaved in Spain as the Spaniards were later to behave, for a much longer period, in the Low Countries. Everything was at their feet. Chièvres, Charles's closest adviser, became Duke of Soria, Admiral of the kingdom of Naples, Captain-general of the navy, General of Spain. His nephew William de Croy, aged 17, acquired the Arch-bishopric of Toledo, while John Carondelet received the Primacy of Sicily and the Archbishopric of Palermo. Adrian of Utrecht, who was later to receive the Papacy, had to content himself for the time, with the Bishopric of Tortosa and the posts of Inquisitor-general of Aragon and Grand-inquisitor of Castile. Such glorious opportunities blinded the Low Countries. They were even willing to give up their peace with France. They thought of Charles still as a Burgundian prince, and of the Netherlands as the chief of his pre-occupations. And certainly at the beginning he did his best for them. War with Francis I of France led to the capture of Tournai, the episcopal seat whose jurisdiction covered an important part of Flanders. In 1526 Francis I

France gives up Flanders

renounced French sovereignty over Flanders. Everyone was charmed. Charles enjoyed his infrequent visits to his fatherland. He flattered his subjects by his obvious pleasure at being among them and by his unwillingness to depart. They were so overcome that the Estates voted subsidies without their usual hesitation, and took the unheard of step of suggesting that they would have been willing to give more if they had been asked.

We have underlined the tendency, present in the County of Flanders and later in the Burgundian Netherlands, to undermine and try to destroy central institutions and to call in foreign help. This had weakened the power to resist foreign interference and had delayed the creation of a powerful state, such as had happened so many centuries ago in England and a little later in France. Yet when the birth of Charles V, in the Prinsenhof in Ghent in 1500 was celebrated with fire-works and tight-rope walkers suspended between the spires of the Belfry and the church of St. Nicholas, his fellow countrymen saw in him a national ruler. He was the prince who would put them on the same footing as the other national monarchies.

The smaller towns, the countryside and the rich bourgeoisie, on whom the Burgundian dukes had relied, saw Charles and his father as their champions. Together, they could stand up to the great old towns and the gilds. The disintegration of the central institutions had been largely repaired by Philip the Fair and Margaret of Austria. Charles V built on their foundations. The Council was split, after the death of the Chancellor Gattinara in 1530, into three departments, responsible for finance, legislation and administration, and affairs of state respectively. All this meant added efficiency. Any French claims on the Low Countries were removed in 1526—and the final step was taken on a road along which had plodded Ferrand of Portugal, Guy of Dampierre, James and Philip van Artevelde, Philip the Good, Charles the Bold and Margaret of Austria. From this moment onwards, France had no legal right of interference. This did not stop her doing so as the history of the next three hundred years was to show. A further step made the Low Countries for the first time legally one unit. In 1548 they became one political division of the Empire with a single frontier forming the Circle of Burgundy. At the same time Imperial rights over these fiefs were reduced to a minimum, and in the following year the Pragmatic sanction reduced all the rights of succession to a single formula. Each of these steps strengthened the territorial unity and solidity of the Netherlands. Charles also added to them Gelderland, which had for a time experienced the heavy hand of Charles the Bold, but which had subsequently shaken itself free. In spite

The seventeen Provinces

of Francis I's support of Charles of Egmont, this Duchy became the seventeenth province of the Low Countries which were not changed, except to be divided between north and south, until the aggression of Louis XIV in the seventeenth century.

There were still occasional revolts against this centralisation and the increasing demands for money required by the Habsburgs to fight wars on every side. It was perhaps fitting that the last should occur in Ghent. By 1539 urban independence was, in fact, quite out of fashion. Administration, paper-work, accountancy, complicated commercial transactions, money lending, interest rates, were becoming more and more popular as a pastime, while town walls and turrets and military exercises by the urban militia, received less and less attention. But there was a miserable element in society which was still ready to riot at the slightest opportunity. This had not profited from the new economy, and was in fact the victim of the decay of the old ways. The sixteenth century was after all also the century of the vagabond and the vagrant in England, when the only means of dealing with unemployment was an increasingly harsh poor law. In Ghent the effects of redundancy were felt perhaps more vividly than elsewhere because, having been so long in the van of European economic expansion, the town was now so obviously falling behind. As usual the immediate cause of the trouble was a demand for money by Mary of Hungary, the Regent who had followed Margaret of Austria in the Netherlands.

A town against an Empire Immediately there was an uproar. General strikes began. The confirmation of the treaty of Kadzand was torn up and either eaten by the crowd or worn in their hats ! All the rogues and vagabonds from miles around flocked together. But the town walls were in ruins, the artillery rusty. Overtures to Francis I of France came to nothing. Charles V was very cross indeed. On February 14th 1540 he entered his native town and until May 12th lodged in his old home. Coldly and legally the town was found guilty of disobedience, disloyalty, the breaking of treaties, sedition, rebellion and lèse-majesté. All privileges were abolished; the urban artillery, and other possessions of the town were confiscated; Roland, the great bell which had so often called the citizens from the Belfry for some revolt or riot, was taken down; numerous citizens had to beg the Emperor humbly for forgiveness, half the town moat was filled, and a very large fine imposed. While the town was still shuddering from the shock, a decree abolishing the old urban constitution and promulgating a new one was issued. This remained in force until the end of the Ancien Régime. While the gold and silver vessels and furniture of the gilds were being sold by public auction, the town echoed to the sound of the demolition of the Abbey of St. Baaf's and the building there of a new castle, to keep the town in order. Charles, with his Italian architect, had not hesitated to take this step, when after climbing the steps of the tower of the present cathedral, they saw that the Abbey occupied the best position for keeping a firm grip on Ghent. This was the end of urban independence in the southern Netherlands. Later, the old tradition of political domination by the towns was continued in the United Provinces. When in 1555, Charles V, his health broken by incessant work, travelling and over-eating, abdicated in favour of his son Philip, he left the Netherlands strong,

Charles abdicates in favour of Philip II

united, rich and at peace. At the age of 55 he was so racked by gout that he could no longer move without help. In spite of his doctors' alarm he could not curb his appetite. Perhaps because of the unfortunate form of his jaw, he was unable to chew his food, and seems to have been constantly hungry and thirsty. In spite of admonitions he continued to enjoy waterzooi-chicken and vegetables stewed in milk and eel pasties for breakfast, and stewed beef, roast lamb, baked hare, stuffed capons and quarts of wine and beer for his supper. Such a diet undermined even his strong constitution, and whatever his steely determination on other matters, Charles could not control his appetite. Hence by 1555 he was worn out, wished only to retire to the sun of Spain, and spend the rest of his life in meditation.

Charles's son and heir, Philip, returned to the Netherlands in 1555 from an expedition to England, during which he had married the queen, Mary Tudor. She was to spend the rest of her sad life waiting for him to return. Six weeks later in a solemn and impressive ceremony in the palace in Brussels, Charles handed over to him the government of the Netherlands. All the notables of the land saw this little, crumpled figure supporting himself on the arm of William of Orange, who was later to become the arch enemy of his house, put on his spectacles and reminisce about the events which had moved him since, in that same room at Epiphany forty years before, he had been declared of age by his grandfather, Maximilian. The Emperor spoke of his Spanish and Imperial responsibilities, of his innumerable journeys—six to Spain, seven to Italy, ten to the Low Countries, four to France, two to England and two to Africa. He thanked his sister Mary for her wisdom and devotion in ruling the Low Countries for twenty-five years, in his name; asked his subjects' forgiveness for any errors or injustices which he had committed, and presented to them his son, Philip, as his successor. Everyone seems to have burst into tears. Philip was unable to reply personally. He could speak neither French nor Dutch. The spell was broken. It was an unfortunate moment.

Eight months later Charles, with his sisters Mary and Eleonora, sailed for Spain. He had resigned his power over Spain, Sicily and the Indies as well as over the Netherlands to Philip, and later, over the Empire to his brother Ferdinand. The party left through the new canal which linked Ghent with the western Scheldt and Flushing and thence to Spain and the monastery of Yuste. It was the last glimpse for the Low Countries of a prince who had some special feeling for them.

The uncompleted church of St. Walburga in Oudenaarde.

The best evidence of a society and culture is contained in the buildings, pictures, music, sculpture, furniture, books, manuscripts and laws which remain. Egyptian history would be much more shadowy without the treasures of the tomb of Tutankhamen. Until the fifteenth century the history of the Low Countries has to be pieced together from scraps. There are great churches, castles, frescoes, a few weapons, a few coins, some seals, ivories and jewels, but hardly any paintings, almost no domestic architecture or furniture, except a few heavy oak coffers, and a certain range of administrative documents. In comparison with evidence from the fifteenth and sixteenth centuries on which we can draw, all this amounted to very little. Suddenly we are faced with an 'embarras du choix'. There is not only an amazing change in the quality of the cultural treasures of this so-

The wonder of Flemish art

ciety, but in their quantity also. The fifteenth century in the Netherlands saw one of the rare steps forward by western society, such as happened at almost the same moment in Italy, in England in the sixteenth and nineteenth centuries and France in the thirteenth. There are indeed great similarities between Italy and the Netherlands during the fifteenth and sixteenth centuries. But at least until the fifteenth, the Low Countries remained, on the whole, uninfluenced by the south. The Netherlands, and particularly Brabant, became one of the great centres of artistic, as they were of political and economic development. Obviously, these three factors hung together. Artists of all sorts could be indulged because of the great fortunes which were amassed at this time, and which allowed a substantial private subsidy for the arts.

Until the fifteenth century artists had worked almost exclusively for the church. But once the nobles left their country strongholds and became civil servants, they were able to build up huge fortunes in the service of their ruler; the towns no longer spent their entire income on arms, walls and turrets and the salaries of the urban militias, and concentrated more exclusively on business, and an entirely new market for works of art grew up beside the old. There were occasional lapses. The fifteenth century saw its riots, pillage and destruction, but this had become the exception rather than the rule. This peaceful atmosphere was fostered by the house of Burgundy. Until Charles the Bold let his ambition run away with him, the Burgundian dukes relied much more heavily on diplomacy than on battles. The court became immensely influential and its wealth encouraged the production of beautiful objects of all sorts. Hard and fast class distinctions began to melt and become confused. Men of ability, whatever their birth, could find opportunities to take part in these new economic developments, to amass fortunes for themselves which they invested in land and in fine possessions and a high standard of living. Antwerp, a world trading centre, greater than any the west had yet seen, acted as a magnet, attracting to itself economic activity and artistic talent of every sort. Antwerp was cosmopolitan by deliberate urban policy and through natural inclination, and during the long period of peace which it enjoyed, huge fortunes, built up from complicated business transactions, could be spent on pictures, tapestries, furniture, books—everything in fact, which accompanies a leisured, wealthy and cultured way of life.

A cultured way of life

There is, therefore, no scarcity of evidence once we reach the fifteenth century. The problem is then rather one of selection. But there were, in the fifteenth century in the Netherlands, still many traditions which continued. Artists still looked upon themselves as craftsmen. They formed gilds, worked for a patron, were employed sometimes on other jobs. Gerard David, who painted the 'Trial and Punishment of the Unjust Judge Sisames, by Cambyses', in Bruges, was also employed by the town in 1480 to paint the bars of the prison in which Maximilian was confined. John van Eyck went on diplomatic missions for Philip the Good, as when he went to Portugal to paint the Princess Isabelle, his master's future wife. By the sixteenth century artists seem to have aspired to a more general culture and to have been gentlemen rather than craftsmen.

Artists becoming gentlemen

Fifteenth century paintings were, on the whole of two sorts: either religious in inspiration, or portraits. The new subjects, inspired by the classics, creep in only in the sixteenth century. There may have been others. Circumstances ensure, on the whole, that pictures destined for churches are less easily lost or destroyed than those kept elsewhere. Thus, as far as we know, for the most part, the artists of the Netherlands during the fifteenth century were still dealing with religious subjects, such as the Annunciation, the Adoration of the Kings, the Nativity, the Last Judgement. The other tendency affords us a wonderful portrait gallery. These rulers and their wives and children—like Charles the Bold, by Roger van der Weyden, Philip the Good possibly by Petrus Christus, Isabelle of Portugal, by an unknown Flemish artist, Anthony, son of Philip the Good, by Roger van der Weyden, the solemn little girl, Margaret of Austria, at the age of three—live for us in a way not possible for the early counts of Flanders and dukes of Brabant whose characters emerge from their actions alone. Portraits were by no means confined to princes. Rich merchants were also painted. There stands the successful merchant from Lucca,

The Graslei in Ghent.

Giovanni Arnolfini, or the young, secret girl by Petrus Christus, or the doctor by Bernard van Orley. Sometimes the two strands were combined in a single canvas, as in the many religious pictures which also contain the portraits of the donor, his wife, and often their children. Thus we have the splendid portrait of Canon Van der Paele on Van Eyck's 'Madonna with Saint Donatian and Saint George'; or the same artist's portraits of John Vydt and his wife Margaret Borluut, on his 'Mystic Lamb'; or Memling's charming representation of the donor William Moreel with his wife Barbara van Vlaenderberghe, with their five sons and eleven of their thirteen daughters; or Van Eyck's splendid Chancellor of Burgundy, Nicholas Rolin, in the 'Virgin of Autun'.

These great paintings were already admired by contemporaries. Charles van Mander, a sixteenth century critic, describes the crowds which flocked to gaze at the 'Mystic Lamb', in St. Baaf's Cathedral on feast days, just as they do to-

Van Eyck's 'Mystic Lamb'

day. There is something distinctive in the beauty of colour and composition of these fifteenth century paintings. Scientific observation of the greatest exactitude, combines with a mysticism already apparent in the literature of the Low Countries. The minute, patient, painting of the flowers in Van Eyck's 'Mystic Lamb', or that of the jewels in the sceptre held by God the Father, or in Mary's crown, or the town views included by Van der Weyden in his panel of 'St. Luke painting the Virgin and Child', show an incredible degree of technical skill, feeling for colour and inspiration; only in Italy was there anything comparable at this time. There, too, we have a similar minute observation of nature, a comparable series of portraits, and equally glorious colours. The blue distances, the intimate views, through open doors and windows, of streets and courtyards, all contribute to a texture as closely painted as a tapestry is woven. Such painting must have been influenced by the techniques of miniatures and illumination already highly developed in the Low Countries by the fifteenth century and strongly encouraged by the bibliophiles of the House of Burgundy. Gradually miniatures ceased to be so closely bound up with the text and became more like small paintings in their own right, as we can see in the so-called Book of Hours of Charles the Bold. There, perhaps, the prince's daughter, Mary of Burgundy, kneels before the Madonna, in a Gothic nave, while as it were before the window, she again sits reading in her breviary and before her on the window sill lies a wonderful jewel and a glass holding some irises. One of the greatest and last of these miniaturists, Simon Bening, has left us a self-portrait: he must have needed the spectacles which he holds in his hand, for such delicate work.

Such art was also very closely connected with the luxurious tapestries produced in such large quantities in the Low Countries at this time. The Flemish miniaturist, Hennequin de Bruges, working in Paris, produced the cartoons for

The Apocalypse of Angers

the great fourteenth century series of the Apocalypse, now housed in Angers. By the fifteenth century tapestry weaving had become a major industry in the Netherlands, and the fact that many were produced at relatively low prices for ordinary customers is an interesting comment on the contemporary standard of living. Thousands of workers around Oudenaarde specialised in turning out these wall coverings, usually consisting of relatively simple compositions of flowers and leaves, known as 'verdures'. Others, much more complicated and expensive—such as the series still hanging in Tournai cathedral depicting the history of Saints Piatus and Eleutherius—were ordered by more important clients. Charles the Bold's great collection, used in his camp at Morat and captured after his defeat by the Swiss, still hangs in Berne. Others ordered by the Pope from cartoons by Raphael are in the Vatican. Numerous orders were received from abroad. Before the Burgundian princes arrived in the Netherlands, many artists from there served foreign princes. But during the fifteenth century there was generally work enough at home. Nevertheless the greatest sculptor of the late fourteenth century, Klaas Sluter, worked chiefly in France, on the church of the Chartreuse in Dijon, and on the tomb of his master Philip the Bold, with its series of mourners which was completed by his compatriot Klaas van de Werve. He began a tradition which was carried on in numerous statues in wood and stone: in the tomb of Philip Pot, by an unknown Flemish artist, now in the Louvre, in the tomb of Mary of Burgundy by John Borman, Renier of Tienen and Peter de Becker in Bruges, of the misericords in St. Sulpitius's in Diest, in the statue of Mary beside the Cross in the Calvary in St. Peter's in Leuven, in St. Leonard's in Zoutleeuw, in one of the extraordinary series of altar-screens of which the greatest come from Brabant. St. George's altar piece from Our Lady's of Ginderbuiten in Leuven, and the Saluces altar piece, both ascribed to John Borman, are of such complexity and beauty that it seems incredible that they are carved from wood. In Hemelveerdegem the Salome dancing before Herod, while next door, John the Baptist's head is triumphantly held on a plate, has an unpleasant reality about it. It reminds one of a night club rather than of an altar piece. Such work can be traced all over Europe. It was obviously produced for export. Brabant altar pieces appear in France, Germany, Finland, Iceland, Norway, Denmark, Spain and Sweden as well as in the Netherlands. Pictures and tapestries were also exported in great numbers. Memling's picture of the 'Last Judgement' never reached its desti-

A Memling captured by pirates

nation. Ordered by the Medici agent, it was captured on its way to Florence by pirates and given to Our Lady's in Danzig, and so arrived in the east.

Many of these artistic treasures were destined for churches. Others, however, were ordered by those who could afford them to decorate their new homes. One of these new complicated town houses was built by Louis of Bruges between 1465 and 1470. It still stands beside Our Lady's in Bruges—the Gruuthuse. From its oratory the master of the house could watch the service at the high altar without leaving his home. Another, the Achter Sikkel, with its columns and cloister, built in typical brick and white sandstone, is one of the few examples in Ghent of a later more delicate, Italianate, architecture. Perhaps the most splendid example is the home of Jerôme van Busleyden in Mechelen. Many pictures and manuscripts show how these rich houses were decorated and furnished, the fashions favoured by the lady of the house, her plate, her food and her servants. Even smaller town houses began to be built in stone rather than wood. Some very rare examples of the latter still stand—near the Fish Market in Ghent, near Our Lady's in Bruges. Many streets began to take on the aspect which in Bruges, and in smaller parts of other towns, they still retain. The step gables, so typical of the domestic architecture of the Netherlands, still line so many streets—in Bruges, on Antwerp's market place, in Damme and Ghent with the gild house of the Free Boatmen. They bordered new streets, many of which were cobbled. New housing estates, water supplies, rubbish disposal, were provided for in schemes of urban development such as Gilbert van Schoonbeke's suburb of Antwerp.

Antwerp's apotheosis

Antwerp was the centre of this development. The enormous attraction which it exerted speeded up the change in influence and importance from Flanders to Brabant. Antwerp not only had trade, but also industry and the money market. It had freedom, was unprejudiced, and enjoyed the favour of the rulers. It provided opportunities for every sort of craftsman, every luxury trade. Ample credit was available where princes sought their loans. Financial transactions became all the time more complex, and some contemporaries considered, risky. There were great opportunities either to make a fortune or to go bankrupt. Look at the faces depicted by Martin van Reymerswael in 'A Merchant doing his book-keeping' or Quentin Metsijs' 'Money changer and his wife'. There is nothing religious about these pictures. They are typical of the

The town-hall and belfry of Douai, French-Flanders.

The great west tower of St. Rombout's cathedral in Mechelen.

new, hectic, cruel business world. Yet, in the latter, a tiny mirror on the table reflects another typical glance down a town street. Diamond cutting, paper making, printing, silk weaving, the production of cloth of gold, all made their appearance. The printing works set up by the Plantijn family in Antwerp still show the techniques used in the sixteenth century. Germans, such as the Fuggers—Anthony Fugger is depicted on one window in Antwerp cathedral—the Welsers, the Tuchers, Italians such as the Affaitadi of Cremona, and the Frescobaldi; English Merchant Adventurers, and financial wizards like Sir Thomas Gresham all either visited or lived in Antwerp, and its influence and that of the artists and craftsmen of the Low Countries spread across Europe in ever widening circles. A real market in art treasures grew up there. Such luxury and wealth contrasted sadly with the growing number of paupers and vagrants, victims of the economic changes. Yet they were not ignored. Many new charitable institutions were founded, often under lay control. The new rich bourgeoisie felt its responsibilities.

All this artistic development shines against an outstanding series of buildings, both lay and ecclesiastical. Long before, Gothic ideas in architecture had flowed from France, northwards along the Scheldt and the Leie. Gradually they were

Brabant Gothic adopted and developed in a distinctive manner. This development too, is centred on Brabant. The typical local materials—bricks from the Kempen and white sandstone from Brabant and Hainaut, give a special flavour to many of these new buildings. Much was still done in stone, but even then it retained a local character. More churches were constructed in Brabant than in Flanders. Our Lady's in Antwerp, with its tall slim tower, St. Peter's in Leuven, St. Gummarus's in Lier, St. Rombout's in Mechelen, with its square high tower, solid like those of St. Michael and Gudule in Brussels, all show the optimism, breadth of vision and technical skill of these fifteenth and sixteenth century architects. Most of these great Gothic churches rose in the Duchy of Brabant, but there were others like Our Lady's of Sint-Truiden, St. Quentin's in Hasselt, St. Nicholas of Veurne, St. Martin's of Ronse and the new St. Baaf's cathedral in Ghent. Such immense works demanded great technical skill. They were the work of specialists. Some families of architects were responsible for a whole series of

A great dynasty of architects churches and civic buildings. For a hundred years successive Keldermans turned the dreams of the century into stone: St. Gummarus' in Lier, the tower of St. Rombout's in Mechelen, the town halls of Middelburg and Mechelen, and the Broodhuis in Brussels are all their work.

Often the plans were too grandiose and ambitious. Our Lady's in Antwerp only achieved one of her two towers, St. Rombout's never had its spire, St. James's in Antwerp was never finished, St. Michael's in Ghent never got further than the base of its spire. Sometimes, the plans were technically too difficult. Sometimes, the money ran out. The town hall in Ghent shows vividly the effect of Charles V's fines on the town budget, by the change from a flamboyant Gothic to a very sober Renaissance style which occurs in the middle of the building. Yet many town halls were completed. In Bruges the first stone had already been laid by Louis of Male in 1376. On its balcony the new counts of Flanders took the oath to preserve the town's privileges. Originally it was decorated with painted statues, but these were destroyed in 1792. The Poortersloge there, was also built in the fourteenth century, but had to be reconstructed after a fire in the eighteenth. Bruges's close neighbour, Damme, was also still building in the fifteenth century. Troubles would soon come, but first there was a new town hall to be constructed. The size of the square in which it stands allows us to admire it in a manner often impossible in more closely built streets. Moving further east, the Butchers' gild hall and part of the cloth hall in Ghent, the Butchers' gild hall in Dendermonde, the town hall of Oudenaarde, lead us into Brabant, where the town hall of Brussels provides one of the most glorious examples of Gothic architecture in the Low Countries. The two wings were built in the fifteenth century, and the tower added in the fifteen-forties, an indication of the growing importance of the town under the Burgundian dukes. The same Gothic style gives us the Broodhuis in Brussels, Matthew Laeyens's splendid town hall in Leuven, and the present town hall of Mechelen, once the seat of the Great Council. Many more examples could be added, such as the town gates which still remind us of the frequently turbulent past of the towns of the Netherlands: like the Hallepoort in Brussels, the Ghent gate in Bruges, the Rabot in Ghent, built to guard one of the town's precious locks, the Broel towers guarding the bridge in Kortrijk, and the Brussels gate in Mechelen.

In art, architecture, fashion, political and economic development the Netherlands had taken a long step forward in the fifteenth century. In the sixteenth, there were to be many further changes. The Low Countries, whose horizons seemed, in its early years, to be widening, found, under Charles V, that the centre of affairs tended to be where he was, and he was often abroad. On the other hand, the immense influence of the revival of interest in the classics, which permeated all aspects of culture, began to make an increasingly deep impression.

Humanism This new humanism seemed to find a natural home in the Netherlands, with their sophisticated and cosmo-

Damme's town-hall and statue of Jacob van Maerlant.

Town-hall and statue of Margaret of Austria in Mechelen.

politan traditions. The Burgundian rulers were themselves scholars. They enjoyed and encouraged the brilliant and enquiring minds which found at the court the patronage on which they relied. Such an atmosphere was perfect for men like Erasmus. Printing had been introduced by Dirk Martens in the

Printing fourteen seventies and had spread like wild-fire throughout the Low Countries. There was a healthy native literary tradition which had started in the twelfth century with Van Veldeke, continued with the mysticism of Hadewijch and the histories and encyclopaedias of Jacob van Maerlant, and in the fourteenth produced the great mystic and didactic writings of John of Ruusbroec, the chaplain of St. Gudule's, who had retired to Groenendael in the Zoniën wood. This tradition of medieval Dutch was beginning to spread out to a wider public through the Chambers of Rhetoric, clubs dedicated to theatrical productions, singing and a general folk culture, which sprang up like mushrooms throughout the latter half of the fifteenth century and of which some still exist to-day.

One of the followers of Ruusbroec took a step of great importance for the cultural future of the Low Countries. This was Gerard Groote, who founded in Deventer the Brethren of the Common Life. This society was dedicated to teaching and had a great veneration for the classics. They were not interested in native literature. They founded, however, many schools, instructed children in the rules of Latin grammar—with the help of such text books as those by Nicholas Despautère whose portrait hangs in the town hall in Ninove,

Erasmus encouraged printing, and above all, educated Erasmus. His condemnation of both heresy and fanaticism fitted into the history and traditions of the Netherlands, but came at an unfortunate moment. In 1517, the same year that Luther is said to have nailed his theses on the door of the church in Wittenberg, Erasmus seemed to have achieved his heart's desire. This was the foundation of a college in Leuven dedicated to the study of the three languages, Greek, Latin and Hebrew, in order to permit a scientific investigation of Biblical texts. Leuven seemed ideal. A flourishing university seat since 1425, it could have provided the atmosphere he sought. His friend Jerôme van Busleyden put up the money. Erasmus installed himself at its head. His intention was to work within the frame-work of the Catholic church. He disliked Protestant fanatics as much as Catholic ones. But by the twenties the Low Countries were already becoming involved in the merciless dispute between two groups. Erasmus was suspect. His followers were attacked and in some cases, as with the geographer Mercator, charged with heresy. This was no atmosphere for Erasmus. In 1521 he left the Netherlands, for Basle. His College of the Three Languages gradually became a centre of philological studies. This was a sad moment for the Netherlands. The heresy hunt which was to claim so many victims, including the translator of the Bible, the Englishman Tyndale, had begun.

Yet this was the darker side of a still bright picture. The University of Leuven attracted students and scholars from all over Europe. An entirely new scientific look was taken at old disciplines.

Expansion of science Andreas Vesalius taught anatomy, although to be allowed to make dissections without interference he had to retreat to Italy; Rembert Dodoneus, another doctor, produced the first scientific work on botany; Ortelius, a map merchant from Antwerp, under Mercator's influence produced the first world atlas, which ran to twenty-five editions; Simon Stevin from Bruges, wrote about, and taught mathematics; while Mercator, who worked chiefly in Germany was nevertheless born in Rupelmonde. In architecture and painting the classical influence became stronger. The splendid series of portraits continued, but they were now painted rather by very skilled gentlemen than by craftsmen of the Van Eyck tradition. Anthony Moro, whose self-portrait hangs in Florence, painted a great series of princes and rulers, including Philip II of Spain, Mary Tudor, Mary of Hungary, Charles V; Bernard van Orley, who also produced numerous cartoons for tapestries, has given us his versions of Charles V and Margaret of Austria; Quentin Metsijs, a child of the fifteenth century, painted an impressive portrait of Erasmus; John Gossaert produced both a portrait of the young Jacqueline of Burgundy and numerous other portraits. But as well as the continuation of the old tradition of pictures in-

Invasion of Italian fashion spired by Biblical subjects, a new classical series began to creep in. Artists made the grand tour to Italy. Many studied in Italian studios. Some, like Lancelot Blondeel and Frans Floris, who enjoyed a great vogue in the sixteenth century, seem to have lost their individuality in their admiration for everything Italian. In some artists, like John Gossaert, the two tendencies exist side by side. His portrait of Jacqueline of Burgundy, with a sphere in her hand and a little bonnet edged with pearls on her head, is in the old tradition, but his 'Hermaphrodite with Salmacis', or 'Venus and Amor' would never have appeared in the Low Countries in the fifteenth century. Some of the typical old touches are lost. The Holy Family tends to be framed in classical pillars rather than in the old stable with moss on its dilapidated thatch; Mary is visited by the angel in a Greek temple rather than in a northern room, with a basin and towel, standing by a window opening on a street bordered by gabled houses. The old combination of urban and mystical traditions gave way before the new enthusiasm for everything Italian. Some actual Italian treasures were imported into the Netherlands, like the charming Michelangelo statue of the Madonna and Child, presented by John Mouscron to Our Lady's in Bruges.

The Gothic architectural tradition which had held its ground so long in the Low Countries also began to give way before influences from the south. Margaret of Austria's court in Mechelen, which was rebuilt for her by Rombaut Keldermans has a Flemish Renaissance facade. The new Town Hall of Antwerp by Cornelis Floris, built in the sixties, burned down by the Spaniards, and reconstructed in 1579, and the New Exchange show that Antwerp, in spite of its difficulties, remained in the forefront of cultural development. In Mechelen the Fishmongers' gild house 'The Salmon', and the Griffie of Bruges, by Christian Sixdeniers, are on a less mighty scale but strongly Renaissance in inspiration, as is also the splendid mantelpiece of the Franc de Bruges, by Lancelot Blondeel, depicting Charles V standing between his grandparents.

A few escaped this all pervading Italian influence. The church found at least one very literate defender in Anna Bijns, whose dislike of Protestants was forcefully expressed in her native language. In music, Orlando Lassus continued the tradition of Josquin des Prés and Ockeghem. But, yet again, it is the painters

Bosch and Brueghel

who surprise us most. Two, Hieronymus Bosch and Peter Brueghel, entirely disregard any inspiration but their own. Some of the weirdness so typical of Bosch recurs in Brueghel's drawings, and in such a picture as the 'Fall of the Angels'. But he is less of a caricaturist. The beautiful series of landscapes with figures, and such panels as the 'Country Wedding' and the 'Dance of the Peasants' contain faces which can be recognised every day among country people.

He, too, had made the trip to Italy. But in spite of a strong Italian influence and in spite of the fact that he was painting mainly after 1563, when most of his countrymen had adopted the southern style, Brueghel's paintings are purely of the north. His cloudy skies are those of Brabant, his figures the work-worn, bent, peasants of the Low Countries. He is said to have painted the landscape near the castle of Gaasbeek, south of Brussels. Certainly looking out from its grounds to-day, one might be looking into 'The Corn Harvest'. Sometimes the countryside is Italian, as in the 'Conversion of St. Paul', but the composition as a whole has nothing in common with the Renaissance except perhaps the clothes. In his winter scenes, hunters return wearily through the snow under a leaden Flemish sky, while villagers slide and skate near a village church and

Town house of Gerard the Devil in Ghent.

The cloth-hall and belfry of Ypres.

gabled houses, beside a row of poplars. In spite of the snow, his panels give a feeling of comfort, good food and good fires, dancing and feasting. And this while the atmosphere in which he worked was already reeking with the smoke of the heretics' fires.

There is much in common between this flowering of the human spirit in the Low Countries of the fifteenth and early sixteenth centuries and the England of Shakespeare and Raleigh, Drake and Elizabeth I. But while across the channel there was no interference from without, the civilisation of the Low Countries was cut off by neglect and the iron hand of Spain.

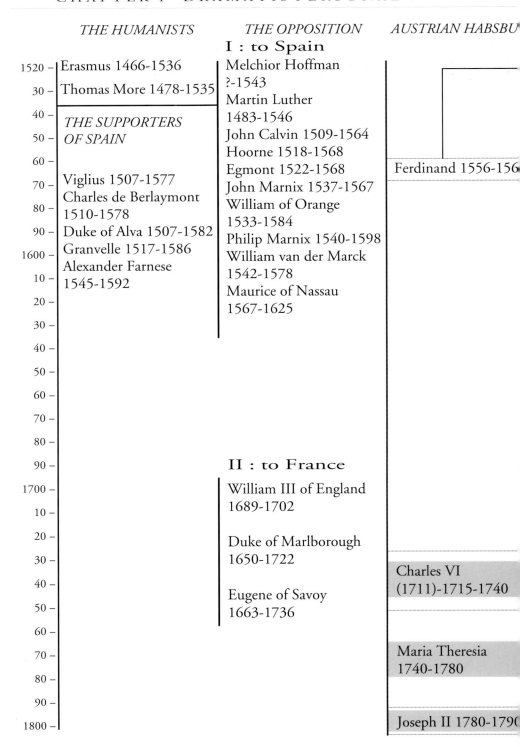

THE HUMANISTS	THE OPPOSITION	AUSTRIAN HABSBU*

I : to Spain

1520 – Erasmus 1466-1536

Melchior Hoffman
?-1543

30 – Thomas More 1478-1535

Martin Luther

40 –

THE SUPPORTERS
OF SPAIN

1483-1546

50 – John Calvin 1509-1564

Hoorne 1518-1568

60 –

Egmont 1522-1568

Ferdinand 1556-156*

70 – Viglius 1507-1577

John Marnix 1537-1567

Charles de Berlaymont

William of Orange

80 – 1510-1578

1533-1584

90 – Duke of Alva 1507-1582

Philip Marnix 1540-1598

Granvelle 1517-1586

William van der Marck

1600 – Alexander Farnese

1542-1578

10 – 1545-1592

Maurice of Nassau

20 –

1567-1625

30 –

40 –

50 –

60 –

70 –

80 –

90 –

II : to France

1700 –

William III of England
1689-1702

10 –

20 –

Duke of Marlborough
1650-1722

30 –

Charles VI
(1711)-1715-1740

40 –

50 – Eugene of Savoy
1663-1736

60 –

70 –

Maria Theresia
1740-1780

80 –

90 –

1800 –

Joseph II 1780-179(*

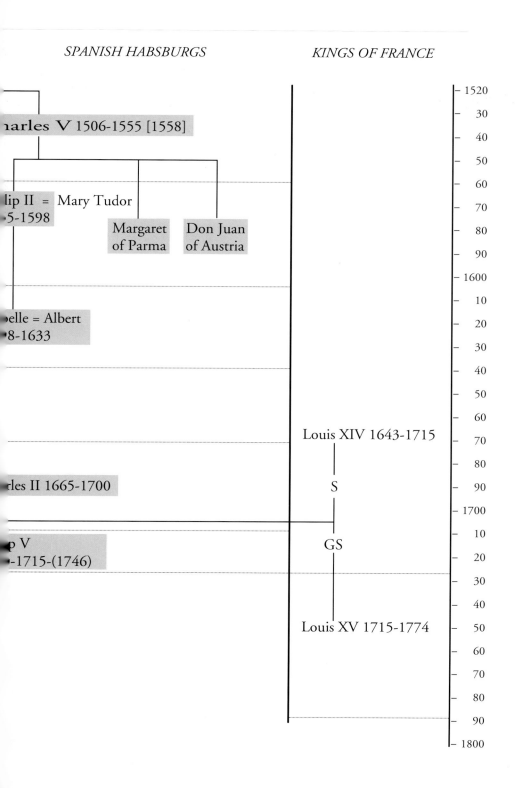

SPANISH HABSBURGS   KINGS OF FRANCE

narles V 1506-1555 [1558]

lip II = Mary Tudor
5-1598

Margaret
of Parma

Don Juan
of Austria

elle = Albert
8-1633

Louis XIV 1643-1715

S

les II 1665-1700

GS

p V
-1715-(1746)

Louis XV 1715-1774

1520
30
40
50
60
70
80
90
1600
10
20
30
40
50
60
70
80
90
1700
10
20
30
40
50
60
70
80
90
1800

Contrarie de Catholicke religie synghende guessche psalmen zoo up straete als zittende ten viere tot grooten schandale ende ontstichtinghe van den volcke... recht doende condemneert u te dienen als forcaire op de galeyen van heurlieden hoocheden den tijt van vijf jaeren...

Ghent, State Archives, Council of Flanders, n° 8594, f° 67-68. 6 July 1603.

The Council of Flanders: 'enforcing the law, condemns you (Gillis Kielmaes), for behaviour contrary to the Catholic religion, singing heretical psalms in the street as well as at the fire-side, causing great scandal and offence to the people... to serve as a galley-slave on their Majesties' galleys during the time of five years...'

Condemneert hem ter causen van onder hem ende tsijnen huyse ghehadt ende gehauden thebben twee Vlaemsche boucken den eenen van Henricus Bullingerus ende den anderen van Petrus Viretus beede heritticquen ende verboden mitsch noch een pernicieus ende uproerich tractaet jeghens den prince ende staet van dezen lande ghemaect... in de boete van tweehondert guldenen sconincx onsen gheduchten heere profyte...

Ghent, State Archives, Council of Flanders, n° 8594, f° 179v°. 19 July 1625.

The Council of Flanders: 'condemns him (Jan van Douvrin, senior) for having and keeping in his house, two Flemish books, one by Henry Bullingerus and the other by Peter Viretus, both heretical and forbidden, and another, a pernicious and rebellious treatise against the Prince and the State of this land... to a fine of 200 guilders to the profit of the King our redoubtable lord...'

The Failed Harvest

1555-1794

O N August 9, 1567, the vanguard of Spanish soldiers commanded by the Duke of Alva arrived in Brussels. Their commander, Philip II's 'best and most intemperate' soldier carried orders from his royal master to destroy urban privileges, to substitute royal for urban officials, to disband local militias, to build citadels in Antwerp, Valenciennes, Flushing, Amsterdam and Maastricht and to raise taxes whether the local Estates agreed or not. He was also secretly ordered to get rid of the Prince of Orange and the Counts of Egmont and Hoorne. In trying to put these orders into effect this cold, cruel, proud man provoked a terrible and bloody war which led to the loss to the Spanish crown of the northern, and to the military occupation and subjection of the southern provinces of the Low Countries. The seventeen provinces which had been unified by the Burgundians and given legal status and a common frontier by Charles V would, owing to his son, fall apart and form two quite separate states.

Philip II's fanaticism The responsibility for this state of affairs must be laid very largely at the door of Philip II who has been called neither 'open, nor intelligent, nor humane'. He had no affection for the Low Countries even at the beginning of his reign. By the end he hated them bitterly. He lacked the common touch so obvious in his father's dealings with his countrymen. In 1555 after his father had abdicated in his favour Philip would have liked to return to Spain immediately. In fact, because of troubles with France he was forced to stay in the north. Four years later however he left, never to return. In spite of frequent requests from the Regent, Margaret of Parma, he never thought it worth-while to spend even a fortnight in his northern possessions. With all his fanatical industry and care for detail, he never understood the situation, or realised the effect of his religious fanaticism in the north. There was a complete breakdown of communication between the Escorial and the Court of Brussels. Margaret herself could hardly believe some of the answers which she received to her reports and requests. While she insisted on the political demands of the nobility, on her own powerlessness, on the sympathy with which the Protestants were regarded by her administration, Philip demanded an even more rigorous enforcement of the terrible edicts against them, and refused to recognise the political pressures so hostile to Spain, which were building up in the Netherlands.

For the revolt of the Netherlands against Spain was far from simply a religious question. It is quite impossible to draw a line on one side of which were the Protestants of the north who fought Spain, and on the other side, the Catholics of the south, who supported them. The nobility, which led the revolt, was centred on Brussels, not on Amsterdam. They were not, on the whole in sympathy with religious revolt. Men such as the

Political, not religious revolt

Count of Egmont, who had headed the political opposition, entered the Catholic camp when forced to make a choice on doctrinal grounds. William of Orange was a champion of the same religious tolerance which had been won in the Empire. He disliked Portestant as much as Catholic fanatics. He did his best to reconcile Lutheran and Calvinist. Even in 1565, when opposition to Spain was already entrenched in the Netherlands, the Compromise of the Nobles, an agreement which was really the charter of the Beggars, or opponents of Spain, was phrased in such a way that it offended no religious convictions. Yet much of the violence of the struggle with Spain certainly came from religious intolerance. When Protestantism acquired a political, as well as a theological programme, as it did from John Calvin, the mixture was highly explosive. The religious pattern in the Netherlands had followed more or less the same lines as elsewhere in Western Europe. It had, perhaps, more than its share of mysticism, but about the same degree of devotion, the same number of heretical outbursts—like the followers of Tanchelm in the twelfth century, and the Flagellants in the fourteenth. Some religious movements originated there, such as the Beguines, whose homes in Bruges, Ghent, Kortrijk, Lier, Leuven and Amsterdam are typical of the Low Countries. They are communities of devout women, dedicated to charitable work who, without taking formal vows, live in a community and support themselves by work. By the sixteenth century the clergy in the Netherlands, was just as deserving of Erasmus's scathing remarks of 'observing with

Religion before the Reformation

punctilious scru-

THE FAILED HARVEST

pulosity a lot of silly ceremonies and paltry traditional rules' as they were elsewhere. The bishops were for the most part political nominees, members of the entourage or family of the Burgundian dukes. Their attention to their ecclesiastical duties was not always whole-hearted, and their morals not always above reproach. The Abbot of the monastery of St. Aubert speaks quite naturally of baptizing the child of the bishop and the daughter of the cathedral's provost. The parish clergy were on the whole ignorant and badly paid. Their congregations were ill-taught and often left entirely to their own devices. This was much the same as elsewhere. Erasmus's attempts to obtain reforms from the inside had never had time to spread to more than a very small area. He had many supporters among intellectuals and the lettered nobility. He had just as little idea of breaking away from the Catholic church as had his friends John Colet or Thomas More. Luther's outbursts were just as unpleasant to them as were the Catholic edicts against heretics. The clergy agreed that there was much in need of reform but that this should come from within. Their temperate, intellectual tolerance appealed to the society of the Netherlands. But it did not satisfy the spiritual need there, or elsewhere. This could only be met by new enthusiasms as violent as the reaction they aroused. The political struggle was led by Humanists. But its violence was augmented by the struggle about salvation, which rent the sixteenth century with such fanaticism. Both Catholics and Protestants wanted to rid the Netherlands of Spain. But the issue was complicated and embittered by religious issues which never coincided exactly with political divisions. It was natural for all Protestants to oppose Catholic Spain. But many Catholics joined them in their struggle against foreign occupation and Spanish mercenaries.

The division of the huge Habsburg dominions between Ferdinand, Charles V's brother, who inherited the Empire, and Philip II, to whom fell Spain, the New World and the Low Countries, was carried out peacefully, thanks to the arrangements which Charles had made about the succession. But the Netherlands provided an obvious base for Philip's ambitions. He saw himself as the champion of the Catholic church, as well as the king of a mighty country. He imagined his duty to lie in bringing back to the church, by force if necessary, the erring heretics. This involved him in armadas against England and campaigns in the Low Countries. His mission included the conversion, also by force if necessary, of his possessions in the New World. And, combined with these attempts to save the souls of so many of his fellows, even if it meant burning them at the stake, was a political ambition to make Spain the greatest and most powerful absolutist monarchy in the world. Such plans left no room for

Lier's beguinage (early thirteenth century and later).

Oudenaarde's town-hall in late Brabant gothic.

tolerance. The Low Countries were an obvious and necessary cog in the Spanish

The Netherlands refuse to co-operate

machine. From them Philip wanted money, troops and a base from which he could strike into England and northern France. But instead of obedience and loans, all he received was defiance and a deficit.

Three weeks after Charles's abdication in 1555 things were already going badly. France was threatening. Philip, as always, needed money. But his subjects in the Low Countries who had always disliked Spaniards, felt quite differently about him than they had felt about his father. The quarrel with France was seen as essentially Spanish. Philip's request for taxes was promptly refused by the States General—it seemed incredible that such a short time before they had responded so generously to Charles V's demands. Even Antwerp's resources were beginning to dry up. Philip's general was forced to send his army home because he could not pay it. Two years later, in 1559, the States softened enough to allow Philip to reform his army, win the battle of Gravelines and finally make peace with France by the Treaty of Cateau-Cambrésis. But there was a very important qualification in their complaisance. They demanded first the redress of their grievances, and that Spain should also make a financial contribution. Such demands must have been intolerable to an absolute ruler of the calibre of Philip II. They had much in common with the demands of the English Parliament which so infuriated the Stuart kings.

Having coped with France, however, Philip was, at last, free to shake the dust of the Low Countries from his feet and leave for Spain. He never came back. To rule for him he left his half-sister, Margaret of Parma, the daughter of Charles V and Jeanne van der Gheynst, the daughter of a carpet weaver from near Oudenaarde. As a girl Margaret had lived in the household of Charles's Chamberlain Andrew de Douvrin, and her education was supervised by both Margaret of Austria and Mary of Hungary, whose accounts show that they gave their charge plenty of toys and pretty clothes. She in her turn sent presents to her mother, when the latter married and produced another baby girl of whom her elder daughter was god-mother. Margaret later married Alexander de Medici and after his assassination, Ottavio Farnese. Philip II controlled her

Margaret of Parma

husband's lands in Italy and, hoping to get them back, Margaret agreed to rule the Netherlands as regent. She was perhaps less brilliant than her two predecessors, but had she been left as free as they had been, the Netherlands might never have landed in the blood-bath which awaited them. The two earliest regents had enjoyed great power and the complete confidence of Charles V. While ostensibly endowing Margaret with full powers Philip left real control in the hands of a secret trio—Granvelle, son of Charles's great minister, the Frisian Viglius, an ambitious jurist, and Charles de Berlaymont. This group was in the hands of Spain. Opposition quickly began to crystallize around the Counts of Egmont and Hoorne and William, Prince of Orange. Their motives were essentially political. Religious issues amalgamated with them only later. Egmont was the rich, showy, brave and immensely popular Governor of Flanders; Hoorne, another leader of the nobility of the Netherlands, who had served both Charles V and Philip II; and William of Orange, 'the Silent', friend

Egmont, Hoorne and William the Silent

of the Humanists, tolerant diplomatist and the richest nobleman in the Low Countries, Governor of Holland, Zealand, Utrecht, Frisia and Gelderland, and Count of Nassau. His father had become a Lutheran but William had been brought up as a Catholic at the court in Brussels, where he had enjoyed the affection of Charles V. He appears to have had no particularly strong religious convictions, but enough will and intelligence to lead the revolt against Spain. It was on his arm that Charles V had leaned when saying farewell to the Netherlands in 1555.

The opposition to Spanish absolutism began in the southern provinces of the Netherlands. It was not the movement of a predominantly Protestant north against a largely Catholic south. This was its result, not its cause, although even after 1585 many Catholics fought with the Protestants against Spain. In fact until the mid-seventeenth century there were less Protestants in the north than Catholics. In Antwerp in 1585, of a population of about 100,000, 44.97 % were Catholic, 14.57 % Lutheran, 28.18 % Calvinist or Anabaptist, 10.86 %

Protestants in the southern Netherlands

unknown and 1.42 % in none of these categories. This is not of course a perfect reflection of the state of the whole country. Antwerp had been allowed more latitude in religious matters than elsewhere, but it would be quite wrong to consider the history of the period, after 1567, as a clear cut battle between a Catholic south and a Protestant north. There has always continued to be a strong minority of Catholics in the northern provinces. It is interesting to note that the percentage of Catholics there diminished very slowly from about 40 % in 1795 to about 38.48 % in 1947. Of the 880 Protestants who died for their faith in the Netherlands in the sixteenth century, 498 met their end in the south. The opposition to Spain was provoked not only by hatred of the Inquisition but by the disregard for national

Béthune (France): belfry and church of St. Vaast.

political institutions and traditions, shown by Spaniards brought up in an absolutist tradition entirely foreign to the Low Countries. It was led by the nobility and the Estates of Brabant, and it failed in the south because of the military might of Spain. It succeeded in the north, not because of these provinces' greater loyalty to Calvin, but because they were guarded from the south by the treacherous waters of the Scheldt and the Maas and by the sluices and flood gates, which allowed the country at any moment to be given back to the sea—a position which was courageously exploited.

As so often happens the last straw was a perfectly reasonable move by Philip II. For hundreds of years a gentle agitation had been going on about the old

The last straw

fashioned and inefficient organisation of the episcopal sees of the Low Countries. If heresy was to be successfully combated, they needed to be in fighting fettle. The church in the Low Countries was still in the framework of bishoprics created by the Franks in the seventh and eighth centuries. They were certainly old fashioned in the sixteenth. They corresponded with no other administrative division in the country. In 1559 Philip II obtained from the Pope a Bull which instead of eight, set up eighteen dioceses, of which three were arch-bishoprics—in Cambrai, Utrecht and Mechelen. He then took the—to him—perfectly normal step, of nominating the new bishops and placing Granvelle in the Primacy of Mechelen. Charles V had often nominated bishops. It had been one of the favourite means by which the Burgundians had obtained good jobs for the princely offspring and ensured loyal support for themselves. But in Philip's hands it became a Spanish incursion into the rights and privileges of the Netherlands. This had always been a danger signal. Even the clergy were outraged. Monasteries which had enjoyed a relative independence saw themselves included in the dowries of the new sees. The new bishops were regarded as Spanish quislings. To Philip they were just one means of fighting the heretics. The other was to enforce the edicts which had flowed from the chancery of Charles V against them. Before 1555, there had been no real question of a Protestant revolt against the state. After 1567 they joined the many other explosive elements united against Spain and the flame of their ardour and fanaticism led to a resounding explosion. But Charles V had himself assumed the role of champion of the Catholic church. Forced to choose

Edicts against heretics

between Protestant and Catholic he had come down with great weight on the side of the latter.

The first edict against the Lutherans appeared in 1520, and was followed by an increasingly savage stream of orders against heretics. But for their enforcement

Charles relied on a number of different instruments—a state appointed network of inquisitors, episcopal courts and the local authorities. The latter, on the whole, hated the harshness of the legislation and quietly tempered justice with mercy. The inquisitorial powers allowed by the edicts were in fact very wide—a commissioner was appointed to name, arrest and imprison heretics, to seize their possessions, to question them, using torture if necessary, free from the usual processes of the law, to condemn, to banish and to execute sentences, against which there was no right of appeal.

The first wave of Protestantism concerned only Lutherans. Their centre was Antwerp. Close connections with Germany, and numerous foreign traders made the town particularly susceptible. The town authorities were against persecution. Many were themselves at least Humanists, if not actually Protestants. They knew, too, that persecution was bad for trade. Many urban authorities throughout the Low Countries refused to take part in the heresy hunt. In Valenciennes and Lille they asked to be exempted from the authority of the inquisition. Yet in 1523 the first Protestant martyrs were burned on the market place in Brussels. Persecution only encouraged ardour. More severe edicts were tried. In 1529 and 1531 they decreed death for anyone other than a theologian who discussed theology, anyone failing to denounce heretics and anyone making or distributing anything disrespectful to God, the Virgin or the Saints. Although, in fact, such edicts were too severe to be applied in the Netherlands, they certainly discouraged the Lutherans, whose faith did not enjoin them to rebel against the state. Many became, however, easy converts for the Anabaptists who entered the Low Countries in about 1529. This was a much

The Anabaptists

more dangerous brand of heresy. It swept through the Netherlands from Emden in Germany where Melchior Hoffman, the leader, had set up his head-quarters. It attacked not only the church but the state and the whole frame-work of society by its advocacy of polygamy and denunciation of property. Everyone, Catholic and Lutheran alike, hated the Anabaptists. At first they were non-violent but under such leaders as John Matthijs of Haarlem and John Beukels of Leyden they took to sterner measures and a revolt broke out in Amsterdam. It was cruelly crushed. After their retreat to Münster, they set up their own form of theocracy which was also barbarously wiped out in 1535, whereupon they rejected further violence. Nevertheless they continued to propagate their faith and to die for it. Of the 880 Protestants who died in the Netherlands in the sixteenth century, 617, or 70 %, were Anabaptists. Nevertheless Charles V, in spite of his hatred of Protestantism, never lost from sight the realities of the situation in the Netherlands. He limited the freedom of printing, burned heretical books, censored school curricula and the plays of the chambers of rhetoric, and even insisted that anyone settling in the Low Countries should have a certificate of good Catholicism, but he was never whole-hearted in his persecutions. He left the nobility alone. He exempted foreign merchants from his regulations on foreigners. He never extended the most severe edicts to Antwerp. A strict enforcement of the anti-Protestant legislation would have ruined the Netherlands, as it was to do in the southern provinces after 1585. Charles did not want to see the massive emigration of the best and most industrious parts of the labour force as happened after the fall of Antwerp to the Spaniards. Philip neither understood nor cared.

In spite of all the legislation Protestantism spread like wild fire. Pamphlets,

Protestantism spreads like wild fire

books and preachers flooded the country. Clandestine sermons were preached. Bibles were ardently studied. But only with the advent of Calvinism did the Protestant cause receive a really solid and efficient organisation. There was nothing sporadic or haphazard about the Calvinistic penetration of the Netherlands. It relied on a framework

Calvinist efficiency

of highly educated preachers trained for the most part in the Calvinist University of Geneva. Its spear-head came from the south. Its strongholds were in the densely populated industrial centres such as Hondschoote, Valenciennes and Tournai. The population sympathised with it. In Valenciennes the authorities, unwillingly going about the long delayed execution of two Calvinists, saw their victims literally snatched from them by the crowd on their way to the fire. Heretics died heroically, singing psalms, and so making converts. Philip II suggested that they should therefore be gagged before being burned as was done in the England of his wife, Mary Tudor. Their fanaticism threatened order and administration.

Margaret of Parma, struggling against one wave after another understood, although she was herself an unshakeable Catholic, that Philip's ways were not going to work in the Netherlands, and refused to see any connection between the political and religious antagonism to the government. She hoped that if Philip would only remove Granvelle, she would be able to rally the nobles, and put a stop to the crisis which men like William of Orange had provoked by refusing to sit in the Council of State until their grievances had been examined. They were in fact on strike. So Granvelle was at last packed off in March 1564 to Franche-Comté to visit his mother. But then the nobles found that government was not so easy after all. The Estates of Brabant did nothing but protest and refuse. The Calvinists were positively praying for the chance to attack the Roman idolaters. William of Orange, who had hoped to get an agreement between Calvinists and Catholics, such as had been concluded in the Empire between Catholics and Lutherans, found that they were unshakeable. They had no desire to agree with the Lutherans either. William was busy searching among the Imperial princes for allies, whom he saw would be essential

Philip's lack of understanding

in a military struggle with Spain. In the midst of such upheavals, such hardening of positions, Philip wrote from Segovia in October 1565, not, as Margaret had hoped, that he was coming north to cope with the situation himself, but that the edicts against heresy should be more severely applied. His only positive suggestion was that heretics might be executed secretly. Six months later Margaret was forced to disobey. The lesser nobility, led by two brothers, John and Philip Marnix, had, under the guise of taking the waters in Spa, drawn up a manifesto to which Protestant and Catholic could alike subscribe, as ostensibly it asked for no more than the end of the inquisition. On April 5th, 1566, it was presented to Margaret, and, she, overawed by the band of armed men at her gate, agreed to reduce the severity of the measures against heresy and to write yet again to Spain. That evening, at a banquet, the supporters of the manifesto dined together and acquired for the first time the pseudonym of Beggars, and took as their emblems the beggar's bowl and the fox's brush,

The Beggars

which were to symbolise the revolt against Spain. Margaret's compliance looked like the defeat of the Spanish party. Although agreement between Calvinist and Catholic tended to become rather shaky, the acceptance by Margaret of the manifesto meant that every hidden Calvinist preacher, every exiled Protestant, felt free to come out into the open. Priests acknowledged their adherence to the new doctrines from the pulpit, sermons were preached at every street corner, churches were demanded for the new cults. The strength of the Protestants was revealed, and it was much greater than even Margaret had feared. Four months after the Beggars' banquet, in Steenvoorde, a small village in Western Flanders, a group of ardent Calvinists listened to a sermon by a fiery young preacher with a black beard, called Sebastian Matte. Encouraged by his words, they rushed to the neighbouring parish church of St. Lawrence and inspired by their hatred for Roman idolaters, destroyed everything they could reach in the church. Three days later Jack de Buyzere, a one time Austin friar, preached in Belle, and St. Anthony's monastery followed St. Lawrence's. On the 14th, Matte was in

The Broodhuis on the Market place in Brussels.

Iconoclastic fury Poperinge and his visit led to the same result. Round Bergues Saint-Winoc, in an area of about 130 square miles, 50 churches were attacked; near Cassel, in an area of about 200 square miles, 55 churches, abbeys and monasteries had their treasures destroyed, images broken, statues decapitated, windows shattered, altar screens smashed, and vestments torn to shreds. By the 20th of August the iconoclasts were in Antwerp. The town administration ordered that they were to be given a free hand. One of their objectives was Metsijs' 'Crucifixion'. In Ghent everything was given an air of legality. The iconoclast Lievin Onghena presented a forged permit from Egmont to the magistrates, and they gave him their blessing. In less than twenty-four hours, 1 collegiate and 7 parish churches, 25 monasteries, 10 hospitals and 7 chapels were dealt with. The 'Mystic Lamb' enjoyed one of its many miraculous escapes, hidden in the attics of St. Baaf's. On August 23rd the iconoclasts were shepherded out of the town to deal with the surrounding villages, of which they visited 46. In Oostwinkel the vicar and his chaplain helped with the work. The violence spread north and east. On the 21st and 22nd it was Middelburg's turn; on the 23rd, Mechelen; from the 23rd to the 29th Tournai. Brussels, Leuven and Bruges escaped. In the north it had all been a little less violent. On September 29th it ended in Leeuwarden. The destruction had been frightful. It had been carried out systematically and often with the blessing of the urban authorities. In Ghent and Tournai the pieces of the broken statues were remitted to the magistrates. To Margaret of Parma as well as to many Catholics, it was an outrage. But to many others it was even worse—it was a threat to the state. Egmont was provoked into saying that this threat should first be dealt with and religion left for later. To the nobility, still clinging to their tolerant humanistic ideals, it was a revelation of religious fanaticism. Margaret, whose army was riddled with Calvinism, was forced to allow freedom to preach, though only in the usual places; to reduce the severity of the edicts still further; to grant a general amnesty and to abolish the inquisition. Freedom of religion seemed to have been established in the Netherlands. But this was not how Margaret looked at it. To her, it seemed that she had grudgingly allowed some concessions, under duress, and that the nobility should have rallied to her to help repair this situation as quickly and thoroughly as possible. She could not bear to see them rushing about trying to establish Protestantism on a footing equal to that of the established church. They seemed traitors both to her and to their faith. She nominated a convinced Catholic as governor of Brussels. Parties began to form up on more strictly religious lines. Those who wanted to stay friendly with both found themselves in impossible situations. Egmont still went to mass in Ghent, but did not remove his hat, and so infuriated both Catholics and Protestants. William of Orange foresaw what awaited the Netherlands at the hands of Philip.

As soon as the worst of the tumult had died away the government had rallied: Margaret immediately announced that only Catholicism was pleasing to God and to Philip II. Egmont took an oath of complete fidelity to the government and started, in Flanders, to destroy Protestant churches and hang Calvinists. German mercenaries were sent to reduce Protestant urban strongholds, except Antwerp, where Orange was left more or less in peace. Valenciennes, where a

Threat of religious war

Calvinist theocracy had been set up, John Marnix, attempted to capture the island of Walcheren, but Flushing and Arnemuiden shut their gates to him. A war of religion was breaking out. Marnix was slaughtered before Antwerp under William of Orange's eyes. It had all come too quickly. Valenciennes capitulated. William refused to lead the revolt without allies. Hoorne took the oath to Philip. Orange retreated to the County of Nassau. Calvinists fled by the thousand—to Germany, to England. The government seemed to have won. Margaret was ready, feeling that she had the upper hand, to be lenient. She wanted to stem the flow of emigration which was bleeding the country white. But they all reckoned without Philip II. Brooding in the Escorial, he alternated between furious outbursts, and utter refusals to listen to any advice. Leniency was certainly far from his thoughts. He had sworn as Catholic defender of the Church and absolute monarch of Spain to deal once and for all with the wretched Low Countries. He had had enough of their independence and their flirting with tolerance. That Catholics and Protestants were united in their hatred of Spain he neither knew nor cared. He had decided to give his possessions a lesson which they would not forget. The result of it was to divide the seventeen provinces into two halves.

'It is infinitely better to hold an impoverished and even ruined country for God and the king by war, than to leave it undamaged in the hands of the devil and his supporters, the heretics', claimed the Duke of Alva. He immediately went

The arrival of
the Duke of Alva

on to put his theory into practice. He did not succeed in holding the Netherlands completely, but what he held he certainly ruined. Between his arrival in 1567 and 1609 when Spain was forced to recognise the independence of the seven northern provinces, the Low Countries were in an almost constant state of war. The result of this struggle was dictated largely by geographical conditions. The fact that Holland and Zealand were maritime provinces consisting very largely of a net-work of islands held from the sea by dikes which could at any moment be cut and the surrounding land flooded, made them able to resist. The older northern provinces such as Gelderland, Drente and Overijssel were essential to their defence on the east. Hence they were amalgamated, often by force. The southern provinces, no less attached to their old traditions, no less Protestant, no less courageous, had no such natural defences. They paid the price of their failure to fulfill the basic requirement of any nation—to defend itself. But in 1567 this was not yet clear. It is essential not to regard the division of the Low Countries into a northern, Protestant republic and a southern Catholic dependency of Spain, as a foregone con-clusion. The first kernel of the Netherlands lay, as we have seen, under the Burgundian dukes, in Flanders and Brabant. To that Philip the Good had added Holland, Zealand and Hainaut. Charles V had insisted on the unity of the Netherlands, had given them a common frontier, a common rule for the succession and had elaborated their common administration. By the accession of Philip II in 1555, these lands were really beginning to see themselves as a unity. The north-eastern provinces—Gelderland, Drente and Overijssel, which later became part of the Republic of the United Provinces, were much less integrated in the Low Countries. Yet it was they and not Flanders and Brabant, which eventually became free from Spain. This was due essentially to

Importance of geography

geographical, not to political or religious causes. Where the two opposing armies laid down their arms in 1609 lay the boundary between the two halves of the Netherlands. The north-eastern provinces were much less affected by Protestantism than Flanders and Brabant. As late as 1580 they in fact attempted to break with the Calvinist dominated Holland and Zealand and to return to the Catholic side. But because they were strategically so essential to the defence from the east, of the heart of the revolt, in Holland and Zealand, they had to be subdued by force. Their distance from the centres of Spanish control made them more vulnerable.

The split came about, however, fortuitously. No-one in 1567 was in open rebellion against the Spanish crown. One of the problems which had to be faced by the States General, and which crippled its effectiveness in opposition, was a possible break with Philip II, who was still regarded as the legitimate sovereign. Men such as the Counts Egmont and Hoorne found this an almost insoluble quandary. Aristocrats, conservative by education and tradition, with strong views about the fealty owed by a knight to his king, they were torn between a patriotic hatred of Spaniards, and their personal duty towards Philip II. The

The Leie in Afsnee near Ghent.

Albert Canal in Riemst.

disastrous consequences of the lack of a native ruling house in the Low Countries appeared here yet again. Egmont's defection and his peculiar shilly-shallying is explained by the awful decision which he had to face. William of Orange had the same problem, but his eye and brain were clearer and his capacity for self delusion less. Yet he continued to stress the unity of the

William of Orange

Netherlands, to try to stop the outbreaks of religious fanaticism, and to draw together all classes in the struggle with Spain. His aim was, as he said himself 'to restore the entire fatherland in its old liberty and prosperity out of the clutches of the Spanish vultures and wolves'. He insisted constantly on religious toleration by both sides. But war conditions forced his hand. Protestant urban authorities claimed that order was threatened by the free exercise of Catholicism. They closed churches and removed statues and priests, in the name, not of Calvinism but of public order. They could do this because they were the active, vigorous element in society. What Alva succeeded in doing by his ferocious punishments in the sourthern Netherlands was to push the energetic, Protestant elements out of these provinces into others which he could not reach. The iconoclasts did not wait to be executed, but fled. Many went abroad. Others took refuge at sea, where they formed fleets of pirates dedicated to attacking Spain. These were the Sea Beggars. This had a dual effect. It meant that the northern provinces gained the most vigorous elements while the south lost them. It would be wrong to imagine that the towns of the northern provinces greeted these harsh bands of Calvinist pirates with open arms. They were in fact very wary about opening their gates. But once the Calvinists were inside, their energy, strength and conviction swept all before them. They gave their authority institutional form, and it proved a solid element in an alarmingly unstable world. They showed that they could provide not only slogans but prosperity.

Thus the opposition to Alva gradually crystallized in the ports and islands of the North Sea shores of Holland and Zealand where boats were more effective than

Opposition to Alva

cavalry and where the Spaniards had to run from the opening of the dikes. The rest of the opposition Alva created himself. His behaviour was so outrageous, his reign of terror so horrible that he pushed many loyal Catholics into the arms of the opposition. The outrages which he and his army perpetrated were the most powerful propaganda for William and the Sea Beggars. He succeeded in making the revolt national instead of confessional. Pirenne says of Alva that 'he advanced, inflexible, among the ruins, his conscience peaceful'. Brueghel probably gives us a glimpse of the disaster in his panel 'The Massacre of the

Innocents', now in Vienna. With nine thousand Spanish troops, Alva treated the Low Countries as hostile occupied territory. His aim was to punish. He demanded victims, and examples. His behaviour showed the tragedy of the situation in the Netherlands where, unlike in the rest of Europe at this time, the ruling house was becoming further estranged from its people. A month after his arrival Alva, whose plans had been previously and secretly laid with his master, who intended to shelter behind him, set up the 'Blood Council'. This com-

The 'Blood Council'

mittee of nine members was controlled by three Spaniards, and presided over by Alva himself, whose signature was necessary on every measure. It took no notice whatsoever of traditions, privileges or personalities. Its aim was the arrest and punishment of rebels and the suppression of disorder. It was not interested in the purely theological side of heresy. That was for the Inquisition. Between 1567 and 1569 the 'Blood Council' executed about 6,000 people and confiscated much property. This made a pleasant addition to the empty Spanish purse. Its most spectacular coup was the execution of Egmont and Hoorne on June 5th, 1568 in the market place in Brussels. They had been arrested the previous September, but kept to await a spectacular occasion. This was provided by Orange's invasion of Brabant. On May 28th, 1568 Alva razed to the ground the Hotel of Culemborg, where the Compromise of the Nobles had been signed, and ten days later Egmont, about whom Beethoven wrote his famous overture,

Execution of Egmont and Hoorne

and Hoorne, showed the people how dangerous disagreement with their masters could be.

Three months later their friend Montigny, who had been sent on mission to Spain, was secretly strangled in his prison at Simancas, according to the plan previously decided upon by the king and Alva. After this the Duke felt that the moment had come to impose a new political structure on the country which would ensure its complete subservience to Spain. No local considerations were taken into account. A general pardon was issued but nearly everyone excluded from it. William's attacks in the north had been ineffective and Alva had shown his metal and that of his experienced Spanish troops by beating William's brother at the battle of Jemmingen in 1568. Flanders and Brabant had not stirred to help Orange. They were still, no doubt, stunned by Alva's retribution. Alva seems to have favoured the simple annexation of the Low Countries to Spain. Throughout 1570 and 1571 Philip hesitated. Gradually the Duke ceased to use the institutions hammered out by the Burgundians. His plan was so to flood all parts of the administration with Spaniards and Italians that finally the

Town-hall and belfry of Arras.

local inhabitants would have no say whatsoever in their own government. This
was exactly what they had always feared. But in his way was one traditional
stumbling block: money. To liberate the administration from dependence on
taxes voted by the States General he attempted to substitute a fixed tax of a tenth
on all commercial transactions. This struck at two tender points at once. Firstly
it was an obvious attempt to undermine the authority of the States General, and
in the second it was a restriction and weight on trade, which in a country
constantly upset and plagued by foreign occupation and disorder, was having
a bad enough time anyway. Yet the States with the exception of Utrecht, voted
the tax. They were so terrified of Alva and his Spaniards, so hopeless of being
able to resist, that their only thought was to avoid the repetition of the massacres
of 1567-70. Orange had been forced to withdraw. Louis of Nassau had been
beaten at Jemmingen. The toughest Calvinists were either at sea with the Sea
Beggars or sheltering in England. What could the Low Countries do except pay
up and make the best of it ?

Everything seemed remarkably gloomy. Yet on March 31st, 1572, William de
la Marcke, Sire of Lumey, a fanatical Calvinist—although later he changed his
mind—and leader of the Sea Beggars, appeared in his little ships before Den
Briel, a small town on the island of Voorne, at the mouth of the river Maas.
These sailors had been turned out of English ports owing to one of Elizabeth's

Capture of Den Briel

constant changes of mind, and were
now looking for a home-port. The
inhabitants of Den Briel were far from glad to see them. Their occupation of the
waterlands of Holland and Zealand was often against the will of the local
population. The clergy and many Catholics fled. But the important point was
that the Beggars had, at last, a foothold on their own home ground. With their
navigational skill and determination they built out from there until their
position became impregnable. When the Spaniards attempted to recapture Den
Briel, the Beggars just flooded the land and the troops had to retreat or drown.
From Den Briel the Beggars went on to take Flushing, and on May 27th
Enkhuizen, in June Gouda and Leyden, in July Haarlem. Sometimes they were
thrown out again. But they always came back. Rotterdam, Schiedam and Delft
opened their gates. Only Amsterdam remained loyal to Spain. Outrages, as
unpleasant as those in the south, were committed by fanatical Calvinists in the
north. William of Orange saw a dangerous gap between a Protestant north and
a Catholic south widening beneath his feet. Yet the leaders of the Sea Beggars
came mostly from the south. By 1575 no Spaniards were left in the province of
Holland. From that moment onwards, triumphant at it was, William's ideal of

a united resistance to Spain became increasingly impossible. Protestant and independent, Holland and Zealand moved from strength to strength. William was himself forced to rely increasingly on these Calvinist supporters. The gap between north and south, even from an economic point of view, grew wider and wider. William's hopes of rallying the south with the help of Huguenots from France was rudely shattered by the news of the Massacre of St. Bartholomew which reached him in August 1572, just as he was marching south. Whereas the northern provinces were starting to organise their own government, public order and trade, in the south everything was in wild confusion. Philip II was tired of Alva. He did not win and he cost too much. Philip made one of his bewildering about-turns and allowed the duke's successor to grant a general pardon, which this time would be really general except that it excluded Protestants, to abolish the 'Blood Council' and to stop insisting on the new tax. Like all Philip's measures for the Low Countries, it came too late. There were

Philip again too late now far too many Protestants to exclude them from a general pardon. By doing so, Philip made agreement with Holland and Zealand impossible. And, as always, he dithered. While his officials in Brussels begged frantically for orders, Philip prayed, distributed alms and asked for choristers to be sent for the royal chapel in Madrid.

Yet the Netherlands in 1576, after the removal of Alva and the death of his successor, were still officially united under the Spanish crown. In fact Holland and Zealand were in the hands of the Calvinists and were beginning to create the urban oligarchies which formed the basis of their new constitution. The southern provinces were still occupied by Spanish troops. Catholics both in the north and south were alarmed by Calvinist pretensions and fanaticism. The nobility, Catholic and conservative, still grasped the hope of compromise between their patriotism and their loyalty to their sovereign. Without William of Orange they had no effective leader, and he was being forced more and more into relying on the northern Calvinists. His own efforts were still aimed vigorously at retaining and strengthening the unity of the revolt of the Netherlands against Spain. What emerged, however, during the next thirty years was the defeat of William's ideals; the hardening of the confessional issue

Division of the Netherlands and, with it, of the territorial division of the Netherlands. We can see in our own day what happens to a country divided on ideological issues. Points of difference were accentuated. Neither Catholic nor Calvinist would give in. Both claimed an exclusive right to the Truth. And

The Gruuthuse mansion in Bruges.

because of the military situation pockets of Calvinism, which was still strong in the southern provinces would be stamped out and the military would become also the ideological frontier. The line which the Spanish troops could not penetrate became the frontier between north and south. This tendency was exacerbated by the Spanish occupying force, which never, in spite of its lengthy service in the Low Countries became in any way reconciled with the local population, and which because of its unruliness, often acted like a boomerang in the hands of its officers.

The situation seemed, however, to have improved for William in 1576. The Spanish army, unpaid and wild, went from one mutiny to another. Something had to be done to defend the population. The States of Brabant took the initiative, called the States General, and began to raise an army. This was open revolt, by the united Netherlands against Spain. The army was led chiefly by Catholics and contained troops of both confessions. Yet during the following months, just when a united opposition seemed to be emerging the religious differences became crucial. For the moment however, they were pushed aside owing to Spanish outrages. Philip had sent his illegitimate brother Don John of Austria, covered with the glory of his victory over the Turks at Lepanto in 1571, to rule the Netherlands. They were an awful grave for military hopes. Don John's command was inaugurated by yet another mutiny by his Spanish troops. This time however, it was on a larger scale than usual. Unpaid by Spain,

The Spanish Fury in Antwerp

the army demanded that it should be paid by the local inhabitants. Completely out of control the soldiers stormed into Antwerp, destroyed a quarter of the town, removed everything on which they could lay their hands, and murdered about 7,000 of the civil population. The Spanish Fury, as this episode in relations between Spain and the Netherlands was called, inflicted priceless damage, and gave a push towards unity in the Netherlands. Religious questions were shelved. The demand by the deputies from Holland and Zealand that only Calvinism should be allowed in those provinces was pushed aside. On November 5th, 1576 the provinces agreed on the proclamation of the Pacification of Ghent, from the balcony of the Pacificatiezaal, in the town hall of that town. It proclaimed a united effort by all the provinces of the Low Countries to expel the Spaniards, to be followed by a meeting of the States General to solve the religious problem. Orange's governorship of Holland and Zealand was confirmed, the edicts against heresy were suspended and political prisoners were released and their possessions restored. This was a manifesto for an immediate united revolt against Spain.

What should have followed was sharp coordinated military action under a skilful general. The whole country could now unite under William against Spain. His personal popularity was enormous. The people looked upon him as their saviour.

Yet his efforts were hamstrung from the first by the religious situation. His most effective troops were the northern Calvinists. They were, however, beginning to feel more and more distinct from the rest of the country and to be interested rather in building up their own new state than in helping their brethren. Those

Defeat of William's ideals

who did return home to the south with William were too fanatical to get on well with the Catholics who had remained at home. Both sides disliked William's own personal tolerance. The States General which should have provided a good army were crippled by their slow procedure and by the fact that even the smallest provinces had as much say in affairs as the larger, who were expected to provide money and men. None of the candidates for the governorship of the Netherlands had the ability or character necessary to provide either inspiration or direction. The Pacification of Ghent had exasperated the Protestants because they were not allowed to exercise their faith except in Holland and Zealand; it exasperated the Catholics because in those two provinces only Calvinists could worship freely. The Netherlands were once more the victim of their own inability to cast off the old ideas of regional independence in order to defend themselves. And just at this moment Philip had a stroke of luck. His appointment of Alexander Farnese, Duke of Parma, son of Margaret, as commander of the Spanish forces in the Netherlands, confronted the forces of the States General with a brilliant general.

Even then, however, they could not really unite. Old traditions of urban independence rose again to the surface. Ghent was of course in the vanguard. Extreme Calvinists set up there what amounted to a theocracy on the Geneva pattern. Catholics were forbidden to worship in public, priests were attacked, churches 'purified'. And then the movement began to broaden on old familiar

Calvinist theocracies

lines. The surrounding country side came in for the same treatment. Parties of fanatics 'purified' country churches and attacked the landowners. Castles, such as that at Ooidonk, were destroyed. Not only ardent Catholics but all property owners were alarmed. Religious peace was possible only when Orange was on the spot and he could not be everywhere at once. Other towns such as Ypres, Lier, Bruges and Breda copied Ghent. There was bound to be a reaction. It came from the south, from the very provinces which had first welcomed

Calvinism, in French Flanders, Artois and Hainaut. After the iconoclasm of 1566, these regions had felt the greatest weight of Alva's fist and the vigorous Protestant elements had either emigrated or been executed. An apathetic Catholic majority was left which above all wanted peace. The best way to obtain it seemed to come to some agreement with Spain. To support William seemed to invite Calvinist violence in the place of Alva's oppression. After Farnese had beaten the Estates' army at Gembloux in 1578 the Walloon regiments had returned to the south. Under their commander, Montigny, they turned on the Calvinists and accused them of violating the Pacification of Ghent. This meant civil war. All William's dreams for a united opposition to Spain were defeated. The two confessional groups formed, on the one hand the Catholic, conservative Union of Arras which included Artois, Hainaut and the areas round Lille and Douai, and on the other the Union of Utrecht which embraced Holland, Zealand and the Calvinist strongholds in Flanders and Brabant. This was not according to the line which would subsequently mark the frontier between the Spanish Netherlands and the United Provinces. In the north east, which had not yet been absorbed by the Calvinists George Lalaing, Count of Rennenburg, commander of Groningen, in 1580 went over to the Spanish side. In the south were still Calvinist urban strongholds. The final division of the country depended on the military campaigns which followed the formation of the Unions of Arras and Utrecht.

After 1579 unity was impossible. William could not control the Calvinist demagogues in Flanders and Brabant. Montigny made peace with Philip and obtained reasonable terms based on the Pacification of Ghent. On the religious question, however, Spain would never soften. The States General packed up and left Brussels for the north. They ceased to include members from the south. William negotiated frantically for help from either France or England. And just at this moment Philip promoted Farnese to the Governorship of the Netherlands. The Duke of Parma was the exact opposite of his predecessor, Alva. He was a brilliant soldier, excellent diplomatist and an attractive person.

The Duke of Parma

In spite of ominous mutterings from the Escorial he got rid, at least in public, of his Spanish suite, and did his best to speak French. He gave important posts to the nobility and in military affairs spared the Netherlands from the frightful bloody vengeance in which Alva had indulged. He had a long frontier to cope with, and a brilliant opponent in Maurice of Nassau, William's son. At first with the troops of the Union of Arras, later with Spanish reinforcements, he advanced against one Calvinist stronghold after another. By means of sieges rather than pitched battles, relying on dazzling engineering feats, new machinery and the persuasion of hunger, he took one town after another. In June 1579, Maastricht; in November 1581, Tournai; in July 1582, Oudenaarde; in January 1583, Ypres; in May 1584, Bruges, in September, Ghent. As each town opened its gates the Protestants were allowed either to leave, after selling up their possessions, or to stay, provided that they did not practice their religion in public. By 1585 Flanders was subdued and Farnese could advance into Brabant. In March, Brussels opened its gates and in August Marnix, in Antwerp, had to capitulate after prodigies of military skill on both sides. Holland and Zealand, free since Orange's murder in Delft in 1584, from any sense of obligation towards the south, sent no help to Marnix in his defence of Antwerp. They merely profited from the town's subsequent economic ruin, when cut off from the sea by the Sea Beggars in the mouth of the Scheldt, the great town's quays rotted in disuse.

The south was under Spanish control. Maurice of Nassau would make inroads later from the north but the great lines of the frontier were drawn. The north had, still, to be subdued. It could be defended and provisioned from the sea. Farnese, who had to cope with Philip's demands from Spain that he should

The south under Spanish control

embark his troops with the Invincible Armada and then, when this proved less invincible than he had hoped, that Farnese would go south and attack France, could not fight on two fronts at once, and exhausted and depressed, died in Arras in 1592, with his work only half done. He had been too independent for Philip. His successors were told to submit to Spain in everything. Philip wanted no more natives in the government.

Yet he was in fact ruminating on a plan which might have worked twenty years earlier. He appointed as Governors of the Netherlands his daughter Isabelle and her husband-to-be Archduke Albert, son of the Emperor Maximilian II. It looked as if the Low Countries might be going to obtain at last what they had been wanting for years—a ruler of royal blood, of their own. After all his attempts to crush the institutions of the Low Countries, Philip II now made a *volte face* and declared that he was making the Netherlands into an independent state. He was of course, much too late. It would have taken more than Spanish promises to make the northern provinces give up the independence they were already enjoying so much, in order to combine with the southern provinces whose independence was more than doubtful. They were quite right in suspecting Spanish promises. The independence was much qualified. The new rulers were in fact tightly controlled by Spain: the succession was regulated; no

Sint-Martens-Lennik in the Pajottenland.

Sluizen in Haspengouw, near Tongeren.

freedom was left over the religious question; Spanish troops were garrisoned in the chief towns; heretics had to be prosecuted; and the Netherlands were firmly excluded from the Indian trade. Although the conditions were patently inacceptable in the north, the fiction of unity was still kept alive. At the solemn recognition in Brussels, of the Archduke, as Governor, in his future wife's place, benches were set ready for delegates from all of the seventeen provinces. Seven of course, remained empty. Yet the others were happy at the thought of their new rulers. When Isabelle entered the Low Countries in August 1599, eleven months after the death of her father, Philip II, she was greeted with great

Albert and Isabelle

enthusiasm. She was conscientious, dignified and determined to do her best. But she was no more free from Spain than Alva and Farnese had been. Once the real business of government began after the festivities of her Joyeuses Entrées, the rift in the lute began to show. Maurice of Nassau was still hovering dangerously in the north. The eternal problem of hard cash faced the Spanish rulers. They called the States General who immediately, as always, demanded first the redress of grievances and then agreed to think about money. The rulers, shocked to the depths of their absolutist souls, declared the money voted and packed the States off home. They would not be recalled for thirty two years. Their presence was

No opposition allowed

incompatible with autocracy. Albert did his best against Maurice of Nassau, who attempted, unsuccessfully to relieve the Protestant garrison of Ostend. Flanders did nothing to help him. Albert was not a very competent soldier and Spinola arrived from Spain to take over from him.

Any nonsense about independence was quickly forgotten. Albert and Isabelle ruled first as Catholics, then as Spaniards and lastly as princes of the Netherlands. Any talk of unity between north and south was becoming ludicrous. It was clear that the situation would have to be accepted. The south would not rise for the Calvinist, Maurice of Nassau. The north would never give up their independence to Spain. The answer was division. In 1609 the independence of the United Provinces was accepted in the Twelve Year Truce. The dreams of the Burgundians had come to this. In just over two hundred years a new state had lived and died.

Thus the home of van Maerlant, of Erasmus, of Brueghel, choked in the stifling piety of the Counter-Reformation. The economic miracle of Antwerp disappeared in the mists of the closed Scheldt. The great Flemish and Brabant towns shrank into demographic and gild-ridden stagnation. The modern centralized administration was wielded by foreigners. The land of tolerance,

Stagnation political innovation and economic experiment became the battlefield for Jesuit and Jansenist, capital drained away from the money market of Antwerp instead of into it, the States General gave way to the Secret Council, and soaring Gothic churches were replaced by Baroque cupolas. This was entirely due to the military conquest by Spain and to her determined grip on the central administration. It also owed much to her firm alliance with the Catholic church. While the United Provinces in the north continued the Burgundian tradition of economic expansion and managed to keep political domination out of the hands of religious fanatics, the south, deprived of any effective say in its own affairs, took refuge in a conservatism which still sometimes appears to-day.

The Archdukes, who were certainly genuinely concerned for the good of the southern Netherlands, did their best to clear up the mess left by more than forty years of war. But they were concerned less with the material wellbeing of the provinces than with the state of their souls. Their overriding passion was the re-establishment and increase of the power of the church. This went of course, hand in hand with the interests of 'le roi très catholique' of Spain, to whom their political decisions were subjected. Even the semblance of independence which Philip II had granted to them gradually disappeared and after Albert's death in 1621 no one even alluded to it any more. In 1616 the southern provinces took without complaint, an oath of fidelity directly to Philip III. He became their immediate sovereign. His successor, Philip IV, even revived the old Consejo de Flandes, instituted in 1588. All foreign affairs and correspondence with Madrid depended entirely on the Secretary of State and War who was invariably Spanish and whose secret correspondence with his master shows where the power really lay. The Privy Council in Brussels which extended its power was dominated by

Spanish control Spaniards and their supporters, who, however ceremoniously, dictated to Albert and Isabelle. The armed forces were in the hands of a Spanish general. None of the real power remained in native hands. Simply by failing to call the States General, the rulers got rid of any organised legal opposition. When they were called by Isabelle in 1632 all the members did was to make fools of themselves by deliberating endlessly about matters over which in any case they had no authority. The only glimmer of independence flickered in Brabant, which in the Joyeuse Entrée possessed a written constitution. When Isabelle died childless, in 1633, any hope which might have existed thirty years before that the southern Netherlands might obtain their own ruling house were finally extinguished.

By the Treaty of Arras, Walloon Flanders had returned to the Spanish fold.

The old cloth-hall, now town-hall of Dendermonde.

Flanders and Brabant had then gradually been won back by Farnese. Calvinists were allowed either to leave or to exercise their faith only in private. This was the end of Calvinism in the south. Such isolated communities as remained, lived quietly without trouble. But the Calvinist republics of Ghent and Ypres and elsewhere, had frightened the nobility. They had threatened not only the Church but the structure of society. Any rebellion might call them again into existence. Hence the nobles lost the taste for revolt. At the same time they were taken in hand by the positive, fighting come-back of the Church, its loins girded for battle. It had been in a bad way. But with the fervent practical support of the Archdukes, and ultimately of Spain, those days were over. Albert and Isabelle were undoubtedly personally devout. They looked upon not only their private lives but their public duties as suitable for ecclesiastical influence. They supported and endowed religious orders in great numbers, re-established pilgrimages and devotions, put back the saints on their pillars. Isabelle, after her husband's death, never again appeared in public except in the habit of the Poor Claires. They mixed government and religion in a way which is apparent in some of the great ideologies of the present. Civil punishment followed religious back-sliding. If children did not attend Sunday school their parents were deprived of certain financial advantages. University students at Leuven had to swear to their hatred of heresy, strenuous efforts were made to improve the educational and financial level of the clergy. A new university had been founded

Interference in all aspects of life

at Douai in 1561 and this was to be a spearhead of the Counter-Reformation not only on the continent but in England as well. But of all the weapons at the disposal of the Counter-Reformation church the most vigorous, intelligent and devoted was the Society of Jesus. It was independent of all authority except that of its own General and the Pope. Once it had a hold in the Netherlands its influence became enormous. In 1586 there were 253 Jesuits in

The Jesuits

the Netherlands; in 1597, 445; and in 1626, 1574. At that date there were only 2962 in Spain itself. They were completely single minded. Everything was aimed at the re-establishment of the Catholic church. The means were manifold. Sunday schools, colleges specialising in the education of the sons of nobles and upper class families, publishing, popularising the Catechism, establishing Congregations of laymen dedicated to the interests of the church. Their activities embraced not only religious, but public and social life as well. Gradually the youth of the southern Netherlands came under their influence or control. Such an all pervasive influence was inescapable. Numerous young men joined the Order. Young women also entered convents in alarming numbers. In 1628 there were 20 women's convents in Ghent alone. The property which the Archdukes and the nobility vied with each other to give to religious foundations was a real threat from the economic point of view. Everything,—art, literature, architecture, drama, —was permeated by this religious influence. Very often it afforded a stifling atmosphere. In the northern provinces the Calvinist fanatics, who would have liked to do the same, never managed it because of the far-sightedness of a few wise men who saw the danger of mingling church and state. But in the south religious considerations dominated everything. There were no comfortable exceptions to the rules as there had been under Charles V. No relaxation of the regulations was allowed for foreigners or for economic considerations. Priests were obliged to report to the state the names of parishioners not performing their Easter duties, and punishment by being sent to the galleys could follow. Midwives had to swear to see that their new-born charges were properly baptized. Every parish had its school, and teachers had to be examined about their religious convictions. Sunday school was compulsory. No theological discussion was allowed among laymen. Only printers licensed by the Archbishop could practise their trade with their own bishop's approval and a licence of orthodoxy. Only books approved by the ecclesiastical authorities could be published. Searches of printing works could be carried out at any time by an episcopal officer. Even the glorious tradition of Plantijn-Moretus, established with their great Polyglot Bible of the seventies, was dimmed.

Religious and secular authority combines

When such regulations were enforced by the secular authority it is not surprising that they succeeded in the south. Their effect was nefarious. Spontaneity and free discussion were simply not allowed. Scholars became involved in fruitless arguments such as the quarrels between the Jansenists and Jesuits. Vernacular literature in the south suffered because all effective writing was in Latin. This was the language of the Counter-Reformation. If the church had not been so militant it might easily have gradually adopted the vernacular, but this was tainted with unorthodoxy. In architecture the Counter-Reformation also developed its own typical style— the Baroque. It marked a complete break with the Gothic tradition, and the black and white marble altar screens and statues cutting across many a soaring nave, illustrate visually the completeness of the break in the artistic development of the southern Netherlands. New churches followed an entirely new plan, like that of St. Charles Borromeus in Antwerp with its cupola instead of tower. Old churches like St. Peter's in Ghent were often pulled down and replaced. Part of the Counter-Reformation, but such a genius that his allegiances are of small importance, was Peter Paul Rubens. Yet in fact his great technical skill, gorgeous colouring and monumental compositions fit into the religious and official art of his time. He needed large spaces, great cathedrals, vast walls on which to display his masterpieces. His exuberance and choice of subjects is completely different from the cosy, middle class art which was developing in the United

Rubens Provinces. His influence, both as a diplomat and as an artist, was very great during his lifetime and his attractive Italian style home in Antwerp shows something of his wealth and importance. He had many pupils. Some of them, such as van Dyck, were of great importance. He received numerous commissions from all over Europe. Even if the southern Netherlands were stagnating, he certainly was not. Other artists escaped the atmosphere by going north. Frans Hals was a Brabanter working in Haarlem. There painting developed a vigorous, much less exclusively religious tradition which culminated in the glorious canvases of Rembrandt.

All this took place against a sombre backcloth. The Spanish Fury of 1576 had cost Antwerp 5 million guilders. Emigration which had begun even before the religious troubles because of difficulties in the Baltic trade, shot up. By 1577, two-thirds of the Merchant Adventurers were trading in Hamburg instead of in Antwerp. Other foreign merchants who had gloried and prospered in the freedom and tranquillity of the old town, left for less perturbed centres. During

Decay of Antwerp Farnese's reconquest of Flanders and Brabant, Antwerp's southern hinterland gradually shrank. Between 1559 and 1596 the number of non-French speaking immigrants from the Netherlands settling in London rose from about 350 to about 1900. Many others had, of course, gone to the United Provinces. Figures of citizens from the south settling in Leyden increased from 69 between 1575 and 1579 (51.49 % of all immigrants) to 440 between 1590 and 1594 (78.33 %) and then to 228 between 1605 and 1609 (54.03 %). Most were Flemings. Many others went to Amsterdam. Between 1578 and 1601 13.9 % of all bridegrooms there came from the southern Netherlands and 788 were from Antwerp alone. Many northern towns extended their urban area to cope with this increase in population. In all, for the figures above concern only citizens, not ordinary workers, about one-tenth of the population of the southern Netherlands, or about 80,000 souls, probably emigrated. Between 1566 and 1612 the population of Antwerp fell from about 90,000 to about 54,000, reaching as low as about 42,000 in 1589. These immigrants were on the

The Jeker in Sluizen.

Gaasbeek castle (Lennik).

whole a worth-while gain for the north. This is how the linen industry came to Rotterdam, how tapestry weaving, and silk, gold, silver and diamond workers, and many skilful and experienced merchants came to strengthen the north. Obviously such losses were felt in the south. This combined with military destruction. The serge production of Hondschoote fell, for example, from 90,000 pieces in 1562 to 59,140 in 1580-81 and after the destruction of the town by the Duke of Anjou in the following year, to 12,843 pieces in 1585-86. This was not caused by iconoclasm but by the military situation, and many emigrated not for religious but for economic reasons. They could no longer make a living in the south. In 1616, 200 Catholic families left Antwerp for the United Provinces.

This was the background to a gloomy political situation. After the expiration of the Truce of 1609, in 1621, hostilities with the north started again, and because of an ominous treaty between the United Provinces and France, in the south as well. The Dutch beat the Spaniards resoundingly at sea at the battle of the Downs in 1639, and thoroughly on land as well, by taking Breda and Hulst and so making themselves masters of the entire left bank of the Scheldt. Having done that, they began to wonder if they were really sensible in allying with France in an attempt to conquer the southern Netherlands and so giving themselves a common frontier with that rather acquisitive nation. They had agreed on either the division of the south, or if the provinces rose spontaneously within three months of an invasion, then to put them under joint protection. By 1648, however, the United Provinces were quite sure they did not want a common frontier with France, and much of their diplomacy throughout the rest of the seventeenth and early part of the eighteenth century was dictated by their strenuous determination to retain a buffer state between themselves and France.

Buffer state The Treaty of Munster of 1648 between Spain and the United Provinces confirmed the provisions of the Truce of 1609. No representatives of the south were present at the negotiations. The Scheldt remained closed. The Dutch retained the ground they had won on its left bank. The south was left with no natural frontiers, ready for the inevitable next invasion. Of the 147 years between 1566 and 1713, the southern Netherlands enjoyed 29 years of peace. After rule by the Spanish Habsburgs, and a short period under Louis XIV's grandson, they were handed by the European powers to the successors of Charles V. Never during this period were their own interests, wishes or views taken into consideration. Trade and peace were sacrificed in the power struggle first between France and the United Provinces, later between France and Austria. By 1648 any brotherly feeling between the two halves of the Burgundian heritage had been completely forgotten. The United Provinces were interested in two points. The first was the maintenance of the closure of the Scheldt and the consequent diversion of the greater part of Antwerp's trade to Amsterdam and other northern ports. Any hesitation on this point by any other power had them immediately up in arms. Closely bound up with this was their determination to keep France out of the southern Netherlands. It had been gradually but vividly revealed to them that their real enemy was not Spain, emptied of energy and money, but France, brimming over with both. The Sun King's piercing eye was fixed on the interesting ports and tempting industries of the Low Countries which had eluded his predecessors for so long. He would certainly open the Scheldt. He would certainly use the Low Countries as a base for an attack on England as so many other ambitious dictators have planned to do. Thus the two tough maritime nations united to bolster up Spain's tottering strength in the southern Netherlands. They made a convenient battlefield where a trial of strength could be held without unpleasant campaigns either in Spain, the United Provinces, or France. But it took a long time and a lot of battles to cope with France. First Louis XIV watched with pride as his armies advanced, as if on a parade ground

French invasions
through devastated Flanders and Brabant, to be rewarded with, among other things, the towns of Tournai, Oudenaarde, Lille, Kortrijk and Veurne. Ten years later he added Valenciennes, Cambrai, Saint-Omer, Ypres and Poperinge. This was very alarming for the United Provinces. It was a brutal war. Louis's great commander Louvois, when asked what should be burned in a village as an example to its inhabitants, replied that the best way to make such people pay their taxes was to burn the whole village. Woods were destroyed, agriculture upset. Further north the dikes were opened and the land flooded. By the end of the century Louis had still not gained complete control of the Netherlands and even France was, in her turn, becoming worn out. It looked as if a precarious balance had been reached. But this was upset by the death in 1700 of the last direct descendant of Charles V on the Spanish throne, Charles II. He had been dying for so long that European chanceries had been busy for years making plans of what should be done with his great inheritance, for he was childless. When however the king's will was read he was discovered simply to have taken no notice of everyone else and to have left all his vast dominions to Louis XIV's grandson, Philip, Duke of Anjou. The temptation was too great for Louis XIV. He accepted the responsibility in his grandson's name. And immediately everyone had horrifying visions of a French empire stretching from Gibraltar to

the Scheldt, if not further. It was obvious that, however loudly Louis might disclaim any part in Spanish affairs, his grandson would remain under his supervision. This was confirmed by the fact that Paris began to send dispatches concerning the affairs of the Netherlands, to Madrid, with instructions that Philip should sign them and send them back by return of post. It made on the whole very little difference in the southern Netherlands. Nobody seemed to mind very much. The fountains in Brussels spouted wine to celebrate the coronation of Charles II's chosen successor. Provided they were not actually the scene of the battle, the southern Netherlands were relieved. The Spanish dynasty, which had cost them so dear, disappeared almost without trace. After causing the fatal division in the Burgundian lands, the Spanish crown had attempted for a short time to reorganise the country on Spanish lines. But the money had soon run out. After the Archdukes no one had really tried again. If the control of external affairs remained in Spanish hands, no serious attempts were ever made to reshape the internal, provincial government. This would have been very expensive and would certainly have provoked reactions which the impoverished Spaniards could not risk. They lived a hand to mouth existence in the Netherlands, never understanding the people over whom they ruled, or appreciating their qualities.

Louis XIV cannot really have expected to be allowed to get away with such a situation. It set up an immediate wave of resistance and fear throughout Europe. The United Provinces, hypnotised by the threat from France, were determined not only to beat her, but to stop anything similar happening again. The southern Netherlands provided just the shield they wanted. But to make the shield effective it had to be strongly defended to the south. This became the constant preoccupation of the United Provinces and dominated their policies even when

Barrier fortresses

there was no longer a threat from France. France's enemies had two aims. One was to stop a single ruler controlling both Spain and France. The second was to beat her armies. This was accomplished very largely on the territory of the southern Netherlands, by armies commanded by the Duke of Marlborough and Prince Eugene of Savoy, ably supported and directed by William III of England, Prince of Orange. The first battle was at Blenheim, in Bavaria in 1704, the second at Ramillies in south eastern Brabant in 1706, the third at Oudenaarde in Flanders in 1708, and the fourth at Malplaquet a few miles from Mons and Valenciennes in 1709. Between these pitched battles the French gradually retreated across Brabant and Flanders so that in June 1706 they surrendered Antwerp, in July, Ostend; in 1708, Lille had to be given up and in 1709 Tournai. While they

The renaissance style Landshuys in Cassel.

The Brussels' exchange built between 1871 and 1873.

Ooidonk castle in Bachte-Maria-Leerne (Deinze).

Cloth-hall of Aire-sur-la-Lys in French-Flanders.

fought their battles in the southern Netherlands the allies insisted that the local inhabitants should pay their troops, provide anything needed by their armies,

Cost of beating Louis XIV

and submit local administration to their supervision. Although these wars may have been less brutal than some others because there was no fanaticism in them, they were an expensive business. Between 1689 and 1694 the damage done by enemy troops in Flanders was calculated at 10,437,871 florins. The maintenance of the allied armies cost 15,887,373 florins.

When in 1713 this series of wars at last ended, the southern Netherlands were divided between the Emperor Charles VI ruling in Limburg, Maximilian Emmanuel of Bavaria who administered Namur and Luxemburg in the name of Philip V of Spain, the Anglo-Dutch who controlled Flanders and Brabant, and the United Provinces who administered Hainaut, the lands ceded by Louis XIV, West Flanders, Spanish Gelderland and the Tournai area. It took six years to re-unite them. They were then assigned to the Austrian Habsburg Emperor, Charles VI.

The Treaty of Utrecht which so casually attributed the southern Netherlands to a new ruling house did not in fact change much. Loyalty towards the Austrian Habsburgs had perhaps never the same quality of that towards the Spanish house in spite of its crimes and mistakes. The internal administration was carried on at least at the beginning much as before. The Scheldt remained obstinately closed. The United Provinces manned their barrier fortresses against an exhausted France. Until about 1750 one-third of the income of the southern Netherlands went to the maintenance of these Dutch garrisons, at Veurne, Ypres, Knocke, Warneton, Menin, Tournai, Namur and Dendermonde. But at least there was peace. Except between 1744 and 1748 when for the first time the southern Netherlands were entirely occupied by France, and the French king Louis XV made a triumphal entry into Brussels, France did not want to provoke England and the United Provinces too far by trying to hold on to the Low Countries. In 1748 they were returned to Austria and in spite of attempts by the Austrian Empress, Maria Theresia, to exchange them for something more interesting, remained in Austrian possession until completely swallowed by Revolutionary France.

Peace was of course, invaluable. Immediately persevering efforts were made to

The southern Netherlands become Austrian

repair the damage, rebuild the economy, squeeze as much benefit as possible within the limits set by the Treaty. Having failed to exchange the southern Netherlands for Silesia, Maria Theresia decided to reform and modernise the administration. She proceeded cautiously and treated the precious privileges with care. Not so her son Joseph II. He, the epitome of the enlightened despot, saw no reason to curb his enthusiasm for the latest bureaucratic techniques, because of the conservatism of his people. He found tradition time wasting and uninteresting. When he made a brief visit to the Netherlands in 1781, instead of making a gorgeous parade of it, which would have appealed so much to this people who revel in processions and festivities, he travelled incognito, refused as much of the fuss as possible, and did nothing but exasperate and disappoint his hosts. He, the enlightened despot *par excellence*, refused to kneel on the special cushion provided for him when watching the procession of the Holy Sacrament in Bruges, tried to clothe Van Eyck's Adam and Eve on the 'Mystic Lamb' triptych in St. Baaf's Cathedral in Ghent, and then tackled the Flemish kermesses. To his prudery we owe the two clothed figures of Adam and Eve hanging near the cathedral's west door. They were painted to replace, for the time being at least, Van Eyck's, which the Emperor found shocking. His attack on the *kermis*, the village festivities so beloved even to-day, by attempting to insist that they should be held all on one day instead of spread throughout the summer, was too much. A collision was bound to come.

Yet in fact things were improving slowly but surely. Peace gave the industrious the chance to work and to rebuild the damage done in the last centuries. The population increased. Agricultural improvements made the Flemish contryside an object of admiration; the little farms which still stud the countryside, and which seem now so old fashioned in their methods, were in the eighteenth century the spearhead of new more intensive cultivation and increased production. The country population grew. In the towns things improved especially in the second half of the century when Joseph's very sensible measures against the exclusivism of the gilds began to take effect. In spite of very little governmental encouragement, great efforts were made to take advantage of any loop-hole in the commercial regulations. The possibilities were sadly limited. Colbert's example in France had inspired Count de Bergeyck at the end of the seventeenth century to encourage trade, to search for new markets and if possible to get on the band-wagon of colonialism. He managed to found a commercial company for trade with India and the Indies. But England and the United Provinces had their eye on things and the plan was abandoned by the government. When later, his plans were revived by the Austrians and the Company of Ostend, drawing mostly on capital from Antwerp, founded, it looked as if at long last the southern Netherlands would have a commercial outlet. But three years after the first three boats bravely left Ostend, the

End of the Ostend Company Company's licence was suspended. The Emperor, trying desperately to obtain European support for his daughter Maria Theresia to succeed him, again preferred not to upset either England or the United Provinces. The value of the Company's shares fell from 1,228 to 470 florins. In 1732 the last boat left for the Indies. In 1785 the Company finally disappeared. The country concentrated on the manufacture of luxury objects such as tapestries, linen, glass, diamonds and lace. They were not bulky and could easily be transported by land. The beautiful lace dress which Maria Theresia wears in her portrait in the town hall in Ghent was presented to her by the Estates of Flanders and made by the town's orphans. Flanders still has its lace-makers. Such over-land trade demanded better roads and canals. Under the Archdukes the old network of canals had been extended and deepened. Between Ghent and Bruges, from Bruges to Ostend and from there to Nieuwpoort and Dunkirk, canals were dug at this time. Bergeyck wanted a new one between Antwerp and the coast, but, typically enough Ghent and Bruges were against it because of the adverse effect it might have on their toll revenues. Many other plans were made but not carried out. A beautifully engraved silver spade

Improvements presented on the occasion of one abortive plan is all that remains of a canal intended to join Antwerp to the Sambre. Leuven was luckier, and was linked with the river Rupel. As for roads, the shatteringly uneven cobbled surfaces were then a subject of intense admiration. From only 40 miles they were increased to 580 miles during the eighteenth century.

But for all these improvements the southern Netherlands were still shut off from the markets which their industry and skill deserved. Joseph II found the closure of the Scheldt extremely exasperating. He had got rid of the barrier fortresses simply by sending workmen to dismantle them which meant that the Dutch garrisons had to go home. He tried something similar with the Scheldt. This time however it was not so easy. His ship, the 'Louis', was fired on by a Dutch frigate as it tried to sail down the Scheldt, and a large saucepan, or 'marmite'

The 'Marmite War' on its bridge was broken—hence the 'Marmite War'! But the Scheldt stayed closed. And Joseph was soon to have greater problems on his hands. His measures were on the whole sensible and liberal. But he imposed them from above without explanation, and without preparation on a people who had become the epitome of conservatism. He supported the papal decision to dissolve the Jesuit Order; he dissolved the contemplative orders; allowed civil marriage; and replaced the scattered episcopal seminaries by a single one in Leuven. This was, however, not enough. While people were still quivering with indignation he brought in a complete re-organisation of the law and the administration. Even the provinces were to exist no longer. All the old regional government for which so much blood had been shed, all the sacred privileges which had been bulwarks not only against improvements, but also against foreign interference seemed to be disappearing under some strokes of the pen in Vienna. Everyone was furious and alarmed. Taxes were refused for the first time since the sixteenth century. Local militias were formed. Even the Joyeuse Entrée of Brabant, the Bible of regional resistance, was suppressed. Everywhere cockades in the Brabant colours of black, gold and red appeared. The church, and the Estates wanted to re-establish things as they had been. The 'patriots' wanted a new more liberal modern government. Even in the southern Netherlands the ideas which were soon to explode in France were in the air. This was 1788. One year later the Bastile would fall. For the first time since 1632 the States General met and on 11 January 1790 declared the southern Netherlands independent as the United Belgian States. But they could not agree among

United States of Belgium

themselves. They had no idea of what to do with power. Foreign policy meant nothing. Having for years had no say in foreign affairs, they had no experience. By the end of 1790 the country was again occupied by the Austrians. They had four years left. In 1794 the southern Netherlands were finally conquered by France from the Austrians and between 1795 and 1796 became part of the French Republic. Once more this looked like the end. In fact it was another beginning.

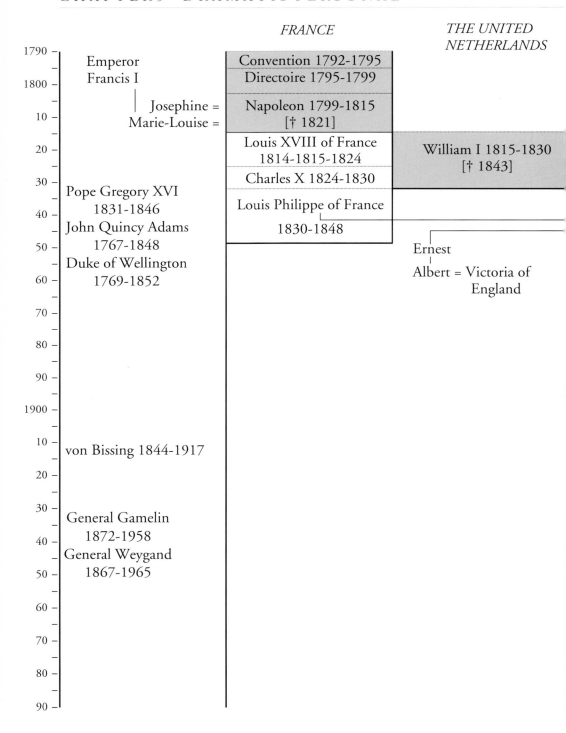

FRANCE

THE UNITED
NETHERLANDS

1790

Emperor
Francis I

1800

Josephine =
Marie-Louise =

10

20

30

Pope Gregory XVI
1831-1846

40

John Quincy Adams
1767-1848

50

Duke of Wellington
1769-1852

60

70

80

90

1900

10

von Bissing 1844-1917

20

30

General Gamelin
1872-1958

40

General Weygand
1867-1965

50

60

70

80

90

Convention 1792-1795
Directoire 1795-1799

Napoleon 1799-1815
[† 1821]

Louis XVIII of France
1814-1815-1824

Charles X 1824-1830

Louis Philippe of France
1830-1848

William I 1815-1830
[† 1843]

Ernest

Albert = Victoria of
England

BELGIUM

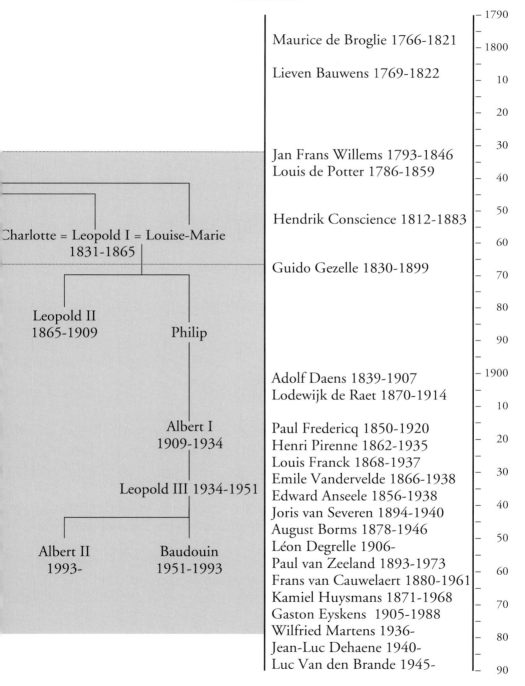

- 1790
- 1800

Maurice de Broglie 1766-1821

Lieven Bauwens 1769-1822

- 10

- 20

- 30

Jan Frans Willems 1793-1846
Louis de Potter 1786-1859

- 40

- 50

Hendrik Conscience 1812-1883

- 60

Charlotte = Leopold I = Louise-Marie
1831-1865

Guido Gezelle 1830-1899

- 70

- 80

Leopold II
1865-1909   Philip

- 90

Adolf Daens 1839-1907
Lodewijk de Raet 1870-1914

- 1900

- 10

Albert I
1909-1934

Paul Fredericq 1850-1920
Henri Pirenne 1862-1935
Louis Franck 1868-1937
Emile Vandervelde 1866-1938
Edward Anseele 1856-1938
Joris van Severen 1894-1940
August Borms 1878-1946
Léon Degrelle 1906-
Paul van Zeeland 1893-1973
Frans van Cauwelaert 1880-1961
Kamiel Huysmans 1871-1968
Gaston Eyskens 1905-1988
Wilfried Martens 1936-
Jean-Luc Dehaene 1940-
Luc Van den Brande 1945-

- 20

- 30

Leopold III 1934-1951

- 40

- 50

Albert II   Baudouin
1993-   1951-1993

- 60

- 70

- 80

- 90

Zij zullen hem niet temmen, de fiere Vlaamse Leeuw,
Al dreigen zij zijn vrijheid met kluisters en geschreeuw.
Zij zullen hem niet temmen, zolang een Vlaming leeft,
Zolang de Leeuw kan klauwen, zolang hij tanden heeft.

Flemish national song, nineteenth century.

They shall not tame him, the proud Flemish lion,
Although they threaten his freedom with chains and clamour.
They shall not tame him, as long as Flemings live,
As long as he has claws, as long as he has teeth.

The New Growth

1794 to the present day

CONTINENTAL history is divided chronologically by the French Revolution of 1789 as English history is divided by the Conquest of 1066. The period before 1789, known as the 'Ancien Régime', was essentially different from the years which followed. This was not just a question of detail. It encompassed the whole structure of the state and of society. These years were the melting pot in which the modern western states were cast. For the southern Netherlands the shock was very great, because they appeared, for twenty years, to have lost their independence and to have been absorbed for ever by their southern neighbour. Yet in 1814 they found themselves free once more. Some of what they had undergone during these twenty years left lasting traces. Most of what had been swept away by the Revolution never returned. Other changes were modified, while still further characteristics of the modern Belgian state had not yet emerged.

Let us look first at what was swept away by the Revolution. In the first place, Austrian rule. An abortive attempt to create a United States of Belgium, on the pattern of the United States of America, had failed in 1790 and the Austrians had returned. They were not popular. The heady whiff of revolution was already blowing strongly from the south and the tentative reforms of the Emperor

What the Revolution swept away

Joseph II had succeeded only in alienating the revolutionaries because they were not fundamental enough, and upsetting the conservatives because they seemed to threaten the establishment. Thus no one was very enthusiastic about defending Austrian rights in the Netherlands, and the French armies defeated them soundly first at Jemappes, a little town in Hainaut near Mons, and two years later, in 1794, at Fleurus, near

Charleroi. Three years later, in the Treaty of Campo-Formio, Austria accepted the *fait accompli* and renounced any claim to the southern Netherlands. Thus the Revolution had swept away the Austrians. The question then became what to do next. The French military governor suggested making the southern Netherlands into a sort of vassal state. This was however not radical enough and it was decided that they should be absorbed by France; that they should in fact become part of the French state. This was, in a way, a logical step, as the history of the relations between the two neighbours had consisted largely of France's continuous attempts to absorb her northern neighbour. The second casualty was, therefore, the southern Netherlands themselves. By their action the

Old divisions destroyed Revolutionaries destroyed all the old traditional divisions—the County of Flanders, the Duchy of Brabant, the Prince-Bishopric of Liège, and replaced them by nine French *départements,* such as covered the rest of their territory. For the first time territories which although often linked dynastically, had never really amalgamated, found themselves together, undefended by the traditions of centuries.

Closely connected with this clean sweep, much else disappeared as well: the privileges of the nobles, the gild organisation and torture in the process of law. Many of these things had been modified or abolished by Maria Theresia and Joseph II but it took a cataclysm like the Revolution to get rid of them completely. Even more overpowering was the complete and sudden laicisation of the country. From the Counter-Reformation onwards the southern Netherlands had never really challenged the power of the church. Joseph II had here also tried a few modifications, but they were, on the whole treated with great circumspection by his subjects. He had introduced religious liberty and civil marriage and attempted to loosen the grip of the church, but with little success. Yet in a few years France abolished nine tenths of the lay power of the church. About one quarter of the land had belonged to religious institutions. This was all confiscated by the state and sold. Buildings, agricultural land, woods, town houses, abbeys, churches and monasteries suddenly became available for development. Golden opportunities for acquiring them occurred as had happened three hundred years before in England when Henry VIII had taken a similar step and dissolved the monasteries. But not every one wanted to profit from the discomfiture of the church. Analysis of the purchasers of these lands and buildings has shown that they were acquired, for the most part, not by the small peasants who farmed the ground, but by the growing middle class of notaries, industrialists, and larger farmers, as well as by the monks and nuns themselves or the nobility, acting through agents. Thus the Revolution swept away all the monastic orders, except a few who served hospitals, and accomplished an enormous change in the ownership of land. It was not, however, content with having done so much, but wanted to sweep away the church itself. This was however, an exaggeration. Churches were closed,

Attacks on the Church

Sundays abolished, priests persecuted and not allowed to wear clerical dress in public, bells were silenced, church and Sunday schools closed. The new 'citizens' were expected to venerate Reason instead, and to devote themselves to studying the 'thoughts of Napoleon'. As if this was not enough, the French attempted to force all clergymen to swear hatred of the monarchy. This, on the whole, they refused to do. Their feelings were further outraged by the French capture of the Papal States and imprisonment of the Pope. All came to a head in 1798 when a Peasants' War broke out in East Flanders and spread

The Peasants' War

to Limburg. From Overmere, where a statue and a museum still commemorate the event, to Diest and later to Hasselt, where they were crushed by the French, hatred of French treatment burst out. Napoleon's Concordat, or agreement, with the Pope in 1802 poured some oil on the troubled waters, and churches were once more opened. But life would never again be as it had been before. The church would never regain its old position. What did the Revolution and the Empire put in the place of all they swept away? How much of it remained after 1815? They replaced the old irregular, territorial divisions of the country by nine *départements*. These later became the Belgian provinces. Among them was one whose presence was significant: Liège.

New administrative machinery

For the first time this territory, which had in fact always been an independent Prince-bishopric became part of France on the same footing as all the others. For the first time this vigorous Walloon, French speaking area confronted its neighbour Flanders in a single political unit. Secondly, depending on the *département,* was a strongly centralised network of local government, of which the members were nominated either from Paris, or by the head, or Prefect, of the *département.* He was rarely a Netherlander by birth and knew nothing of local traditions. Such a framework did not survive. It was too strange in the Low Countries. The church's monopoly of education went the same way. As in other spheres, Maria Theresia and Joseph II had founded new schools under lay control, but with little success. Under the Revolutionaries new schools based on entirely new programmes, and

The gothic cathedral of Our Lady in Antwerp.

replacing religion with Reason also found few supporters in the Low Countries. Napoleon compromised to some extent by allowing some religious instruction, and a return to the old teaching methods, although a Napoleonic catechism was included in the curriculum. But his schools were also intended to form a loyal, efficient and pro-French ruling class, and were concerned only with middle or upper class children. They were, moreover, a strong weapon in the spread of the French language. Napoleon did not like universities. He did nothing therefore, to replace the University of Leuven suppressed by the Revolution.

The judicial system, on the other hand, formed the basis for the later system. The new legal Codes, like the metric and decimal system for weights, measures and money, remain. A further lasting result of the revolution and the domination of France, was the encouragement of a middle class strongly attached to French ideas and French culture, and not only in the parts of the Netherlands which had always been French speaking, but in Flanders as well.

The importance of the French language

It had been foreshadowed by an increase in French influence at the court in Brussels under the Austrian Empire, and after 1789 was encouraged by economic considerations. Many members of the rising middle class had acquired their start from land or property bought cheaply from a government which was actively insisting on the spread of French, and the disappearance of Dutch in their new territories. Anyone who wanted to get on in the new regime had to speak French. This was unfortunate in Flanders for it meant that there was no extensive Dutch speaking middle class, and that a gulf widened between rulers and ruled. This was a lasting result of the French occupation and annexation.

Such a vast upheaval was bound to have very far reaching economic results. Between 1792 and 1800 the southern Netherlands suffered terribly. First there were the troops and the resulting disruption of trade and agriculture. Then the Revolutionaries flooded the country with paper assignats, which were officially equivalent to gold, but which were in fact worth next to nothing. Furthermore they deliberately ransacked the country. Agents were appointed 'for the extraction of articles of trade, agriculture, science and the arts from conquered territories'. Hence innumerable artistic treasures from the Netherlands in French museums. After about 1800 things improved. At least until 1814 there was no more fighting on Belgian soil. Everyone hurried to make the most of the peace while it lasted, and of the wide market offered by the whole of France,

French acquisitions

freed from customs barriers. Antwerp profited rather less than towns such as Ghent, for although the Scheldt was officially open, English gun-boats were always lurking threateningly in its mouth. Napoleon saw its value as a naval dock-yard, and many war ships were constructed there. One dock, the Napoleon dock, still bears the emperor's name. Elsewhere there were wonderful opportunities. The loss of the English market was more than compensated by the opening of France, and further afield, of the countries conquered by the Napoleonic armies. Capitalism had already appeared in the Low Countries in the eighteenth century, but all the new opportunities offered by the sale of church property and the introduction of machinery stimulated it enormously.

Sale of church property

Lieven Bauwens from Ghent managed to smuggle out of England not only the pieces of a spinning jenny but some workers from Manchester who could use it. In the old convent of the Chartreuse in Ghent he was soon employing three thousand textile workers. Large scale capitalism had arrived. There was a negative side to this new prosperity. It embraced only the middle class. The workers, in spite of the triumphs of the Revolution, were worse off than before. Those in the countryside who had supplemented their agricultural earnings with piece work, found that they were not needed after machines were introduced into textile manufacture. They tended to flock to the towns in search of work where they only depressed wages in general. Women and children had to work in order to eat, and wages again suffered. Workers were forbidden to form unions, forbidden to strike and only allowed to work if they had a permit which had to be signed by their employer before they could work elsewhere. Revolutionary equality did not apply to the working class.

Much that is fundamental in the modern Belgian state did not exist as yet under either the Revolutionary or Napoleonic governments. They were much too centralised and authoritarian. For all their dogma about freedom and equality,

What the Revolution did not bring

they succeeded rather in creating a police state dominated by the middle class, and entirely omitting democratic principles. There was no place for Parliament, universal suffrage, for urban self-government, for free elections, a free press, or the right to form trade unions. Furthermore, the form of the state would be radically altered, first in 1815 when the southern Netherlands, freed from France and united with the kingdom of the Netherlands were part of a constitutional monarchy; and fifteen years later, in 1830, when at last they enjoyed their own constitutional monarchy combined with much more extensive Parliamentary control and much wider, although not yet complete, freedoms.

As part of France, the Low Countries had to play their part in the last difficult years of the French Empire. From about 1810 onwards the military situation became so critical that the machinery of government started to break down. Taxation shot up. In one year it increased threefold, and was accompanied by endless military requisitions. Conscription, which had always provoked resentment became so exigent that even the sons of noble families who

The decline and fall of the Napoleonic Empire

had previously bought exemption were forced to go, and young men were called up from groups only due years ahead. Thus the military and financial burdens grew heavier. Meanwhile the economic situation was less than brilliant. The blockade of the coast by the allies, and the loss of markets in Spain because of the Peninsula campaign, meant a decrease in prosperity.

Even Lieven Bauwens went bankrupt. And dislike of the French certainly did not diminish. Opinion was outraged by Napoleon's annexation of the Papal States in 1809, and his divorce of Josephine and marriage with Marie Louise the daughter of the Emperor Francis I. Few made much effort to resist the allies, after their victory over Napoleon at Leipzig in October 1813. Russians and Prussians entered the Low Countries. By May 1814 the French evacuation was complete.

Napoleon was beaten—or so it seemed. The question which had to be tackled was the reorganisation of Europe. To do this the allies, Prussia, England, Austria and Russia met in Vienna and decided, usually without consulting the countries concerned, on the future of the Napoleonic Empire. One of their chief

Congress of Vienna

preoccupations was what to do with the Low Countries. While Cossacks and Prussians roamed the streets, and the Netherlands enjoyed yet another military occupation, diplomats manœuvred and danced far away. As during the earlier period, they were influenced by an absolute condition—that the Netherlands should form a barrier against France. Various means to achieve this were canvassed. No notice was taken of the wishes, or even the history of the inhabitants. In the south a strong party formed under church leadership which favoured a return to Austrian rule and the old system from before the Revolution. Their request was however refused by the Austrian Emperor whose interests lay more in Italy and Eastern Europe. Prussia would not have refused. Two of her commissars headed the temporary government. But England did not want to exchange an ambitious France for an ambitious Prussia. No one

Premonstratensian abbey of Our Lady and St. John the Baptist in Averbode.

Memorial to allied service men missing in the first World War, the Menin Gate in Ypres.

seems to have suggested that the southern Netherlands should become independent. The other alternative was to club the two parts of the Low Countries together, building a barrier against France by combining the northern and southern halves of the old Burgundian inheritance. There was even an obvious candidate for the crown. In 1813 the northern provinces had revolted against Napoleon who had been proclaimed their emperor and welcomed back William, prince of Orange, descendant of William the Silent, as their ruler. To the diplomats in Vienna he could easily take over the southern provinces as well. Such a proposition astonished both north and south. The two hundred years of separation which had followed the Treaty of Münster of 1648 had simply been ignored. The southern Provinces could not believe that the solution was

What to do with the southern Netherlands

intended seriously. How could they be expected to live harmoniously in one state with a people who were largely Protestant, under a Protestant king, who had closed the Scheldt in 1648 and insisted on the Barrier Treaties ? The Dutch, on the other hand, found it inconceivable that they should share their hard won colonies and live in a state with a Catholic majority—for the population in the south was larger than in the north,—and accept the French culture which predominated in the south. It was in fact an unwise arrangement. Neither north nor south wanted it. Both heartily disliked and distrusted the other. But it had at least one whole-hearted supporter in the Prince of Orange, William. It has been said of him that he was 'one of those clever men who constantly do foolish things and one of those obstinate men who support one bad measure by another, worse'. With a very difficult task in front of him—the real amalgamation of the two parts of his kingdom—he succeeded by his tactlessness and impatience, in making it impossible. The Congress of Vienna had laid down eight points which were intended to help such an amalgamation. They were to form the basis of a constitution. They limited the royal power by insisting on religious liberty, equal commercial rights for all the provinces, divided the two national debts equally, and insisted that all the provinces should have 'suitable representation in the States General.' Such limitations did not really appeal to William, who supported the old theory of benevolent despotism. However, a crown made some sacrifice worth-while. At this point, while the affair was still being discussed and William was still without his crown, Europe's hand was forced. On March 1st 1815 Napoleon landed at Cannes in the south of Provence. Fourteen days later William took the title of King of the Low Countries. Events had been precipitated by the probable need to defend them yet again from the French. Three months later the French armies again crossed the frontier.

Louis XVIII in Ghent

Louis XVIII, restored to the throne of his late brother, fled to Ghent. He and his court ate and danced in the d'Hane Steenhuyse house in the Veldstraat and gallery tickets were sold to the local inhabitants to watch the gout-ridden monarch stiffly take the first dance steps which would allow the ball to begin. They had acquired a taste for international affairs during the previous year, when the delegates arranging a peace treaty between England and the United States of America had argued in the old Chartreuse convent. The American headquarters were in the Lovendeghem house also in the Veldstraat, while their chief delegate, John Quincy Adams, was lodged in a hotel on the Kouter. Later in the same year Tsar Alexander was escorted to the town hall by a procession headed by the Butchers gild in their gala uniforms. Ghent had recovered the importance which she had enjoyed in the fourteenth century as one of the biggest and most prosperous towns of Western Europe.

Napoleon was sure to tackle the Allied armies in the Low Countries and not wait for an invasion of France. Wellington set up his headquarters in Brussels and for weeks the town scintillated with the amusements of the allied troops. In an area south of the town near the village of Waterloo, Napoleon made his last bid. Wellington watched and directed operations from Mont St. Jean; Napoleon, at first, from near La Belle Alliance. Later on the evening of June 18th he moved

The Battle of Waterloo

up with his Guard which he threw against the English and Dutch massed before him. By 8 p.m. he was himself being attacked by the Prussians under General Blücher on his right flank and an hour later Wellington and the Prussian general were meeting in La Belle Alliance to discuss the pursuit of the remnants of the French army over the Sambre. Something like 45,000 dead and wounded remained on the battlefield, where earlier in the day the two armies had manœuvred. Yet another decisive European battle had been fought in the Low Countries.

Napoleon was finally defeated and the Netherlands had their king. The southern frontier of his kingdom was fixed and has subsequently remained unchanged. The province of Liège remained in the new state. William settled to the task of 'amalgamating' the two parts of his kingdom according to the

'Amalgation'

principles laid down by the Congress of Vienna. He first had to have a constitution. This, if it was to have the least chance of success, had to treat the two parts on exactly the same footing, for William as a Dutchman by birth and disposition, had to overcome the fears of the south that he was prejudiced against them. The pity of it was that William was just that. He disliked and distrusted the French culture, fashions and religion of his southern subjects, just about as much as they disliked and distrusted him as a Protestant and a Dutchman. However, a group of nobles chosen by William from both north and south worked out a constitution. This retained many of the characteristics of Napoleonic government. It was in no way democratic. The States General could only vote taxes, not introduce legislation. Ministers were responsible to the Crown, not to the States. Much of the old administrative framework was retained, although the provinces obtained more power. The Congress of Vienna had decided that there should be religious liberty and that the debt should be divided equally between north and south in spite of the fact that it amounted in the north to 599 million florins and in the south to only 27 million. There could be no discussion on this point. The trouble arose over another point set down by the Congress. This said that the two parts of the country should be 'suitably' represented in the States General. This implied that representation should be according to population. But this was awkward for William, as he had about 2 1/2 million subjects in the north and close on 4 million in the south. He decided that each part should have 55 representatives. Any illusions which the south may have retained about their position in the new state were dissipated.

William felt, nevertheless, fairly sure of obtaining approval for his new constitution because he took care that only the propertied classes should be consulted, and their interests he had sincerely in

William versus the Church

mind. He had, however, counted without the church. The most powerful element in the southern Provinces had been overlooked. As soon as the constitution was published it went into action under the leadership of Maurice de Broglie, bishop of Ghent. He really would have liked a return to the Ancien Régime with the church as the most powerful force in the state. Although that was clearly impossible, he was determined not to accept a Protestant king with absolute power over religious affairs, and control of education and the press. By claiming that William intended to impose Protestantism by force on the south—which he certainly did not intend—the church could arouse an almost unlimited opposition to the new king and constitution. Just how powerful this opposition could be appeared when the acceptance of the constitution was defeated by 269 votes in spite of William's careful choice of voters. The king was forced to cheat again. He declared the constitution

Cheating ?

accepted by claiming that 280 abstentions were in fact

Plantijn-Moretus Museum in Antwerp.

favourable votes and that 126 unfavourable votes had been cast for religious reasons which invalidated them. The south was very bitter. From that moment onwards there was really no hope of amalgamation. The idea was defeated from the outset. The story of the next fifteen years is really a matter of how the two different threads in the opposition, on the one hand the liberals who disliked William's despotism, and on the other the church, which disliked his Protestantism, gradually forgot their differences and united against him.

William did not improve things by being inaugurated in Brussels in September 1815 as economically as possible. The crowd was disgusted to find that the medals which were then distributed were of copper instead of gold. In fact William was a good economist and set out to help industry and trade in both north and south. The latter had lost the valuable French market. William's insistence on freedom of trade, his establishment of credit facilities and his public works, such as the extension of the canal north of Ghent as far as Terneuzen on the Scheldt, were all excellent. The attention he paid to education was also good. But here he was treading very delicate ground, for education was looked upon as one of the preserves of the church. Elementary schools in the south hardly existed. Under William the Dutch system of secondary schools was extended south, and attempts were made to tackle primary teaching. Three new universities were founded, at Ghent, Leuven and Liège. The great hall of the University of Ghent still bears the Dutch royal arms. William was being really

Good economic measures

provocative however, in insisting that all clergy should receive a year's state controlled teaching in a college of Philosophy in Leuven. Closely connected with his educational programme was William's insistence on the use of Dutch for administrative purposes. It might seem that this would appeal to the Flemish parts of the country. During the two hundred years that north and south had been divided the dialects spoken in the south had diverged from the Dutch spoken in the north. But even more importantly, Dutch was seen as the language of Protestantism. Thus we have the curious picture of Flemish peasants encouraged by their vicars to resist the spread of the Dutch language. For the middle and upper classes French had become the accepted language both in Flanders and Wallonia. In 1823, however, William imposed Dutch as the only official language in Flanders, Brabant, Antwerp and Limburg. The Walloons saw this as ominous. All these threads of opposition found a leader in de Broglie. His stand was firm. He simply refused absolution to anyone taking the oath of loyalty to the constitution, which was necessary for any public appointment. William said he was endangering the security of the state, and de Broglie prudently retired to France. He was, in his absence, condemned to deportation, and public indignation was thoroughly roused when his condemnation was publicly exhibited in the market place in Ghent between two thieves standing in the pillory. The final break with the church came in 1827 when William signed a concordat with the Papacy. This allowed the creation of dioceses in the north, and the south had the impression that William's attitude over the religious question was becoming more supple. When his plans were published however, they found that all the old state controls and the College of Philosophy were still retained. This completed the fashioning of one prong of the opposition to William and his united state.

The other prong had started with the opposition to the constitution from liberals who saw it as the expression of old despotic traditions—which it was. There was no really democratic opposition. The liberals were for the most part middle class.

Their leader was Louis de Potter. They were opposed to the abitrary power of the king, to the fact that his ministers were not responsible to the States General,

Liberal opposition

and the fact that he controlled the press and the bench. William quickly sued any author criticising the state. He felt that he knew what was best for everyone and should be allowed to carry out his ideas in peace. Judges could be removed at pleasure in spite of constant agitation to make them independent. Basically, as liberals, this group was opposed to the church, but differences were buried in a common hostility to William and the Dutch. When once these two groups combined, William's days as king of the Netherlands, were numbered.

William did not know what to do. No European power wanted to risk a new general war for his sake. In July 1830 Paris was again in uproar. Events there always had repercussions in the southern Netherlands. The overthrow of Charles X and his replacement by Louis Philippe, whose power was to be strictly limited, encouraged similar thoughts in Brussels. Opposition to William crystallized in two movements. On the one hand the constitutional and legal feeling expressed by the southern members of the States General; on the other the popular agitation behind the young Catholic and Liberal leaders. The members of the States General wanted a real application of the constitution and a limitation of royal power, the Catholics wanted freedom for the church from lay control, and the Liberals wanted Parliamentary government through responsible ministers. Everyone wanted to get rid of William and the Dutch. On August 25th, 1830, there was a performance of the opera 'La Muette de Portici' in the Muntschouwburg in Brussels. Crowds had gathered during the

Sint-Truiden: the abbey church (burnt down in 1975), town-hall and church of Our Lady.
Beguinage of Our Lady Ter Hoye in Ghent.

'La Muette de Portici' day in a rather aimless fashion. There seems to have been no plan of action. When however the tenor sang his aria 'Amour sacré de la patrie', the tremendous applause inside the theatre sparked off the crowds outside. They started to demonstrate and break windows. Everyone seemed to have sashes and cockades in the colours of Brabant. The excitement spread. The crowds began to get out of hand. French agitators encouraged them. The French tricolour appeared, although a plaque at the corner of the Grasmarkt and the Heuvelstraat in Brussels commemorates the place where the first Belgian flag was made. The crowd started to pillage and break up machinery and the middle class took fright. They formed themselves into a guard to preserve order and stop vandalism. The Dutch garrison fired a few shots and then withdrew to the royal palace. They were not any more enthusiastic than the Belgians, about preserving the union. King William still thought the whole affair unimportant but

Dutch lack of enthusiasm nevertheless sent a few regiments under his son's command to Brussels to keep an eye on things. The citizens were furious and refused entry to the Dutch troops. Prince William was allowed to enter the town alone but felt the atmosphere so hostile that he put spurs to his horse and took refuge in the palace as quickly as possible.

Four days later, on September 3rd he left with the garrison, promising to do his best to explain the position to his father. By this time it was obvious that the only solution was partition. The provinces were moving in to support Brussels. Although the south did not say so explicitly, it was in fact independent. The situation recalls the time when the earlier William of Orange had avoided formal revolt against Philip II of Spain. William still did not know what to do. In Brussels more violent elements were taking over and barriers of paving stones and furniture were being erected across the streets as they had been in Paris. Early in the morning of September 23rd the first cannonade from the Dutch was fired against Brussels. They were showered with all sorts of rubbish and heavy objects from upper windows as they advanced towards the palace. Peasants from Flanders under the leadership of their vicars started to join bands of miners from Liège in coming to the help of Brussels. Instead of making straight for the palace, the Dutch took refuge in the Park opposite where they could easily be sniped at if they tried to get out of the gates. They had no enthusiasm for their task. On the 27th they quietly melted away in the dark and went home. They were followed by most of their compatriots stationed elsewhere in the south. By the beginning of October they had given up Lier and retired to the citadel in

Dutch retire northward Antwerp. That night their ships bombarded the town from the Scheldt. But no-one wanted a general war. On October 4th the southern provinces were declared independent by their provisional government.

In 1830 the nine provinces of the southern Netherlands found themselves for the first time in their history alone in a single unified state—Belgium. The revolution had been led by a French speaking ruling class consisting of both Catholics and Liberals united in their determination to establish their country's

Belgium independence. Belgium's subsequent history followed the same broad lines as that of other European countries— widening democracy, industrialisation and social reform. It had to cope, however, with one additional problem which emerged gradually with the growth in political awareness—the separate consciousness of the two groups of people of which it consists: on the one hand the southern, French speaking, Walloon provinces of Namur, Hainaut, Liège, Luxemburg and southern Brabant; and on the other the northern, Dutch speaking, Flemish provinces of East and West Flanders, northern Brabant, Limburg and Antwerp. What divides them is known as the language frontier. Brussels, the capital is a case apart. These two parts of modern Belgium came to be known as Flanders and Wallonia.

What was necessary in 1830 was a constitution. Liberals and Catholics combined in drafting one which ensured the freedom of the press, of meetings

The Constitution of 1831 and of religion, and which fixed the constitutional limi- tation of the monarchy and the responsibility of ministers to Parliament for which the south had revolted against William. They agreed, almost unan- imously, that the new state should be a constitutional monarchy, and the throne was offered to Leopold of Saxe-Coburg, widower of Princess Charlotte, the daughter of George IV of England, and uncle of Queen Victoria. He could choose between the thrones of Greece and Belgium and having chosen the latter took the oath to the constitution on July 21, 1831. The column of Congress in Brussels commemorates the work of these men who gave the new state one of the most modern constitutions in Europe—so modern, in fact, that the Pope was only with difficulty persuaded not to put it on the Index. Liberals and Catholics then settled down together to make it work, under the suspicious eye of the great powers.

The framework they had created may have been modern but it was far from democratic. The franchise, as elsewhere in Europe at that time, was based on a property qualification. At first only 1 % of the population had the right to vote. Gradually this was extended. The revolutionary wave which swept across

Extension of the franchise

Europe in 1848 and which avoided Belgium, led to a lowering of the property qualification and a moderate increase in the electorate. A growth in political awareness followed, and changes in the attitude of the old political groups to social questions. There was also, inevitably, a split in the Liberal party into a radical and a central wing; of the Catholic party in the same manner; and the emergence of the Socialist party. Political divisions became sharper. By the 80's Catholic and Liberal were opposing each other strenuously but, under Socialist stimulus, had begun to see that social reform was a matter for legal intervention and not for appeals to the moral principles of employers. The Pope's acceptance in 1891, in the Bull 'Rerum Novarum', of social progress, led to the formation within the Catholic party of less conservative groups, such as the one led by the clergyman, Adolf Daens. His Christian People's Party aimed at offsetting the rigid French speaking upper class core of the party. In 1890 the Farmers Association (Boerenbond) had been formed, as well as other Catholic trade unions. Radical anti-clerical popular agitation found expression in the new Workers' Party. Its formation followed a long development during which attempts had been made to get into contact with the actual workers. They were, until the middle of the nineteenth century, in such a miserable state that it was almost impossible to establish any sort of contact with them. Ignorant, starving, overworked or out of work, they remained a mass largely unknown to the lower middle class, and the craftsmen, among whom the first vestiges of organisation appeared. The wave of revolution of 1848, and an entirely unsuccessful attempt by a tiny group of revolutionaries to invade Belgium from across the French border, crushed first attempts at organisation. When the alarm had died away the movement revived, and because until 1865 trade unions were forbidden by law, worked as a sort of co-operative association.

The First International

A more revolutionary group took an active part in the First International, but not to much practical purpose. Even at this early date a difference emerged between the methods advocated by workers from the different parts of the country. The Flemings favoured political agitation through parliament, whereas in the south more radical solutions were popular.

Meanwhile the new socialist party was emerging. One group, founded in Ghent in 1877 by Edward Anseele, united with a Brabant group in 1879, and in 1885, at a meeting in the Swan in the Market Place in Brussels, where earlier Karl Marx

Premonstratensian abbey of Our Lady in Tongerlo.

had argued with his friends, an agreement was reached with the Walloon group, and the Belgian Workers' Party created. Violent agitation in the coal mines of Wallonia, led on the one hand to social legislation limiting hours of work,

The Workers' Party

and improving conditions, and, on the other, to further electoral reform which in 1893 gave every man of 25 the right to vote, and which heralded the first Social members of Parliament in 1894. Property qualifications, however, still gave the right to additional votes. This system of proportional representation with plural votes, continued until 1919 when one man one vote became the rule. In 1948 women were added to the electoral role.

This political development, common to most of western Europe and characterised by a widening of the franchise owing to social pressure, was accompanied in Belgium by a growing antipathy between church and state. This had necessarily been pushed aside in the more pressing business of getting rid of William, but once the threat from Holland had been finally removed by his acceptance of a peace treaty in 1839, the alliance between Catholic and Liberal began to wear a little thin. Philosophical differences counted once more. Liberals wanted the state to be completely free from church influence, while Catholics preferred freedom for the church and the right for it to interfere in the state. Such views were bound to clash. The church had at first been very doubtful about the Belgian constitution itself. Pope Gregory XVI was indignant about its claim that all power comes from the people. The hierarchy looked with suspicion on the oath demanded from all state officials, on the claim that all denominations had equal rights, and on the insistence on civil as well as religious marriage. Many Catholics found the hierarchy too old fashioned. But everyone, Catholic and non-Catholic alike, wished to educate his children in schools of his own choosing. The question as to the extent of church intervention in

The school question

education split Belgian politics for a hundred years, until it was settled in 1958. Sometimes the battle was fast and furious, sometimes there was a lull. Often it was quite ludicrous. First it involved the church's claim that education in general should conform to religious principles, and whether, for example, a teacher, whose book had been put on the Index, should be allowed to continue teaching. Then it moved on to how far a father's choice of a school for his children should be influenced by the state—by for example, providing free education in state schools and granting no subsidies for church schools, which in fact meant applying economic sanctions. The battle raged backwards and forwards, and hardened the attitudes of the political parties. The different tendencies were headed by the universities. Two, at Ghent and Liège, depend directly on the state. The Catholic University founded in Leuven in 1425 had been suppressed in 1797. Under William I a state university had been founded there, and in 1834 a Catholic one in Mechelen. In 1835, however, the old tradition was revived, the state university of Leuven discontinued and the **Universities**   Catholic brought there from Mechelen. A 'free' or anti-clerical university was started, inspired by Theodore Verhaegen, largely through masonic patronage, in Brussels, in 1834. The church which still looked back nostalgically to the good old days before the Revolution of 1789, when it had dominated the southern Netherlands, had still such great power that it had to be treated carefully. As party lines hardened, the more extreme elements on either side took over and drew up their forces for the hard fought 'School War'. After eight years of rule by the Catholic party from 1870 to 1878, a radical government dedicated to the realisation of a completely lay state came to power. It wanted even to cut out the 'Te Deum' from state occasions. Its radical measures to reform primary schools envisaged more state control over teachers, less support for free schools, and no religious instruction during school hours. That the measure was voted in the Senate by a majority of one vote cast by a member who had himself been elected with a one vote majority shows that the fight was by no means over. The church retaliated vigorously. The Sacraments were refused to teachers in the state schools and to parents who sent their children there; many parish schools were started, supported by the funds of the faithful. The result was that especially in Flanders, many state schools were almost deserted. The government became really peevish, refused to allow church buildings to be properly repaired, and even started weighing the candles !

In 1884 the Catholics resumed power and reversed the policy but were a little more ready to compromise. Each borough was allowed to organise its own primary school and teachers no longer needed a state diploma—which allowed the church again to draw on its large reserves of manpower. Each borough could decide on religious education, and if twenty fathers asked for an alternative, it had to be provided. In Flanders, church schools were immediately re-started by the boroughs; in Wallonia such new church schools were mostly provided by private charities.

There was then a lull. Feelings still ran high but Parliament took no specific action. The big increase of grammar school pupils after 1944 caused the next major battle. State schools received higher subsidies than church schools and to that extent the choice of the pater familias was not completely free. In 1952 there were 890,000 children in Catholic, and 634,000 in state schools. Parliament decided that all teachers with diplomas should receive the same salary, while non-lay personnel were to receive 50 %. The return of the Socialists to power in 1954 hotted the issue up again. They dismissed more than 100 teachers who held Catholic diplomas, from state schools—about half were later taken back; new state schools were set up; and Catholic children were to be sent before a jury rather than being able to receive their school-leaving diploma from their own

The school pact

school. The radio was enlisted to support this new plan. It could not, of course, last, once the Catholics were back in office. But everyone was getting rather tired of the whole business, and the three parties agreed to sign an armistice—the School Pact of 1958. It provided that every recognised school should receive the same state subsidy; that all qualified teachers should receive the same salary; and that more state schools should be provided especially in Flanders, as well as a free bus service for the pupils. At last the pater familias really had a free choice of school, and one of the time honoured themes disappeared from Belgian politics.

These political movements—the extension of the franchise, the growth of political parties, the search by the church for its place in society went on during a period of economic development which in Flanders particularly, was often bitter. The end of the eighteenth century, under Maria Theresia and Joseph II had been relatively prosperous, with the Austrian rulers keeping a benevolent, if distant, eye on trade and early industrial development. The French Revolution brought chaos and high taxes, devaluation and the systematic plundering of the Netherlands. Under Napoleon at least there was more order, and the absorption by France meant extended markets. The union with the northern Netherlands in 1815 meant a dramatic shrinkage of the home market but this was compensated by the Dutch colonial empire which particularly suited the Flemish textile industry. But in 1830 the good days were over. The Dutch colonies were suddenly forbidden; the Scheldt was again closed; the

Economic depression in Flanders

home market was further reduced. These circumstances hit Flanders terribly. Her textile industry, once the reason for extraordinary prosperity, was old-fashioned. The old structure of country industry on which it was based, could not possibly hold its own against the huge output of new English factories. Between 1835 and 1850 the export of linen was cut by half. Workers in flax diminished between 1846 and 1896 from 60,000 to 22,900. Between 1845 and 1849, the worst years in Flemish history, one third of the population was on poor relief. Epidemics of typhus and

The early gothic church of Our Lady in Lissewege.

cholera were followed by a potato disease which destroyed the poor's chief food supply. Physically the Flemings long bore the traces of these years of misery, starvation and unemployment, or work so hard and unremitting that it demanded a twelve hour day from children six years old.

That the luxurious land of Philip the Good, of the turbulent weavers of the fourteenth century, of James van Artevelde negotiating with the king of England, should come to this ! Many Flemings emigrated—some to the mines of Wallonia, others to northern France or America. In Wallonia the situation was a little less gloomy. Coal and iron still found a market. Wages were higher than in the textile industry. While the situation in Flanders deteriorated after 1830, in Wallonia it improved. By 1858 the population in Flanders had diminished; in Wallonia it was rising. Later in the nineteenth century Flanders would start to recover; coal was found in 1901 in the Flemish Kempen; the textile industry was gradually modernised and revived. But those terrible years left a mark on Flanders which has only recently been cast off.

The economic situation more than anything else high-lighted the difference between the two halves of Belgium. Against this sombre background, the two groups—Flemings and Walloons—had to work out methods to live in one centralised state. Their previous connection with each other had consisted

Language differences chiefly in sharing a common ruler. That they spoke different languages made the difficulties sharper. Yet in the early years this did not emerge. For everyone, who was anyone, spoke French. This was not something which began in 1830, or even in 1794. It went back much further into the Ancien Régime. The eighteenth century was the great age of French culture, when fashion in dress, in literature, art, scientific research, and manners, was inspired by French models. Administration was carried on in French, legal texts and mathematical treatises published in it, parents struggled to have their children educated at colleges in France, or to employ French tutors, so that they could hold an honourable place in the Establishment. But insistence on French was not a government policy until the Netherlands were occupied by France in 1794. Then it became the deliberate intention of the government to use the French language as a unifying force.

The division of the Netherlands in 1648 had had a double effect on the Dutch language. In the northern Provinces it became the official language, not only of

Difficulties of Dutch during the Counter-Reformation the state, but of Protestantism. It went through a golden age of literature and was cared for like a valuable and flourishing plant. In the south the repression of the Counter-Reformation, censorship and fear, choked all intellectual activity, while Dutch itself was feared as the weapon of Protestantism, and nothing, therefore, done to maintain or strengthen literary contacts with the north. The Dutch language in the southern Netherlands gradually deteriorated in purity, grammar, and structure into a series of local dialects empty of intellectual pretension, and often almost incomprehensible from one region to another. The language which had been used to publish some of the most advanced scientific, learned theories of the sixteenth century, was used to publish almost nothing but books of devotion. It suffered in fact from two sides: it was itself terribly impoverished, and it carried the social stigma of being used only by the illiterate and unambitious who had neither the ability nor the ambition to 'get on'.

This fitted, of course, closely into the economic pattern. Tendencies which had appeared in the eighteenth century, were aggravated by the misery of the nineteenth. A region which had a third of its inhabitants on poor relief and innumerable others forced to emigrate in order to eat, could not bother with schooling and literature. This was particularly true when the upper class spoke another language, French, and when it was clearly in their interest to retain a large, simple, uneducated and undemanding working class. Large fortunes were entirely in the hands of the nobility and the bourgeoisie. We have stressed that it was not the peasant who profited in Flanders from the distribution of church

The infiltration of French

property which followed the suppression of the religious houses at the end of the eighteenth century. The nobility and professional classes who did profit were closely attached to the masters from whom they had acquired their new wealth—and were wise to speak French. They educated their children in French, sent them to French boarding schools, employed exiled Frenchmen as their tutors, read French papers and magazines, and dressed their wives and daughters in French frocks and hats to go to French plays and parties. The contrast was enormous between this small class and the mass of Flemish peasants or urban workers, forced not only to work, for example in the counts' castle in Ghent, which had been turned into a textile factory, but to live in it too, so that their employer could close the great door and be sure they were under his hand. The church, which maintained its contact with the Flemish people in the Flemish dialects, used French once the village pastor was left behind.

This frenchification was deliberately accelerated between 1794 and 1815. The central administration was entirely in French. By 1800 French had been imposed in administration and justice, the new schools taught only in French, papers which had until that time appeared in Ghent and Bruges in Dutch, became bilingual, and books which would have appeared in Dutch were suppressed. In addition, conscripts in the armies of Napoleon lived under French speaking officers and were wise to understand their orders. Many Flemings were bilingual: the upper crust in order to give orders to their servants, the middle classes because their business contacts demanded it, although they did their best to hide this knowledge when 'in society'; and minor officials to a certain extent because their reports had to be written, often painfully, in French. Thus in Belgium, a Walloon could become Prime Minister without knowing a word of Dutch, but a customs' official in Flanders had to know French in order to draft his reports.

This situation could not go on forever. But while only the rich had political power, there were no practical results possible from an agitation which was at first carried on largely on literary and philological grounds. While only a few Flemings were interested in the purity of the language, no really Flemish movement could get under way. Only when they widened their activities to include social, economic and political questions could they hope for popular support. Under William I official policy was reversed and Dutch became the favoured language. But this period was much too short, and William much too unpopular to penetrate the deep, long established French preferences of the upper class. His foundation of the University of Ghent in 1817 was in fact of great significance for the future of the

Foundation of the University of Ghent

Flemish movement, but this did not emerge for a long time and courses were given in Latin. The generally low level of intellectual activity in the southern Netherlands, in whatever language, is however illustrated by the difficulty which the new university had to find any professors ! Only the medical faculty found staff easily. In science and mathematics, two Germans, one Frenchman and one Dutch professor were nominated, and in the Arts, two Dutchmen, one Luxemburger and one Frenchman. In 1830 the right to vote depended on property qualifications. Most voters were therefore French speaking. The representatives of Flanders in Parliament were also French speaking. Thus the extension of the franchise was essential if Flanders was ever to recover the full right to use its own language. When more Dutch speaking people gained the vote, and could show in Parliament that their language meant something to them, then the movement could gain momentum. From being a theoretical, learned problem, the question of the use of the Dutch mother tongue in

Veurne's town-hall.

Flanders was seen to involve the whole economic, social and cultural framework. The Flemings were fighting against being treated as second class citizens. Their troubles stemmed very largely from the fact that Belgium was not cut neatly into two equal halves each with its own language, and of equal economic viability, but into one prosperous entirely French speaking half, and the other in which a desperately poor working class was controlled by a French speaking bourgeoisie. Awareness of this situation in which in 1846, in Flanders 22,134 spoke French, of a total of 1,959,672, and in 1910 there were 47,000 French speaking citizens out of a total of 2,935,000, was fostered by the Flemish movement.

The Flemish movement

The movement had literary roots. Writers, who had remained faithful to the old literary tradition transmitted by the chambers of rhetoric sounded the alarm about what was happening to the Dutch language in Belgium. Many were philologists, such as Jan Frans Willems, and sought contact with writers in the north in order to explore problems of grammar and vocabulary. Gradually their influence spread and in the hands of a popular writer such as Hendrik Conscience, began to link up with Flemish historical traditions. His novel, about the Flemish victory of the Golden Spurs of 1302, helped to remind many Flemings of their glorious past. In West Flanders a learned clergyman, Guido Gezelle, showed that in his hands Dutch—although retaining a special regional flavour—could express delicate shades of poetic feeling.

This was the beginning. Meanwhile others began to formulate a wider programme. This was officially published by a Commission for Flemish Grievances in 1857. It enumerated the following points: that of 382 civil servants of the central administration only 22 were Flemings; that tax forms were only printed in French; that French speaking officials refused to issue birth certificates in Dutch; that laws providing for the use of Dutch in education were not applied; and that judges hearing cases in Flemish courts understood no Dutch. Gradually these points were dealt with: Dutch was allowed in Flanders in legal matters in 1873; in the administration in 1878; in grammar schools in 1883; and at last in 1888 the first speech in Dutch was made in Parliament. But such laws were not always enforced. Children at school were punished for using Dutch; and when the pupils in the episcopal seminary in Bruges asked permission to use their own language on Sundays and holidays, it was firmly refused.

Until the eighteen seventies the movement was largely literary. Later political questions began to count. At about the same time, social and economic considerations were recognised as an essential part of the problem of the fight to enable Flanders to stand on its own feet. One of the greatest leaders of the Flemish movement, Lodewijk de Raet, saw that language and economics were inextricably intertwined: that while the only language of more than eighty percent of the Flemish population was ignored or treated with contempt, economic revival was impossible. From this moment on the Flemish movement began to have a popular appeal. Insistence on the right to use Dutch in every aspect of life was seen as the means to obtain economic and social fulfilment. But

Popular appeal this would be impossible while all control, all the best jobs in Flanders, remained in the hands of a rich, powerful and exclusive French speaking minority. What was necessary was a highly educated, technically equipped, Dutch speaking upper class who would put an end to French speaking colonialism in Flanders. In every plan with this aim, education was obviously of major importance. The spear-head of such a movement should be Flemish universities. There were two: in Ghent and Leuven. But since the early eighteen thirties all teaching there had been in French. In 1911 some courses in Dutch had begun in Leuven and they were subsequently extended. Ghent University was a stronghold of the French speaking coterie. Everyone in the Flemish movement saw that their biggest guns should be aimed at this state university, but the leaders differed as to how their aims should be accomplished. Some thought that it would be enough to give some branches in Dutch but to go on teaching the sciences in French. De Raet realised that this would be to spike his guns at the outset. All real power, both economic and cultural, would remain with the French speaking group. What was necessary was to get rid completely of French as a teaching language and replace it by Dutch. Mass meetings, processions, newspaper articles and pamphlets gradually worked on public opinion until by 1914 the outlook was rosy. When, for the first time in the twentieth century the German armies rolled across the Belgian frontier, a bill for making Dutch the official language of the university of Ghent was before Parliament.

The war split the Flemish movement and put back the clock fifteen years. One group of Flemings, a sprinkling of whom were pro-German, co-operated with the German occupying forces as a means of obtaining strictly Flemish ends. They—the Activists—obtained a Dutch speaking university in Ghent in 1916. By far the greater number of members of the Flemish movement refused all co-operation with the Germans, and many university professors made public their disapproval of the whole affair and refused to teach. This was done at

Water-mill on the Witte Nete in Retie.

Lier's town-hall and belfry.

considerable risk to themselves. But the Germans had created a bitter situation which was used for years as a stick to beat the members of the Flemish movement. Into arguments about a Dutch speaking university crept the accusation of collaboration. A witch hunt after 1918 tried to brand everyone who had supported a Dutch university as a pro-German collaborator, and unscrupulous politicians were careful not to distinguish between the two. So-called and real collaborators were pursued, and many old scores thus paid off. Such exaggerations could only end in a wave of disgust, and many in Flanders came to feel that the guilt was not being fairly apportioned. The government did nothing. The whole question of an amnesty was so hot that they dared not touch it. When, however, in 1928, Dr. August Borms, an Activist who had been

Election of Borms

condemned to death, was elected in a by-election as Member for Antwerp, with a huge majority which could not possibly be made up entirely of Flemish extremists, the government realised that Flemings in general were getting impatient with the witch hunt, and that they could not continue to dismiss every demand as a symptom of collaboration. The affair was not a party issue. A bill to make Dutch the teaching language in the University of Ghent was supported by the Socialist, Kamiel Huysmans, the Catholic, Frans van Cauwelaert and the Liberal, Louis Franck. It was accepted with a majority of 96 in the Lower House on March 5th and 80 in the Senate on April 2nd, 1930. The opposition did not try to deny existence to a Dutch speaking university in Ghent. They wanted to continue the system begun in 1923 by which some courses would continue to be given in French, as well as free courses in French and alternative teaching in French in the Ecole des Hautes Etudes, which had been created to double courses given in Dutch in the university. They wanted, in fact, to make a completely French education in the university still possible. This was seen, quite rightly, as the thin end of the wedge, which would mean that every one not a convinced and vigorous supporter of the Flemish movement, or anyone wanting to succeed among the French speaking upper class, would not study in Dutch and the whole aim of the movement would be lost. In Parliament the opposition pleaded that 'the torch (of French culture) should not be put out: that would be a crime', or as the French speaking Fleming, Amelot put it, in a nut-shell, 'Science is only for the few, and instruction only the right of the élite'. The whole affair was highly dramatic, occasionally punctured by a glancing blow from Huysmans. Some Walloons in Parliament tried to turn it into an attack on Wallonia, or even on culture itself. 'In carrying out such a measure' they claimed, 'a few educated elements in that backward region may be pleased but what is even more certain is that a lighthouse will be replaced by a candle'! And finally that 'each time the Barbarians have seemed to triumph over civilized peoples, they have concentrated on the destruction of the latter's achievements. Their excuse was

The 'wicked work' that they did not understand what they were doing. The wicked work which the House has done is of this sort'. This seems rather an overstatement of the case. The university bill of 1930 was followed up by others which officially recognised the language frontier for the first time. On one side is Dutch speaking Flanders, on the other French speaking Wallonia, in the middle bilingual Brussels. Administration was doubled and a system of a ten yearly census introduced to decide on any necessary adjustments in the language frontier. This was

Bilingual Brussels supposed to regulate the language regime to be followed in areas on, or very near, the language frontier, in which the ratio of inhabitants speaking each language might easily change. This and the bilingual regime for Brussels and other boroughs with more than a 30 % language minority, has subsequently caused great difficulties. The census held in 1947 in what seem to have been very dubious circumstances—in some areas near the frontier French had increased by as much as 33 % in 10 years !—was not published until 1954. The new census due in 1960 was not carried out by hundreds of Flemish local councils, supported by the big Flemish towns and cultural organisations. Finally in 1966 the language census was stopped and the language frontier was fixed by law. The year 1932 saw also a new law on education: schools, both state and free, receiving official subsidies and awarding official diplomas were to use the language of the region: thus every child in the Walloon part of the country was to be educated in French, in Flanders in Dutch. To this extent the old principle of the father's freedom of choice was sacrificed, this principle led also to bitter quarrels concerning Leuven. Three years later, in 1935, the language in legal cases was also fixed according to region although certain exceptions were made to which Flemings objected. From the early thirties onwards the nature of the language problem in Belgium changed. From being one of obtaining complete recognition for Dutch in Flanders, it became one of discarding bilingualism, getting rid of French, and fixing the language frontier. Flanders insists on the acceptance of Dutch by every class in every sphere, including the highest. This has been only partially successful in unofficial life. There is still a conservative, traditional group faithful to the use of French in social contacts, but it is no longer supported by the use of French officially. The spread of Dutch however, even among these classes, was helped by the economic improvement of Flanders. By 1938 the trend in population figures had changed in spite of the loss of Flemish workers to Wallonia. Between 1797 and 1801 the absolute population figures for East and West Flanders fell, although by 1806 they were rising again. Between 1831 and 1913 there was an increase of 54 % in East Flanders, 46 % in West Flanders, 175 % in Brabant as a whole, 191 % in Antwerp, 105 % in Liège and 140 % in Hainaut. Between 1840 and 1870 much of the increase in Wallonia consisted of Flemish émigré workers. Between 1930 and 1938 the recuperation of Flanders was beginning to show in an overall increase of 250,559 while in Wallonia the population fell by 32,713. In Brussels it rose by 76,703. By 1946 Flanders had reached 4.5 million, Wallonia 2.9 million (excluding Brussels). By 1991 the population of Belgium had reached 9,978,681, of which 22.5 % live in Brabant, the most densely populated province. 57.8 % of the total live in Flanders, 32.6 % in Wallonia and 9.5 % in Brussels. Between 1947 and 1991 Flanders' growth has been swifter than that of Wallonia and Brussels.

The language problem highlights differences between the two parts of Belgium. We have stressed the importance of the economic depression in Flanders at a time when the industrialisation of Wallonia was having a favourable effect. Basic political differences also exist, and emerge in action at critical moments. The Catholic Party had its stronghold in Flanders. In 1865 three-quarters of the Flemish seats went to the Catholic Party; this was the same in 1900, while in

Party strongholds 1946 it had changed to two-thirds. In Wallonia on the other hand three quarters of the seats in 1865 were Liberal, in 1900 two thirds Liberal or Socialist and in 1946 more than two-thirds Liberal, Socialist or Communist. In 1991 the CVP (Christelijke Volkspartij) still polled most votes in Flanders while the Socialist party had a big majority in Wallonia and the Liberals in Brussels. Both parts of the country have an extreme element, but the south is more quickly violent, an easier prey for agitators.

Between the two world wars there was a real threat to democracy from extremists particularly from the Right. In 1944 the threat was from the Left. It was very tempting in the thirties to blame the Parliamentary system itself for all the corruption, mismanagement and downright inefficiency of these years. More autocratic policies seemed to some to offer the only answer to the inexplicable economic chaos into which the world had fallen. While argumentative and sometimes stupid politicians failed to find a solution, others were tempted to think that a firm hand could put everything in order.

Ship-building on the Scheldt in Temse.

Berlaymont building of the EEC in Brussels.

The university hall of Ghent.

Opposition from the Left had begun first among theoretical middle class groups which had failed really to establish contacts with the workers; later the democratic, radical group which worked through the trade unions and later the Workers' party saw the growth of a much more revolutionary group. Belgian Socialists were active in the First International in London in 1864. Overt anarchists with revolutionary aims celebrated the fifteenth anniversary of the Paris Commune in 1886. The early Socialist leaders were Emile Vandervelde, Edward Anseele and Louis Bertrand. In 1921 the Belgian Communist Party was founded. Its greatest successes followed the second world war when, in 1946, it obtained 46 Parliamentary seats. Many feared a Communist take-over. After

Danger from the Left

1944, when the country was in turmoil, the highly organised Communist party was able to make the most of the hunt for collaborators. They managed to forget the Russo-German alliance of 1939-41 and give the impression that the Right contained nothing but collaborators and the Left nothing but patriots. Until 1947 they retained several ministerial portfolios— there were 4 Communist ministers in the Socialist government of 1946, but the Cold War froze them out.

The thirties and forties were a dangerous time for democracy. Extreme movements were not confined to the Left. One government crisis after another made many wonder if Parliamentary government had not had its day. The country often seemed ungovernable. The economy, as elsewhere in Europe, was on the point of collapse. In 1935 a 28 % devaluation was carried through. An improvement in efficiency was brought about not by the political parties but by a national union under the leadership of Paul van Zeeland, vice-governor of the National Bank and not a politician. Under his guidance, and because the situation was itself improving, exports increased 100 % and unemployment fell by two-thirds, but the democratic structure was still very shaky. It was attacked very vigorously from the Right. Most such attacks were launched by lower middle class groups, with a sprinkling of the professional classes, and were born from a dissatisfaction with the workings of existing political institutions. Few showed admiration for Hitler; some for Mussolini. Some, such as the Légion Nationale, whose support came chiefly from Liège, were fascist and wanted to wipe out the existing regime completely; others drew on the hostility between Wallonia and Flanders, and wanted either federalism, or closer links between all Dutch speaking peoples. Of these the two most important were the VNV

Threat from the Right

(Vlaamsch Nationaal Verbond), a political party set up in 1933 to unite Flemish nationalist organisations, and dedicated to freeing Flanders from the clutches of the Belgian state and to setting up an authoritarian government; and the Verdinaso, a Flemish nationalist movement under the leadership of Joris van Severen, a theatrical figure murdered in France in 1940. In 1936 the VNV obtained 168,000 votes. Some of its leaders collaborated with the Germans in 1940 but most of its members were really exclusively interested in Flemish questions. For the French speaking Belgians an authoritarian party, the Rexists, under the leadership of Léon Degrelle gained much success. In 1936, one French speaking Belgian in 6 voted for this party, not because they were fascist but because they wanted a political clean-up. It was a one man show, however, and when Degrelle challenged the existing system in the person of Paul van Zeeland, supported by the church, in a by-election in 1937, he was defeated by a majority of 80 % and the movement gradually petered out. Degrelle himself collaborated with the Germans, and was even awarded the Iron Cross for his services on the eastern front where a Flemish and a Walloon regiment also fought. The peace of 1944, which had begun in such a rosy glow, disappeared under clouds of gloom. Belgium's faith in international treaties and organisations had received one severe blow after another. Yet 80 % of Belgians polled in 1984, 1986 and 1987 were positive about European unity and only 8 % against it. Her geographical vulnerability, so often shown throughout her history, was illustrated twice in less than forty years. The first occasion was on August 4th, 1914. Once the German offer of independence after the war, in return for a free passage to the Channel, had been refused in 1914, Belgium

First German invasion: 1914

was treated as an enemy, and invaded. On August 20th German troops entered Brussels; a counter attack from Antwerp failed and on October 9th the town fell. The Belgian army withdrew with British, Canadian and Australian support to the IJzer river where under the command of King Albert it dug in and remained entrenched until the end of the war. Clever manipulation of water levels and locks put an impenetrable morass between it and the Germans. The cost of this movement to the coast and the fighting in 1917 on this front can be counted in the scattering of war cemeteries round Passchendale and Roeselare, by the endless record of Commonwealth names on the Menin Gate in Ypres, and by the complete destruction of that town under bombardments. 15,000 Belgians were killed or wounded; 500,000 fled. The whole country with the exception of the tiny IJzer area disappeared under the pall of enemy occupation, once again. Government inside occupied Belgium was ensured by a German Governor-general except in areas near the front which came under military command. The Belgian government was in exile near Le Havre. Industry was at a standstill and most people were hungry. Some went voluntarily to work in Germany; 120,000 were deported—among them the scholars, Henri Pirenne and Paul Fredericq, and the burgomaster of Brussels, Adolf Max. To avoid complete starvation American Relief was organised. By 1918 prices on the black market had risen 1,000 %. A small group of activists saw the Germans as the answer to all their problems, as the saviours of Flanders. They supported the Dutch language in the University of Ghent set up by the German Governor von Bissing, and set up a Flemish Council in 1917 intended to govern Flan-

The von Bissing University

ders after the division of the country into two halves. They were however, declared illegal by the Belgian bench, which resulted in the deportation of some judges and the replacement of Belgian by German courts. A pocket of strong Flemish feeling grew up in the Belgian army on the IJzer. By far the greater number of soldiers were Flemings and many felt themselves misunderstood and badly treated by their French speaking officers. It was a dreadful time. By September 1918 however, the end was in sight and after yet more bloody battles for the Flemish hills round Tielt and Torhout, King Albert entered Ghent on the 13th, Antwerp on the 19th, and Brussels on the 22nd of November. The liberation had cost 3,500 Belgian dead and about 30,000 wounded.

There followed a bitter period of economic upheaval and political weakness, but also a more hopeful one of reconstruction and faith in international organisations such as the League of Nations. By the midthirties such optimism was obviously misplaced, and Belgium claimed a right to her own independent foreign policy. This

Second German invasion: 1940

did not help much against the German tanks which rolled over the frontier early in the morning of May 10, 1940. Precautions and plans were thrown into complete confusion as the enormous weight of armour poured across the country. The King, Leopold III, had, like his father Albert in 1914, joined his troops. The Constitution made him their commander-in-chief. Two days later the Belgian army was placed under the command of the French General Gamelin, whose contribution to the war was the loss of Sedan. Two days later Holland, which had hoped to avoid involvement, as she had managed to do in the first World War, capitulated to the Germans, and Gamelin ordered the Belgian army to retreat to the south. Leopold refused, choosing rather to try to keep the Channel ports open for the retreating British army. At this point, General Weygand,

Church of St. John the Baptist in Afsnee.

Guido Gezelle's birthplace, now a museum in the Rolleweg in Bruges.

Gamelin's successor, ordered a counter attack from north and south, in which the Belgian army, which had no suitable weapons, was to cover the British. The attack failed and the British withdrew via Dunkirk. The Belgian army was left in a loop of ground between the sea, the river IJzer, the river Leie and Bruges. Into that space, which usually contained 242 people per square kilometre, refugees, soldiers and inhabitants were now squashed at the rate of 1250 per square kilometre. Retreat south was cut off by German troops who had swept through the Maginot line, Sedan and Amiens and were tearing north through Arras to Lille. All communications were choked. Leopold, after informing the French and British of his intention, surrendered unconditionally on May 28th, 1940. The Belgian army had fought for eighteen days. Leopold was later accused of having been beaten on purpose, although it is difficult to see how he could have avoided the fate of the armies of the United Kingdom and France. The country was occupied by the Germans for the second time in a generation.

In 1914, however, King Albert had retained a small slice of territory on the IJzer. In 1940 the occupation was complete. The Belgian administration continued under German military commanders who were replaced in 1944 by Nazis. The Germans again did their best to exploit antipathy between Flemings and Walloons, this time by sending home Flemish prisoners of war and keeping Walloons. 13,000 political prisoners died in Germany. Meanwhile the Belgian government, which had disagreed fundamentally with the attitude taken up by Leopold III in remaining in Belgium, had fled to London, where a government in exile was set up. Leopold, who refused to leave the country with his ministers but chose to remain instead with his troops,

King Leopold III took up a position in relation to Germany which many found equivocal. He never seemed convinced that the Allies would win in the end. He had become increasingly doubtful about Parliamentary government throughout the thirties when he saw one after another tottering on the brink of collapse. His idea of the royal prerogative no longer coincided with that of his ministers. He felt he could still do what he thought best and that his governments should be guided by this advice. He, no doubt, had Belgian interests at heart, but his methods of achieving them were sometimes arguable. His refusal to leave Belgium in 1940, his visits to Germany and interview with Hitler, his remarriage while many of his subjects were divided from their families, his friendship with one noted collaborator, and above all his failure to be obviously on the allied side, made his position after the war extremely delicate. For the king's behaviour was used after the war as a political weapon of the sharpest sort. On June 6th, 1944, the day of the Normandy landings, he and his family were deported to Germany. By November 1944 Belgium was free from German occupation but still had to meet the von Rundstedt offensive in the Ardennes, and the bombardment of Antwerp by V 1's and V 2's. The next seven years were, as after 1918, a bitter period of political instability and the threat of violence. Between September 1944 and July 1951 there were ten governments, three general elections and one referendum. Two big issues divided the country: the punishment of collaborators and the position of Leopold III. While he remained abroad and his brother acted as regent, Leopold's part during the war was pushed into the political limelight by Socialist

Attacks on Leopold

governments with strong Communist support. The king decided to explain and defend his behaviour. Attacks on him were both personal and violent. All the old quarrels re-emerged as to who had collaborated most—Walloons or Flemings. Finally it was decided to settle the royal question, which cut across ordinary party lines, by a referendum. This showed that the country as a whole favoured the king's return by a majority of 57.68 %; in Flanders 72 % wanted him back; in Wallonia only 42 %; Liège and Hainaut, strongholds of the Socialist party, voted against his return by 59 % and 64 % respectively and Brussels by 52 % while Brabant was equally divided.

Leopold came back. Socialists and Communists immediately organised violent demonstrations against him, especially in Wallonia. Near Liège three demonstrators were shot by the police. It is possible that Wallonia at this moment seriously considered independence. To avoid more violence Leopold was replaced on August 11th 1950 by his son Baudouin, who, on July 17th 1951, took the oath as king. The ceremony was interrupted by the Chairman of the Communist Party shouting 'Long live the Republic'. A week later he was shot

Accession of King Baudouin

dead in his own home. Thus against the will of a small majority and under the threat of violence, Leopold III had been forced to give way. It took a long time for tempers to cool. In 1950 collaborators were still being chased. The war had done nothing to assuage antipathy between Walloon and Fleming. The language problem, complicated by all sorts of political overtones remained. To it had been added a new element: the dispute about Brussels.

Flanders had come an immense distance since 1830. How had this progress been achieved ? Not through revolution but through democratic parliamentary action and the rule of law. The Flemish movement has always been essentially democratic. Noisy mobs have given tongue, but Parliament has always had the

The old and new tower on the IJzer in Diksmuide.

last word. Each great step has been achieved not through violence, military coups or changes in the regime, but through the democratic institutions created in 1831. Although all forms of political agitation have been used—propaganda, marches and demonstrations, the Flemish movement has avoided violence. Although between the wars political extremists aimed at changing the Parliamentary regime and replacing it with an autocratic government, they

Holding on to democracy

failed. Even in 1936 when the extreme parties, the Communists, VNV and Rex had their biggest success, they polled only 24.61 %. By 1939 this had fallen to 18.06 %. Democracy may have seemed occasionally on its last legs but it has always staggered to its feet at the last minute, possibly sustained by the long history of democratic institutions embedded in the changing framework of the Netherlands.

Sometimes during the terrible gloomy days of the Counter-Reformation or the poverty and misery of the nineteenth century it may have seemed that the glorious Flemish artistic tradition was lost forever. But it was not so. Once the worst was over the old rich individualism and delight in the wide skies of Flanders returned. A new school of painters drew their inspiration from the slow broad rivers and the rolling hills, from the heavy, simple peasants and the change of the seasons. Unlike many of their predecessors they were not concerned with princes and courts, but with farmhouses and farm animals, with landscapes under snow and the sea under grey northern clouds. In this they go back rather

New Flemish school of painters

to Brueghel than to Van Eyck, to van der Goes than to Metsijs. On the curving willow lined banks of the river Leie, in the moist air which gives to every colour a richer glow, in the villages on the river Leie, Afsnee, Latem and Deurle, all near Ghent, they lived, often in groups, in simple cottages, enjoying each other's company and revelling in the beauty of the Flemish landscape. Under the benevolent eye of the painter Albinus van den Abeele, burgomaster of Latem, the first group formed in the eighteen nineties round Valerius de Saedeleer, whose exquisite detailed landscapes and particularly his winter scenes often recall Brueghel and who painted near the Leie and later further south in the hilly country round Ronse. He was joined by the two brothers van de Woestijne, Gustaaf and Karel, painter and poet. Gustaaf painted the picture of the 'Holy Virgin with St. Dominic' which hangs behind the altar in Latem church and the terrible 'Crucifixion', said to be a portrait of his dying brother, in the Museum of Fine Arts in Ghent. With them lived George Minne, a sculptor whose art centred on the relationship of mother and

child. Later they were joined by Constant Permeke, much of whose work hangs in his home in Jabbeke and whose canvases of Flemish peasants or fishermen are so close to earth and sea that they seem to become part of the elements. Such paintings—the 'Sower', the 'Beggar', the 'Farmer with his spade', the 'Engagement', give a feeling of the immensely hard work and patience of the Flemish peasant. While James Ensor in Ostend painted his strange masked figures and his 'Entry of Christ into Brussels', Albert Servaes joined the group in Latem and set in motion with his 'Holy Evening' and 'Burial of the Poor' the whole movement of Flemish Expressionism. Later with his controversial series of 'Stations of the Cross', which at one time were forbidden in religious establishments, he became the grand old man of the Flemish painters, until his unfortunate political involvement in the second world war. During this early period these painters and poets were poor, half educated in many cases, unrecognised and extremely happy. When they were hungry they ate Servaes's samples (he was a traveller in colonial goods), begged money from the local vicar, or quickly stretched a long strip of canvas round a room and painted it together in order to get it done quickly—they cut pieces off the roll to sell !
This group was broken up by the first World War during which many of them fled to Wales, where Lloyd George offered them hospitality on a rather unaccustomed scale. Most of them were terribly home-sick for Flanders and could not paint, although one, Leon de Smet, whose gallery can still be visited in Deurle, was lionised and painted portraits of Shaw, Hardy and Galsworthy. In the twenties they became well known; Queen Elizabeth visited the area; a museum of their work was opened in Deinze. And towards the end of the forties they gradually disappeared. One of the most impressive characteristics of Flemish art has always been its individualism. In spite of innumerable attempts at cultural domination particularly by France its core remained untouched. This is also the case with Flemish literature. Perhaps the strength to keep it alive through years of neglect and worse, could only come from such individualists. It has certainly heightened their awareness of language. Even the group which began in the last years of the nineteenth century to publish the literary magazine 'Van Nu en Straks' worked from the most diverse points of view. They, like Brueghel, who, after undergoing all the influence of an Italian tour, returned to Flanders to paint the most personal and unfashionable pictures, have stuck to their own themes, their own language, and, very often, to the inspiration of their own landscape. Many of the motives in Flemish art recur in Flemish literature. The intimacy of household scenes even in such pictures as the 'Mystic Lamb' return, for example, in Stijn Streuvels' farmer who watches impatiently while

the rain streams down outside when he wants to get on with his spring sowing. Intense love of their landscape which made Flemish painters unable to paint when they were exiled from Flanders appears in the poetry of Karel van de Woestijne. The peculiar dream-like quality of the bosses in St. Baaf's Abbey or night-mares of Bosch turn up again in the novels of Johan Daisne, or Hubert Lampo, or Ivo Michiels. A deep religious awareness sometimes expressed in biting criticism runs through the novels of Gerard Walschap and Paul Lebeau. While Maurice Gilliams' poetry and prose reach inwards like some of the earlier masters of literature in Dutch.

Before the First World War Flemish literature maintained its strongly personal element. A few writers, particularly Cyril Buysse, mirrored the misery of the small-holders living always on the edge of starvation, but it was only after the war that many writers began to look more at society than at their own personal reactions. Perhaps because of Flanders' many years of powerlessness, heroes like Timmermans' 'Pallieter' and Walschap's 'Houtekiet' created a world in which all problems can be solved, all unhappiness dismissed. But actual, real difficulties in personal relationships emerged in the work of such writers as Walschap and Willem Elsschot, who, in a dry and laconic style described the disillusionment of ordinary life; Marnix Gijsen whose lucid style analysed the immense difficulties of living together or Karel Jonckheere in the frame-work of his obsession with the sea. The earthiness of Brueghel's 'Land of Cockagne' combines, in a writer like Louis Paul Boon with an exuberant ability to tell a good story, while the experimental poets—of whom some, like Hugo Claus are involved also with plays, films and novels—hark back to Paul van Ostaijen. Translations of classic authors as well as poetry have been published by Anton Van Wilderode, and biographies about such important figures as Hadewich have also appeared.

In the nineteenth century when French influence reached its peak, some Flemish authors such as Maurice Maeterlinck and Emile Verhaeren chose to write in French and achieved international fame.

Flanders, because of her geography and history, stands to-day at the heart of European life, as she did throughout the Middle Ages. Now, as then, she is at the crossroads, not only of economic, but of social and political routes. The two great motorways, E 40 which will eventually link Ostend with Istanbul, and E 17 between Lisbon and Stockholm, cross on the outskirts of Ghent. The backwardness, caused by the Counter-Reformation and the isolation which followed, has been shaken off by a gradual revival of self-awareness and confidence. Belgium is in an excellent position to profit from the growing ideal

Canal Ghent-Terneuzen.

of European unity to which she can contribute an age-old tradition of receptivity and variety. She is enthusiastic in supporting the Common Market and all its subsidiary organisations, as well as the North Atlantic Treaty Organisation. By nature and history awake to every new development, she has behind her an invaluable tradition of hard work and adaptability. In all this Flanders takes her part. Population growth is slow. In Flanders it increased

Increase of Flemish population

between 1970 and 1992 by about 373,500, in Wallonia by about 116,000, while in Brussels it has decreased by about 120,000. 5,794,857 lived in Flanders, 3,275,923 in Wallonia and 951,217 in the Brussels Region.

Flanders has evolved dramatically from the pre-war agricultural and semi-industrial society to an economy based on the most modern technology. As elsewhere the percentage of women working outside the home has grown markedly, and continues to do so. The Belgian gross national product lies about half-way on the European scale. In Flanders very great changes took place from about 1960 onwards when the economic balance in Belgium swung in its favour. This was caused by an important pool of labour which attracted foreign investment, the excellent infra-structure, a peaceful social climate and relatively low wages. This was based on the triangle Antwerp-Ghent-Brussels, and led to the growth of the Flemish economy to a point higher than the European average. Wallonia, on the other hand, suffered bitterly from its out-dated heavy industry which needed constant subsidies. These were not popular in Flanders. Industrial production has, for example, grown in Flanders from index 100 in 1980 to index 138.6 in 1991, while in Wallonia it rose from index 100 to 135.3. Between 1985 and 1987 unemployment in Flanders fell by 10.3 %, in Brussels by 14.4 % and rose in Wallonia by 0.4 %. The great strides which Flanders is making can best be appreciated by a good look at the huge industrial area with dock installations and the biggest sea-lock in the world, near Antwerp—this area, of about 3,000 acres provides work for about 40,000 people—or along the canal linking Ghent and the western Scheldt, which has

Expansion of Antwerp

been doubled in width and along which have sprung up some of the most modern factories in Europe. They, like the atomic central at Mol, look to the whole of Europe. The development of such industries in Flanders is of the greatest significance. We have traced the effects in Belgium of the industrialisation of the nineteenth century, when the promising sectors such as fuel, metal and chemicals expanded round the Walloon coal and iron mines, while Flanders struggled out of the old fashioned trammels of the textile industry. The change in fuel from coal to oil and the importation of iron ore from overseas have largely offset the purely economic advantages enjoyed in the past by Wallonia. Flanders now finds her coastal position of the greatest value, and is exploiting it to the full.

The extensive exhibition space created near Ghent, and known as Flanders Technology is a symptom of the vigorous development typified on many levels, especially in genetic and electrical engineering, medicine and bio-chemistry.

Thus the fight for Flemish identity and Flemish prosperity set in motion in the nineteenth century, and pursued first on a cultural and later, under such men as Lodewijk de Raet, on an economic level, has achieved successes which must sometimes have seemed unattainable. Because of the list of successes the average income in Flanders has risen and the average taxable income per head has capped Wallonia. And in Flanders the regional gross product per head rose more quickly than elsewhere. There have been a few large scale attempts to mobilise Flemish capital for Flemish development. Industrial enterprises are financed from all over Europe, America and Japan. This continues a trend already obvious after the discovery of coal in the Kempen in 1901. By 1928, 40 % of its capital investment was in Belgian, though non-Flemish hands; 55 % was in French and 5 % in German possession.

The change from a French to a Dutch language regime in the University of Ghent in 1930 was a great step forward for Flanders, as King Baudouin publicly declared in 1967, and the penetration of Flemings into management has been vigorous and successful. Groups such as the Flemish Economic Society (Vlaams Economisch Verbond) insist on the use of Dutch in economic life; while individuals, such as the late Fernand Collin, the President of the Kredietbank, who refused the Presidency of the Belgian Banking Federation unless it was clearly understood that he would continue to use his mother tongue in that capacity, have done much to make business circles realise that Flanders is no longer only a pool of cheap labour; moreover the active encouragement of art and culture provided by a maecenas like the late Maurice Naessens of the Bank van Parijs en de Nederlanden is very precious.

Art Sponsorship for art, music and architecture is possible for prosperous firms and institutions from both inside Flanders and abroad. Flemish artists take part in all modern movements. Many, such as Panamarenko, from Antwerp with his fantastic air-ships, Marcel Broothaers and his mussels, Alechinsky's mesmerizing panels, Paul Delvaux's dreams of women, Vic Gentil's wooden fantasies, Octave Landuyt's nightmares and Paul Van Hoey-

The partly medieval castle of Laarne near Ghent.

Bornem with the park and rebuilt neo-gothic mansion of Marnix van St. Aldegonde.

donck's man-in-the-moon, Bijl's transformed art galleries, Deleu's engineering fantasies and Denmark's dead archives are internationally well-known. Whether they are typically Flemish is another question. In opera, ballet with Anne-Theresa De Keersmaeker, ceramics like those of Frank Steyaert, sculpture by Hilda Van Sumere, architecture and restoration, Flanders shows the artistic diversity typical of the country, no longer restrained by poverty. Underground stations and new hospitals can temper their utilitarianism with wall-paintings while fine new museums like the one in Deinze or the open-air sculpture park of Middelheim near Antwerp mean that no-one is obliged to visit museums only in the capital.

Equivocal rôle of Brussels

By 1993 the number of female undergraduates in Flanders had reached 49.2 % of the first year student population. There were, in 1993, 61,231 students in Dutch speaking and 61,716 in French speaking universities. About five times more young people were studying in Flanders than in 1960. About 8 % of students studying in Belgium are foreigners. Many students receive grants of differing sorts. Flanders has now a pool of highly trained young men and women to fill the demanding tasks which its investment in high technology has opened up.

Many of these jobs are still in Brussels. The capital's international rôle has led to a large increase in banking, legal services and accountancy as well as all the administrative work involved. It is officially a bilingual city although the number of languages used there is infinite. It has not always been popular in Flemish eyes because it was seen as an hostile francophone city which treated half the country's population as second class citizens. The change in economic balance has done much to improve this. Feelings about Brussels certainly contributed to the growing desire to create a Belgian federal state, and its position has complicated negotiations between political parties, pressure groups and language communities from the outset. Belgium is a rare example of a country moving away from a unitary, towards a federal state. The process has been going on since 1970 and has involved interminable negotiations which have highlighted the patience and willingness to argue endlessly rather than resort to violence, characteristic of the country. Flemings are determined to organize their own affairs themselves. Belgium is now divided into two Communities, the French and the Flemish, and three Regions, Flanders, Wallonia and Brussels. [The small German speaking group makes up part of the French Region]. The first constitutional change divided the country into four language areas: Dutch speaking, French speaking, German speaking and bilingual Brussels. Three cultural councils (Kultuurraden) were set up, of which two, the Dutch and French were given law-making powers over a limited number of matters. Their members were members of the national parliament and their powers covered culture, the use of language and aspects of education. Their decisions were carried out by the national civil service and financed from the national budget. The three Regions: Flemish, Walloon and Brussels were created at the same time. Nothing was done to put the Brussels Region into effect. An attempt in 1978, called the Egmont Pact failed to solve the Community problem and was followed in 1980 by a second constitutional change. The three cultural groups became Communities each with its own executive to carry out decisions taken by the Flemish or French Regional Council (Gewestraad). In Flanders the Region and Community combined in one Flemish Council with a single Flemish executive. No direct elections were foreseen. National taxation was divided to a considerable extent according to its place of origin, and a new law court, the Court of Arbitration was created to decide on arguments about competence. Nothing happened concerning Brussels until 1993.

Education had not yet been federalized and Flanders considered the financial arrangements unfair but the new constitution has coped with most of these matters. Brussels is now a Region with a status slightly different from Flanders and Wallonia.

Belgium remains a constitutional monarchy although this institution was jolted by serious disagreements on the law about abortion in 1990. Many legal details have still to be effected, and the existence in some areas particularly round Brussels but also near the language frontier of what are called 'facilities' is provocative and seen by many Flemings as a subtle but determined attempt by French speaking Belgians to take over Flemish areas. These facilities allow citizens of one language group, if numerous enough, to demand services in their own language in areas officially belonging to the other community. Round Brussels this happens extensively in Flemish areas attractive for commuters and in an area north of Liège called the *Voeren* has led to a certain amount of irritability and unrest. When, however, the complications of the situation are taken into account progress towards federalism has been remarkably smooth.

The political parties

Since the Second World War Belgian political parties have tended to split into two sections, according to language. Thus the Liberal Party founded in 1846 split in 1971 into a Flemish wing *(Partij voor Vrijheid en Vooruitgang: PVV)* and a French speaking wing *(Parti Réformateur Libéral: PRL)*. The Catholic party created in 1884 from associations of electoral clubs became in 1968 two independent parties: the *Christelijke Volkspartij (CVP)*, and the *Parti Social Chrétien (PSC)*. Two Socialist parties also exist: *Socialistische Partij (SP)* and *Parti Socialiste (PS)*. Their foundations were laid in 1885. Regional parties such as the Flemish *Volksunie* (VU), and more extreme *Vlaams Blok* and in Brussels and Wallonia the *Front National* as well as green parties also appeal to voters. Flanders is basically more conservative but the strength of radical left parties has decreased markedly in recent years throughout the whole country. National governments are always coalitions because of the system of proportional representation. Polls have shown a very substantial and increasing majority in favour of European unification.

The importance of the rôle played by the universities in the economic, social and cultural development of Flanders cannot be overemphasised. One of the two Belgian state universities is in Ghent where all courses are given in Dutch. The other, in Liège, teaches exclusively in French. Most students in Ghent come from the provinces of East and West Flanders. The provinces of Antwerp and Limburg are less well represented, probably because they are further away. Antwerp has recently obtained its own university whose structure is complicated by the existence of the Faculty of St. Ignatius
Leuven founded previously by the Jesuits. Kortrijk, moreover, now houses an offshoot of the University of Leuven. Each of the two non-state universities of Leuven and Brussels became double—each with complete teaching in both Dutch and French. Since the thirties Leuven had possessed a complete double programme, in Dutch and in French. It is a Catholic university under the control of the Belgian episcopate, although most of its resources is provided by the state. The town of Leuven is Flemish. Professors and staff from the French speaking section, nevertheless, demanded special facilities, such as schools in French for their children, which Flemish public opinion found irritating. After a good deal of agitation the French speaking university of Leuven decided in 1968 to move to Ottignies in Wallonia, while the Dutch speaking university remains in Leuven itself. The atmosphere became explosive following a proclamation by the Belgian episcopate, and signed by Cardinal Suenens, known abroad for his liberal views, which completely disregarded advice offered by a special commission set up to study the matter, and which announced categorically that the university was to remain unified, and in Leuven, and that staff who did not like it, could simply go elsewhere. Everyone was very cross. The repercussions of this statement reverberated for a long time, but the present situation is now considered normal.

Flanders is a rich treasure house. The Flemings tend, perhaps, to take their brilliant and turbulent history for granted. Hurrying every day between beautiful buildings, with art galleries and museums always at their disposal, stuffed with pictures, sculpture, manuscripts and carvings, they are casual about the things with which they have always been familiar. Yet since 1958 the Festival

The Festival of Flanders

of Flanders, which belongs to the exclusive European Association of Music Festivals, has revealed not only Flemish treasures but a rich and varied programme from all over the world. Ballet, opera, concerts and theatrical productions from the oldest to the most modern follow each other in a whirl, each year throughout Spring, August and September. Historic buildings and modern concert halls are all drawn into the enthusiastic presentation, when orchestras and artists of the highest quality provide a real feast, typically Flemish in its lavishness. To watch and listen in the great hall of the counts' castle in Ghent to the music of Dunstable, Dufay and Binchois, while ballet dancers dressed in the costumes of Philip the Good's court, revive a fifteenth century princely ball, must awaken pride in the past. The festival has already widened out from Ghent to include the towns of Brussels, Leuven, Bruges, Antwerp, Tongeren, St. Truiden and Kortrijk and many other castles, villages and towns. It is very impressive and beautiful to sit in the Gothic nave of the cathedral in Ghent while before the altar screen rises the mighty golden idol and the Burning Fiery Furnace of Nebuchadnezzar, and the choir, singing one of Benjamin Britten's scores, appear out of the shadows of the aisle, dressed in monks' habits: or to watch and listen in the Baroque castle of Ooidonk, encircled within its moat among the quiet pastures beside the river Leie, to German and English lieder: or in the richly decorated town hall of Leuven a concert of beautiful, old songs of the Burgundian court by the Alarius Ensemble, or to yet more music in the intimacy of the courtyard of Gruuthuse in Bruges, or to the glory of Händel's Messiah in the town hall, looking out over the town's very heart.

List of Buildings and Works of Art mentioned in the text

ANTWERP

ARCHIVE AND MUSEUM
OF FLEMISH CULTURE
Minderbroedersrui 17. Literature, music, sculpture, documents about the Flemish movement.

CASTLE [Steen]
Very early foundations; rebuilt XVI to plans by R. Keldermans and D. de Waghemakere; restored XIX.

CATHEDRAL OF OUR LADY
Choir and ambulatory, 1352-1472, Gothic; later XV additions, tower by H. de Waghemakere et al., finished 1521-1530.
Stained glass window showing Anthony and Jan Jacob Fugger, 1538.
'Crucifixion' by P.P. Rubens, 1610.
'Descent from the Cross' by P.P. Rubens, 1612.

MAYER VAN DEN BERGH MUSEUM
'Mad Meg' by Peter Brueghel, 1562.

NEW EXCHANGE
1531; reconstructed according to original plans, 1868.

PLANTIJN MORETUS MUSEUM
XVI-XVIII.

ROYAL MUSEUM OF FINE ARTS
'Portrait of Margaret of Austria' between 1515-20, copy of original by Bernard van Orley.
'Entry of Christ into Brussels', by James Ensor.
'Burial of the Poor' by Albert Servaes (oils).

RUBENS'S HOUSE
Bought by Rubens, 1610; extended by him; right wing Baroque; badly damaged, restored 1939-46.

ST. CHARLES BORROMEUS CHURCH
1614-24 by F. Aguilon, Peter Huyssens, Baroque.

ST. JAMES'S CHURCH
1491-c. 1533 and 1602-1656 by H. and D. de Waghemakere; late Gothic.

TOWN HALL
1561-65 by Cornelis Floris de Vriendt; Renaissance;
1576, partially destroyed and rebuilt; several partial restorations.

ARRAS

ABBEY OF ST. VAAST
[containing museum]
Original buildings entirely destroyed;
rebuilt XVIII and restored after First World
War.

LA GRAND-PLACE AND LA PETITE-PLACE
TOWN HALL
1502-1505; late Gothic, and 1572,
Renaissance and XIX; rebuilt after 1918.

BELFRY
1463-1554; restored XIX, rebuilt after 1918.

HOUSES
XVII, except n° 49 (1460); Flemish style;
many rebuilt after 1918.

BERGUES

ABBEY OF ST. WINOC
Square tower, lower part XII; octagonal
tower restored 1818.

BELFRY
Original XVI; rebuilt and simplified 1961.

MONT-DE-PIÉTÉ
1629-1633; Flemish style gable.

BOKRIJK

PARK
Reconstructions of typical houses, mills etc.

BRUGES

BELFRY
By 1280, 2 lower rectangular floors in brick
or stone surmounted by wooden bell tower
which burned 1280; 1389-95, important
restorations; new windows in upper
rectangular floor, 1394-95; clock face 1449
or 50, battlements of gallery, 1493; upper
octagon, 1482-86; frequent additions and
changes.

CHURCH OF OUR LADY
XIII-XV; brick tower finished 1297; various
restorations.
*Tomb of Mary of Burgundy, by P. de Becker
between 1495 and 1502.*
*Statue of Madonna and Child, by
Michelangelo; gift of John Mouscron, 1514.*

CLOTH HALL
Early XIII; c. 1240 some buildings in brick
or stone; by 1280 had ground floor arches
and windows; various additions later.

GHENT GATE
1402.

GRIFFIE [office of the Law Courts]
By Christian Sixdeniers to plan by Jean
Wallot, 1534-37; Renaissance; many
decorations destroyed 1792.

GRUUTHUSE MUSEUM
Built for Louis of Bruges, 1465-70; some
parts earlier; restored XIX.

HOUSE VAN DER BUERSE,
Schouwburgplaats n° 35
First mention of family 1257; house partly
reconstructed 1452; modernised 1838;
reconstructed to original plan 1948.

HOUSE OF THE EASTERLINGS,
MEMLINGPLAATS
By J. Van der Poele, 1478; much damaged
XVIII, restored.

HOUSE OF THE GENOESE MERCHANTS,
Schouwburgplaats n° 33
1399; rebuilt 1720.

LAW COURTS
Mantelpiece of the Franc de Bruges by
Lancelot Blondeel, 1529-31; chimney and
alabaster frieze by G. de Beaugrand et al.;
restored 1850.

POORTERSLOGE [now State Archives]
XIV; rebuilt and extended after fire 1855;
restored 1899-1903.

ST. SALVATOR'S CATHEDRAL
Lower part of tower XIII; choir and nave XIII
and XIV, ambulatory XV; upper tower XIX.
Misericords, c. 1450.
Portrait of Charles the Good, XV; restored
XVIII.

ST. JOHN'S HOSPITAL
c. 1188; extended XIII; church XV and XVI.
'Mystic Marriage of St. Catherine' by Hans
Memling, 1479.
Shrine of St. Ursula by Hans Memling,
finished before 1489.

TOWN HALL
Begun 1376 and extended XV-XVII; restored
XIX; original painted statues destroyed
1792, present ones XIX; important Gothic
hall.

TOWN MUSEUM [Groeningemuseum]
'Trial and punishment of the unjust judge,
by Cambyses' by Gerard David, 1498.
Moreel triptych, by Hans Memling, 1484.
'Portrait of Philip the Good' copy of picture by
Roger van der Weyden.
'Virgin with George van der Paelen' by John
Van Eyck, between 1434 and 1436.

WOODEN HOUSE
Behind church of Our Lady.

BRUSSELS

BLACK TOWER, St. Catherine's Place
Part of first town wall, XII-XIII; upper part,
XVI; restored XIX.

CINQUANTENAIRE MUSEUM
St. George's altarscreen from Our Lady's of
Ginderbuiten in Leuven by John I Borman,
1493.

COLUMN OF CONGRESS
By Joseph Poelaert, 1859.

HALLE GATE [Arms museum]
Remains of second town wall, c. 1381;
rebuilt XIX.

MARKET PLACE
Gild houses rebuilt after bombardment of
1695; many by W. de Bruyn; Baroque.

MUSEUM OF MODERN ART
'The Engagement' by Constant Permeke.

ROYAL LIBRARY
Miniature of Philip the Good, receiving
manuscript of the translation by John
Wauquelin of the Chronicle of Hainaut from
Simon Nockart 1446, possibly by Roger van
der Weyden.

ROYAL MUSEUM OF FINE ARTS
'Fall of the Angels' by Peter Brueghel, 1562.
'Justice of Otto' by Dirk Bouts, 1468-75.
'Knight with the Arrow' by Roger van der
Weyden, 1460, possibly portrait of Anthony,
illegitimate son of Philip the Good.
'Portrait of a doctor' by Bernard van Orley,
1519.
'Venus and Amor' by John Gossaert, 1521 (?)

ST. MICHAEL'S CATHEDRAL
[previously Ste. Gudule]
Choir XIII, early Gothic; nave and façade XV,
Brabant high Gothic.

TOWN HALL AND BELFRY
Wing to left of belfry, begun 1402
by J. van Thienen; wing to right, begun
1444; belfry
by J. van Ruysbroek, 1449-54; burned
down 1695; various restorations.

TOWN MUSEUM
[Broodhuis or Maison du Roi]
Rebuilt 1515-32 by R. Keldermans; burned
down 1695; restored XIX.
*Saluces altarscreen ascribed to John Borman,
early XVI.*
*Silver spade presented in connection with
Antwerp-Sambre canal, 1699.*

DAMME

CHURCH OF OUR LADY
Nave and tower XIII; choir partly rebuilt XVI;
restored.

TOWN HALL [Town museum]
1464

DENDERMONDE

BUTCHERS' GILD HALL [Museum]
1460.

TOWN HALL
1330, belfry 1376; additions XVI; interior
burned XX, restored.

DIEST

ST. SULPITIUS CHURCH
Misericords, 1491.

DUDZELE

OLD TOWER
Lower part, XII.

GAASBEEK

CASTLE
Medieval, but reconstructed XIX; bailiff's
house also restored.

GHENT

ACHTER SIKKEL
Patrician dwelling, XV, Flemish
Renaissance.

BELFRY
Late XIII and early XIV, by J. van Haelst and
P. van Beergine; 1338 work stopped below
corner towers; completed 1911-13; various
bell towers.
*Stone Men, copies of only remaining original
in St. Baaſs Abbey Archaeological Museum.
Dragon, first 1379, others later.*

BIJLOKE MUSEUM
Cistercian foundation XIII; refectory XIV
with brick gable c. 1325.
*Brasses of William Wenemaer († 1325) and
Margaret de Brune († 1352), earliest in
Belgium.
Monument to Hugh II, Castellan of Ghent
(† 1232). Frescoes XIV.*

CLOTH HALL
By Simon van Assche, 1425-44; completed
1903.

COUNTS' CASTLE
Earliest X; main buildings 1180 et seq.; later
additions; restored.

FRIDAY MARKET
Statue of James van Artevelde by P. de Vigne, 1863.

GERARD DUIVELSTEEN
[now State Archives]
Town house of Castellan of Ghent, 1216.

GRASLEI
Gild hall of Free Boatmen, 1531,
by Ch. Van den Berghe;
Grain measurer's house, 1698;
Receiver of grain toll, 1682;
Grain staple, c. 1200;
Free Masons' house, 1600;
Angel, XVI; etc.

D'HANE STEENHUYSE, Veldstraat n° 47
Occupied by Louis XVIII in 1815.

HOUSE VAN DER SICKELE
c. 1200.

MONT-DE-PIÉTÉ
By W. Coeberger, 1622.

MUSEUM OF FINE ARTS
'Crucifixion' by G. van de Woestijne, 1928.
'Burial of the Poor' by Albert Servaes (drawing).

RABOT [fortified lock]
1489; restored 1860 and 1872.

ST. BAAF'S CATHEDRAL
[previously dedicated to St. John]
Crypt XI; choir XIII; completed XVI.
'The Mystic Lamb' painting by John Van Eyck, 1432.

ST. BAAF'S ABBEY
[now Archaeological Museum]
Founded by St. Amandus, c. 631;
demolished by Vikings, rebuilt X;
demolished by Emperor Charles V; ruins XII
and later, lavatorium c. 1177.

ST. MICHAEL'S CHURCH
XV-XVII; tower unfinished.

ST. NICHOLAS'S CHURCH
West door Romanesque; nave and transept
early XIII Scheldt Gothic.

ST. PETER'S ABBEY
Restored abbey buildings containing Centre
of Applied Arts.

ST. PETER'S CHURCH
Formerly church of St. Peter's abbey;
present church, 1629 by Huyssens;
Baroque.

TOWN HALL
Hoogpoort side, 1518-35 by
R. Keldermans and D. de Waghemakere,
Gothic; statues XIX; Botermarkt side, 1595-
1620, Renaissance; corner of Hoogpoort
and Stadhuissteeg, Baroque; Police station,
1750.
Pacificatiezaal, Troonzaal.
*Portrait of Maria Theresia in lace dress
offered by Ghent, 1743, by Meytens.*

UNIVERSITY HALL
By L. Roelandt, 1819.

UNIVERSITY LIBRARY
*Autograph manuscript of the Liber Floridus,
encyclopaedic work by Lambert of Saint-
Omer, 1120.*

VLEESHUIS
Butchers' gild house, 1408-17.

WOODEN HOUSE
Behind Fish Market.

HASSELT

MONUMENT OF PEASANTS' WAR OF 1798

ST. QUENTIN'S CHURCH
Tower 1250; nave c. 1300; chapels and choir XIV and XV.

HEMELVEERDEGEM

CHURCH OF ST. JOHN THE BAPTIST
'Salome dancing before Herod', part of carved wooden altar screen, 1515-25.

JABBEKE

PERMEKE MUSEUM
'Farmer with his Spade' by Constant Permeke, 1930.
'Beggar' by Constant Permeke, 1931.
'Sower' by Constant Permeke, 1933.

KOKSIJDE

TER DUINEN ABBEY
Founded c. 1127, Benedictine; 1138 becomes Cistercian, destroyed XVI; excavations show extensive parts of old abbey buildings.

KORTRIJK

BRIDGE AND BROEL TOWERS
Southern tower, lower part XII, upper XIV; northern tower built with bridge 1411-13.

LAARNE

CASTLE
Old entrance XII-XIII; main entrance XVI; additions XVII.

LEUVEN

BEGUINAGE CHURCH
1305 et seq.

ST. JAMES'S CHURCH
Romanesque tower c. 1225; nave late XIII-XIV; transept XV; and later.

ST. PETER'S CHURCH
1425-1527, to plans by S. van Vorst, M. de Laeyens, J. Keldermans etc.; crypt probably XI; sacrament tower, 1450; towers by J. Metzys, 1507 et seq.
Calvary ascribed to John II Borman, XV.
'The Last Supper' by D. Bouts, 1467.
'Martyrdom of St. Erasmus' by D. Bouts, 1466.
Monument to Henry I, Duke of Brabant, c. 1235.

TOWN HALL
By M. de Laeyens, 1448-63.

LIER

BEGUINAGE
Founded XIII, most present houses XVII,
Renaissance entrance, XVII; Church,
Flemish Renaissance, XVII, XVIII.

ST. GUMMARUS'S CHURCH
Nave and choir, 1540 to plans by H. Mys,
Keldermans family and H. de
Waghemakere; stained glass; tower 1377-
1455.

TOWN HALL AND BELFRY
Belfry, 1369 by H. Mys; top changed 1411.
Town hall, XVIII, Renaissance by J.-P. van
Bauerscheit; remarkable Rococo staircase by
L. van Everbroeck, 1775.

LISSEWEGE

BARN OF TER DOEST ABBEY
c. 1280.

LOMBEEK

CHURCH OF OUR LADY
Life of the Virgin, altar screen, 1512-16.

MALE

CASTLE OF COUNTS OF FLANDERS
Originally XIV; rebuilt 1954.

MECHELEN

BRUSSELS GATE
Remains of medieval town wall, upper part
restored XVII.

FISHMONGERS' GILD HALL 'THE SALMON'
By W. Van Werchtere, 1534.

HOME OF JEROME VAN BUSLEYDEN
[Town Museum]
1503-1508, by A. and R. Keldermans;
various restorations.

PALACE OF MARGARET OF AUSTRIA
House of John Laurin, 1508, transformed
for Margaret by R. Keldermans, 1517,
Flemish Renaissance style; 1609-1791:
meeting place of the Great Council;
XIX restored.

ST. ROMBOUT'S CATHEDRAL
Begun XIII; continued XIV, XV, XVI; tower
begun 1452, by A. Keldermans, unfinished.

TOWN HALL
Old Cloth Hall, 1311, unfinished;
part Gothic, 1526-XX, plan by
R. Keldermans.

MIDDELBURG

TOWN HALL
1506-1513 by A. Keldermans; restored
after 1944.

MONTREUIL

CASTLE
Begun 1567.

NINOVE

TOWN HALL
*Portrait of Nicholas Despautère XV, unknown
painter*

OOIDONK
[Bachte-Maria-Leerne]

MEDIEVAL CASTLE
Destroyed and rebuilt on old foundations
XVI, Spanish-Flemish style; XIX restauration.

OOSTKERKE

ST. QUENTIN'S CHURCH
XIII; blown up 1944 and rebuilt with
original materials.

ORVAL

ABBEY
Stations of the Cross by Albert Servaes,
on stone.

OUDENAARDE

CHURCH OF OUR LADY OF PAMELE
Scheldt Gothic by A. de Binche, 1235.

TOWN HALL
1526-1537, by H. van Pede, surmounted
by statue of Little John, the Fighter.

RONSE

ST. HERMES'S CHURCH
Romanesque crypt; XIII-XIV.

ST. MARTIN'S CHURCH
XIII; Gothic.

SAINT-OMER

CHURCH OF ABBEY OF ST. BERTIN
Founded VII, ruins 1326-1520, burned
1830; tower 1431-1520, collapsed 1942.

SINT-MARTENS-LATEM

ST. MARTIN'S CHURCH
'Holy Virgin with St. Dominic' by G. van de
Woestijne, 1900.

SINT-TRUIDEN

CHURCH OF OUR LADY
xiv, xv; tower rebuilt 1847.

TONGEREN

MOERPOORT [now Military Museum]
1379.

TOURNAI

CATHEDRAL [with museum]
Tapestry of the 'Legend of St. Piatus and
St. Eleutherius', Arras work, 1402.

VEURNE

ST. NICHOLAS'S CHURCH
1494-98; tower end XIII; restored 1891.

VORSELAAR

CASTLE
Corner towers c. 1275; rest 1670-1756;
restored 1850-60.

YPRES

CLOTH HALL AND BELFRY
1200-1304; completely destroyed in First
World War; rebuilt.

MENIN GATE
British war memorial of First World war,
by Reginald Blomfield, 1923-27; c. 50,000
names.

TEMPLARS' HOUSE [now Post Office]
Part XIII; partly destroyed 1914.

ZOUTLEEUW

ST. LEONARD'S CHURCH
St. Leonard's altar screen, by Arnould, 1478.
Dancing David.

Index of Persons and Places

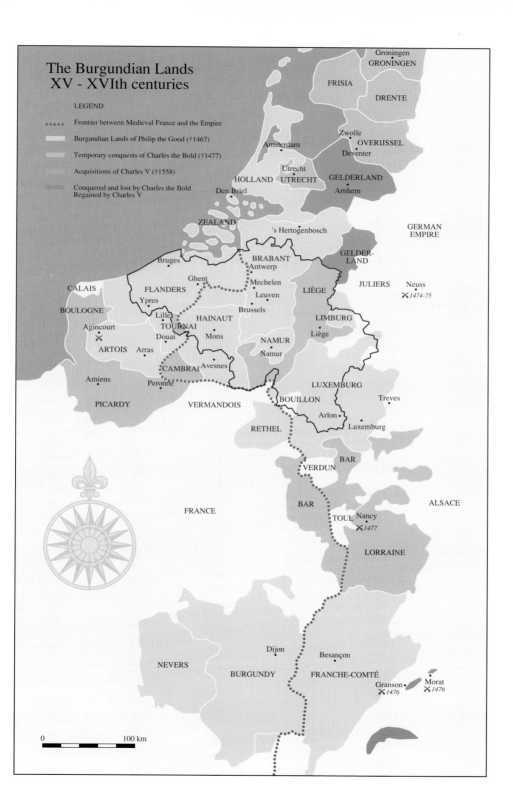

The Burgundian Lands
XV - XVIth centuries

LEGEND

········· Frontier between Medieval France and the Empire

      Burgundian Lands of Philip the Good (†1467)

      Temporary conquests of Charles the Bold (†1477)

      Acquisitions of Charles V (†1558)

      Conquered and lost by Charles the Bold
      Regained by Charles V

Groningen
GRONINGEN

FRISIA

DRENTE

Zwolle
OVERIJSSEL
Deventer

Amsterdam

Utrecht
UTRECHT

GELDERLAND

HOLLAND

Arnhem

Den Briel

ZEALAND

's Hertogenbosch

GERMAN
EMPIRE

BRABANT
Antwerp

GELDER-
LAND

Bruges

Ghent

Mechelen

JULIERS

Neuss
✕ 1474-75

CALAIS

FLANDERS

Leuven

LIÈGE

Ypres

BOULOGNE

Lille

Brussels

LIMBURG

HAINAUT

Agincourt
✕

TOURNAI

Liège

ARTOIS

Douai

Mons

Arras

NAMUR

LUXEMBURG

Amiens

CAMBRAI Avesnes

Namur

Treves

Peronne

BOUILLON

Arlon

PICARDY

VERMANDOIS

Luxemburg

RETHEL

BAR

VERDUN

ALSACE

FRANCE

BAR

TOUL Nancy
✕ 1477

LORRAINE

NEVERS

Dijon

Besançon

BURGUNDY

FRANCHE-COMTÉ

Granson ·
✕ 1476

Morat
✕ 1476

0   100 km

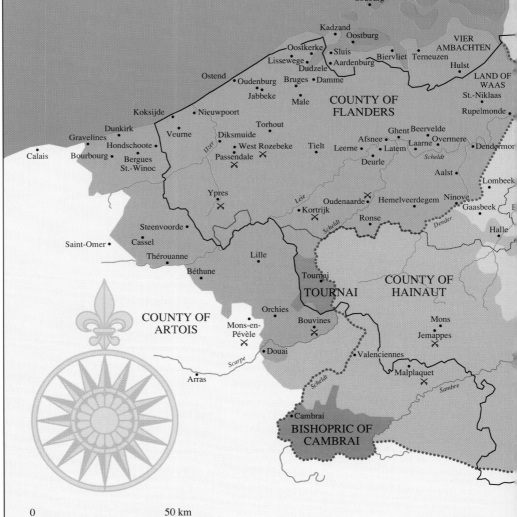

The Southern low countries in the later Middle Ages and present-day Flanders

LEGEND

∘∘∘∘∘   Boundary between lands held from France en from the Empire

···········   Dutch-French linguistic frontier

Den Briel

Burg op
Schouwen

COUNTY OF ZEALAND

Middelburg
Souburg

Kadzand

Oostburg

VIER AMBACHTEN

Oostkerke

Sluis

Biervliet Terneuzen

Lissewege

Aardenburg

Hulst

Dudzele

Ostend

Oudenburg Bruges Damme

LAND OF WAAS

Jabbeke

Male

COUNTY OF FLANDERS

St.-Niklaas

Koksijde

Nieuwpoort

Rupelmonde

Dunkirk

Torhout

Ghent Beervelde

Gravelines

Veurne

Diksmuide

Afsnee

Laarne Overmere

Hondschoote

West Rozebeke

Tielt

Leerne Latem

Dendermo

Calais

Bourbourg Bergues
St.-Winoc

Passendale

Deurle

Scheldt

Aalst

Ypres

Lombeek

Steenvoorde

Lete

Oudenaarde Hemelveerdegem Ninove

Saint-Omer Cassel

Kortrijk

Ronse

Gaasbeek

Thérouanne

Scheldt

Dender

Halle

Béthune

Lille

Tournai

COUNTY OF HAINAUT

TOURNAI

Orchies

Bouvines

Mons

COUNTY OF ARTOIS

Mons-en-Pévèle

Jemappes

Douai

Valenciennes

Scarpe

Malplaquet

Arras

Scheldt

Sambre

Cambrai

BISHOPRIC OF CAMBRAI

0   50 km

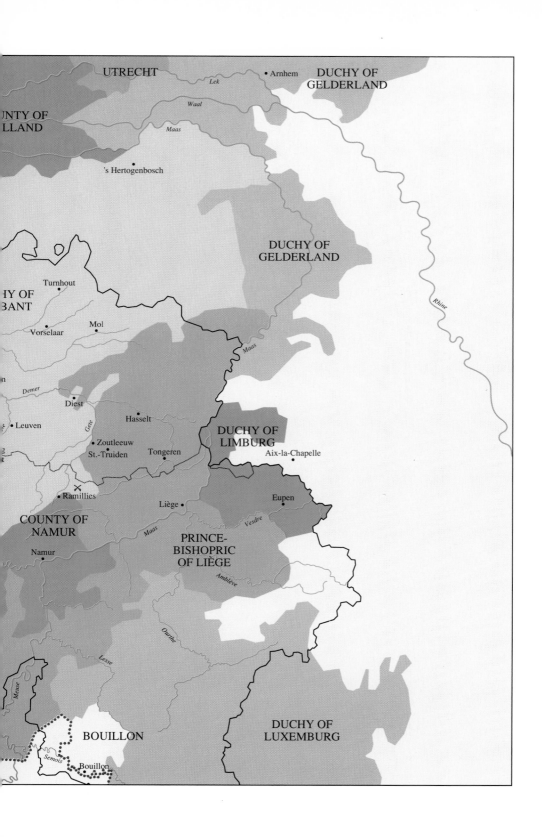